THE BASSET HOUND

POPULAR DOGS' BREED SERIES

Ch. Fredwell Varon Vandal, 1960

Ch. Rossingham Amber, 1953

THE BASSET HOUND

GEORGE JOHNSTON

POPULAR DOGS

London

POPULAR DOGS PUBLISHING CO LTD
3 Fitzroy Square, London W1

An imprint of the Hutchinson Group

London Melbourne Sydney Auckland
Wellington Johannesburg Cape Town
and agencies throughout the world

First published September 1968
Second edition revised November 1969
Third edition revised August 1972
Fourth edition revised December 1974

Printed in Great Britain by The Anchor Press Ltd
and bound by Wm Brendon & Son Ltd
both of Tiptree, Essex

ISBN 0 09 122110 2

For
C.M.J. and G.A.J.

ACKNOWLEDGMENTS

I gratefully acknowledge the valuable assistance and information given to me by the following societies and individuals. The co-operation I received was such that a mere acknowledgment does not seem ample recompense.

The Kennel Club, American Kennel Club, *Société Centrale Canine* and *Société de Vénerie* for their help and permission to publish the breed standards and registration details.

Mrs. M. Seiffert, secretary of the Basset Hound Club.

Mrs. J. Groom, secretary of the Masters of Basset Hounds Association.

Mrs. J. Newby-Fraser, secretary of the Basset Hound Club of South Africa.

Monsieur Jean Rothéa, president of the *Club du Basset Artésien-Normand*.

Monsieur Hubert Desamy, secretary of the *Club Griffon-Vendéen*.

All gave me much assistance and information on their respective breeds and clubs.

Mr. Asa Lees, a canine historian without peer. His delving into the breed's past yielded priceless information on early British hounds.

Lieutenant-Colonel E. F. S. Morrison, M.C., M.F.H., for kindly supplying details and information on the Walhampton hounds and the 'English' Basset.

My thanks are due to Mr. Lionel Woolner, M.H., for his generous contribution on the Hunting Basset, an integral part of the book, and to my overseas friends for their assistance ungrudgingly given—Mrs. Ruth Turner and Mr. Carl Smith of the U.S.A., Mr. Peter Warby of Australia and Mme A. Gondrexon-Ives-Browne of Holland.

I am in debt to you all.

G.I.J.

CONTENTS

ILLUSTRATIONS

IN THE TEXT

AUTHOR'S INTRODUCTION

My father had a kennel of Basset Hounds and a host of friends who, like him, were devotees of the long, low hounds, so all my life I have been surrounded by Bassets and have enjoyed the company of people who loved the ancient breed. This intimate connection with the Basset need not have led to the point of 'like father, like son', but I am glad to say that it did. It would please me very much if one day I could see my son taking an interest in the Basset Hound. He would quickly discover that the breeding and rearing of these unique hounds is a fascinating, absorbing hobby and the source of much enjoyment. In a clumsy way I am trying to show that the breed has a past, a present and a future.

No breed can boast a finer past than the Basset, which evolved as a true hound during the *belle époque* of hound-breeding in the very cradle of venery, France. It was there that the Basset's reputation as a hound was founded, and it was apparent that the little hounds had many other qualities. These we are fully aware of—charm, docility, loyalty and dignity, the attributes which are largely responsible for the popularity of the Basset today when more are being hunted, exhibited, and kept for companionship than ever before. Yet in this period of the Basset's history there lies the greatest danger: commercial breeding and the demands for changes in the conformation of the breed. The Basset must not be altered in order to make it more acceptable to the dog-buying public. We should feel proud to breed and own a breed which has proved itself capable of performing so many functions in so many differing conditions and eras and has yet remained basically the same.

In order that future generations of hound-lovers can enjoy and appreciate the Basset Hound let us ensure that it passes through our era unspoiled.

1968   G.I.J.

In this second edition the errors—fortunately few but irritating—in the first edition have been corrected, and the appendices brought up to date. I hope that the book is now made more enjoyable and informative.

1969   G.I.J.

To Mr. Gerald Austin I am very grateful for the opportunity he has given me to revise this book. This was last done in 1969 and inevitably some changes, deletions and additions were necessary. These have been attended to and appear in the relevant chapters and appendices, thus bringing the book up to date again.

1972   G.I.J.

Once more I must thank my publisher for giving me the chance of making the revisions necessary to keep this book up to date. I am also grateful to Mrs. Mildred Seiffert for kindly checking through the list of champions.

Wigton, 1974.   G.I.J.

I

Origins and Evolution

ONE has only to look at the Basset Hound to see that it is a very odd form of canine life. The species of long-bodied and low-standing dogs is an unusual and very ancient order, and even among contemporary breeds the Basset stands alone. To the casual observer it must appear grotesque and bizarre—the distinctive head, full of nobility and expressing reposeful dignity, and the long, low, heavy body set upon very short legs, the front legs being crooked almost to the point of deformity.

The word 'Basset' is French, and means 'low-set', 'stunted' or 'dwarfed', and that is in fact what we have, a 'dwarf-hound'. Small wonder that many people should be puzzled by the Basset and often ask how and where it originated and why such a breed was evolved.

In answer to these questions we can offer detailed proof of the Basset's existence in 1585, but before that date no authentic record of the Basset Hound as such can be found. I say 'the Basset Hound as such' because there is ample evidence to show that a short-legged and long-bodied race of dogs was known to man as early as 2200 B.C.

Wall-paintings have been found in Egyptian tombs depicting strange little dogs. In the tomb of Beni Hassan (2200–2000 B.C.) a painting shows a group of elegant, finely made dogs accompanied by a small short-legged dog. The same type of dog is shown also on the tomb of Thotmes II (2000 B.C.) and legend has it that the little dog was, in fact, the Pharaoh's favourite.

The ancient civilisations of Assyria and Egypt attached much importance to their canine companions, and they are often shown on paintings and recorded on the scrolls. The purpose of the large dogs is obvious, because they are shown in all the

B

phases of the chase, hunting the desert game, gazelle, antelope and so on. This was hunting that required swift hounds with great stamina. Such ancient hounds are held to be the fore-runners of the modern breeds of gaze-hounds (hounds hunting by sight) which they strongly resemble: the Saluki, Afghan and Greyhound.

Unfortunately, the small dogs shown on the same paintings do not seem to be performing any useful or sporting function, and therefore we can only guess at their purpose. It is, of course, possible that they were kept purely as household pets and children's companions. They could also have been terriers and used for controlling vermin—but all this is pure conjecture.

Many breeds of dog have a body structure not unlike the Bassets; I am thinking of the Dandie Dinmont and Skye Terriers, the Dachshund, and the Clumber and Sussex Spaniels. Their construction is long-bodied, short-legged, and in the main of some substance. In view of these general similarities I cannot see how we can dissociate these breeds from those whose line of descent we believe to have originated in ancient Egypt. The process of evolution through the centuries accounts for the different types and characteristics found among the low-set breeds, but I feel that up to a certain un-identifiable point all the short-legged breeds I have mentioned were one and the same order. Naturally, certain groups be-came isolated, geographical and climatic conditions affected them, and certain features exemplified each group. Eventually they became different breeds sharing a common ancestry. The same order of events applies to man, flora and fauna.

From the ancient lands of the Middle East the distribution of the small dog seems to have been in a northerly direction and then dividing, one group going east and the other group turning westwards. The eastern group seems to be the fore-runner of the small Tibetan and Chinese dogs found in Budd-hist monasteries and Mandarin palaces. The western group was distributed over Europe, and the Romans had little terriers—the word is in fact Roman in origin, *terra*=earth. When the Romans penetrated the lands of Gaul and Germany they found dogs of similar build providing food, by hunting game, for the nomadic tribes of early Europe. These dogs ran the game by scent, *Canis Sagaces*, a scent-hunting dog.

It is more than likely that these early French dogs were the ancestors of the early hounds known as St. Huberts. These hounds were bred by the monks in a monastery established in the Ardennes by Hubert (A.D. 656–727), son of the Duc de Guienne. Hubert, like most of the nobility of the period, was extremely fond of hunting, and legend has it that he was converted when a stag with a cross between its horns confronted him during a hunt on a Sunday. Hubert apparently devoted the rest of his life to God, but did not cease breeding his hounds.

The hounds of St. Hubert were noted for their hunting ability, and well known throughout France. There was no St. Hubert breed inasmuch as they were all of one type. The strain was established, but the hounds in the strain were varied.

A most reputable chronicler of canine affairs, George Turbeville, says in his *Art of Venerie* (1576) that 'the St. Huberts are mighty of body, legs low and short, not swift, but very good on scent', and that 'they come in all colours'.

Turbeville also records how the various colours were sought after for different purposes, the white hounds for stag, and the black hounds made the best Bloodhounds.

Writing in the same year as Turbeville, Dr. Johannes Caius, a less truthful observer, states in his *Of English Dogges* (1576): 'We may know these dogges by their long large and bagging lips, by their hanging ears reaching down both sides of their chappes', and: 'they come in sundrie sorts'.

Turbeville drew attention to the short legs of the St. Hubert hounds, and his observation is verified by the definition in an early French-English dictionary (1632). It says: '*Chien de St. Hubert*, a kind of strong short-legged hound, and deep-mouthed'.

The St. Hubert hounds are occasionally referred to also as Talbots, probably an English applied misnomer for Taillebois, who was Abbot of St. Hubert's Monastery after A.D. 727.

Because of their superiority over most other hounds of early France, the St. Huberts were distributed to the kings and aristocracy, and were most welcome additions to their kennels.

Due to this wide distribution to all parts of France, the St. Huberts played a major role in the development of the numerous French hound breeds. By breeding their St. Huberts with their own native breeds, and culling undesirable colours and types, the noblemen eventually established *chiens courants* (hunting dogs) of distinct breeds, such as *d'Artois (artésiens)*, *d'Ariège (ariégeois)*, *de Bretagne (bretons)*, *de Bresse*, *de Franche-Comté*, *de Gascogne (gascons)*, *de Normandie (normands)*, *de Poitou*, *de Saintonge (saintongeois)* and *de Vendée (vendéens)*.

As in the early evolution of breeds, once again geographical isolation and gradual selection eventually established the differing type and colours of all these descendants of the St. Hubert Hound. An example of what climate and local conditions can do to affect colouring is found in the Blue-Mottled Gascon Hound. Zoologists have found that the mottled colour is produced because the pigmentation of the skin is affected by the sun and the soils of the Midi, the dry area of France where the Gascon hound is bred.

The hounds I have listed were all bred for stag-hunting and consequently larger than the St. Huberts. Nevertheless, they all carried the genes of the low-set St. Hubert and throwbacks to this type were often produced, and most authorities agree that this is the origin of the true Basset we know today.

In the early days each French hound breed was found in three versions, regulated only by size. In other respects—colour, type, voice, etc.—all were identical, and they were:

1. *Chiens d'ordre*. Full-sized hounds, standing upwards of twenty-three inches. Hunting: stag, boar, etc.

2. *Chiens briquets*. Hounds standing between fifteen and twenty-two inches. Hunting: smaller game, hare, roe deer, etc.

3. *Chiens bassets*. Low hounds, under fifteen inches in height. Hunting: small game, and used as terriers.

To give an example, the *Chien d'Artois*, a noble-headed tricolour hound, would be found in each of the three stages, *Chien d'Artois*, *Briquet d'Artois* and *Basset d'Artois*.

The Basset order was subdivided further by the degree of crook of the forelegs, and these subdivisions were:

Basset à jambes droites. Straight-legged Basset.

Basset à jambes torses. Full crooked forelegs.
Basset à jambes demi-torses. Half crooked forelegs.

The straight-legged hounds are recorded as being used as running hounds, hunting hare and rabbits, and the two crooked varieties were used underground as terriers and truffle-hunting dogs.

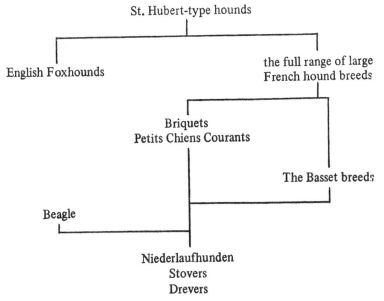

FIG 1   Basset Hound's line of descent

M. Léon Verrier of Rouen, France, the author of the classic work devoted to Bassets, *Les Bassets Français et leur Utilisation* (Paris 1921), supports the theory that the Basset is descended from the hounds found in the *chien d'ordre* size. M. Verrier says that the first Basset probably appeared in a litter of *chiens d'ordre*, and was therefore a throwback to the ancient low St. Hubert Hound. This theory is most feasible, especially now that we know that the reverse procedure can take place, i.e. a Basset bitch may produce a puppy of the large hound type. (This has occurred in France, U.S.A. and Britain.) Out of curiosity the breeders of the 'first dwarf hounds' retained them, and by means of inbreeding and always selecting the lowest hounds eventually managed to produce *chiens bassets* corresponding in all except stature to the large 'parent' breed.

Another eminent canine authority, M. Pierre Pichot, a Director of the *Jardin d'Acclimatation* in Paris, wrote in 1875: 'The Basset in my opinion sprang from the different local breeds of large hounds and is therefore connected with the *Vendée, Saintongeois, Artois* and *Normandie* types.'

The first mention of the word 'Basset' appears in 1585 in Jacques du Fouilloux's early classic *Vénerie de Jacques du Fouilloux*. This author devoted several pages to Bassets and their work as badger dogs. Two types are recognised by du Fouilloux, the crooked-front (*torses*) and the straight-front (*droites*), and he states that the crooked-legged Bassets go to ground better, and in general are short-coated, whereas the straight-legged dogs often have the rough coat (early Griffon Bassets) and often run game above ground as well as doing terrier work. Du Fouilloux gives advice on the training of Bassets for this occupation, and believes that unless the hound is entered between eight and ten months old, it proves difficult to train. Du Fouilloux was obviously a gentleman who enjoyed his sport to the full. He recommends that the *charrette de chasse*, or hunting cart, should be furnished with 'a sprightly lass of sixteen or seventeen to scratch his head so as to while away the weariness of the journey'. Small wonder that on one occasion when this 'gay old sportsman' met the King of France he was accompanied by his fifty sons, of whom only one was his legitimate offspring!

Du Fouilloux attributes the original home of the Basset to the regions of Artois and Flanders, and another contemporary, Leverrier de la Couterie, agrees with this and adds the information that the Artois type were courageous and good below ground, but that he preferred the quicker-witted and fiery Flanders type.

The text of du Fouilloux's book is illustrated by a charming woodcut by Sigmund Feyeraband, and shows a bearded gentleman, presumably du Fouilloux, setting out in his *charrette de chasse* to enjoy a day's badger-digging. The springless carriage

is very well furnished with wine flagons and the necessary
tools for digging out the badger. The cart is pulled by two
sturdy horses; two other hunters, or servants, accompany du
Fouilloux. Completing the merry entourage are a couple of
portly-looking Bassets.

They are substantially constructed, with heavy-boned, short
front legs, round hindquarters and well-bent stifles. Their head
tends to be rounded and the ears are long, but set high on the
skull. Both hounds are moving with the head carried low. One
of the brace carries his tail in true hound fashion, whereas the
other dog, probably a little fatigued, is letting his tail down
slightly. Their whole appearance is typical of modern Bassets
in motion; the Basset today usually carries the head low and
ears high when moving.

As I have said, du Fouilloux was the first to call the hounds
'Bassets', and Feyeraband's woodcut is perhaps the earliest
known illustration of the breed. Incidentally, the illustration is
adjusted in later editions of the book to include the 'sprightly
lass' du Fouilloux was so fond of!

Although du Fouilloux mentions the use of straight-legged
Bassets as running-hounds, there seems to be little doubt that
during this period (1585–1632) the Basset was regarded as an
earth-dog. The *French-English Dictionary* (1632) defines:

Basset . . . a Terrier or Earthing Dog.

and de la Blanchère, in his complicated *Table of French Breeds
and their British Counterparts*, lists:

Bassets et Terriers
Bassets à jambes droites . . . Bull Terriers
Bassets à jambes torses . . . Scotch Terriers

Not only was the Basset a sporting dog in every sense of the
word, he was also most adaptable to the changes taking place
in medieval sport. In 1682 the Basset was attracting attention
and praise for the ability it showed when used by shooting
men enjoying *chasse à tir*, shooting with the aid of hounds.
Jean de Sélincourt, in his *Le Parfait Chasseur* (1682), says: 'The
Basset is a most useful dog for gentlemen hunting with the
arquebus' and continues to explain why the Basset, especially
the *torse* or full crook type, is superior to other hounds in

chasse à tir. Because of its diminutive size the Basset was able to penetrate the densest undergrowth and flush out the game to the waiting guns. The construction of the *Basset à jambes torses* prevented them pursuing the quarry quickly; nevertheless they were extremely sure on scent and most diligent hounds. The quarry, usually deer, hare or rabbit, was therefore chased on slowly and unhurriedly, and because of this presented a much better target for the waiting sportsmen than a fast-moving animal would have done. The early shooters needed all the available time in order to present, aim, fire and possibly re-load their heavy, unwieldy guns and muskets. Game pursued by larger hounds moved too fast and gave the guns little chance of bringing it down.

Although the game hunted by Bassets, and the *chasse à tir* method, was usually confined to the smaller deer, hares and rabbits, larger quarry was not beyond the Basset's scope. The hounds occasionally hunted wild boar and wolf. The former, known in France as the *Bête Noire* (Black Beast), is a dreadful adversary, and it needs brave men and even braver hounds to face one. The Basset did not lack courage and had considerable success in controlling the numbers of boar and wolf when used by the *Louvetier*, a government-appointed warden whose duty it was to control these two pests, which caused much destruction to crops and stock. So dreadful and yet so compelling is the wild boar that most hounds, when on its scent, are inclined to run mute (fail to give tongue). In order to counteract the silence, and aid the hunters in pinpointing their hounds' position, small bells, or *grelots*, were fitted to the collars worn by the dogs. Many early illustrations of Bassets show the hounds wearing the bells.

The *chasse à tir*, or shooting with hounds, is not to be confused with *la chasse*, which is the orthodox form of shooting over gundogs, or *chiens d'arrêt*. The *chasse à courre* or *chasse au chien courant* is hunting game with a pack of hounds. Before the French Revolution and the Napoleonic Wars (1789–1815) hunting in France was at a high premium, and much thought was given to the scientific breeding of hounds. The whole order of venery was a medieval pageant of pomp, dress and etiquette; the forests resounded with the stirring 'Hallalis', the music of the French hunting-horns. Needless to say only royalty, aristocracy and the landowners could afford time and money for hunting, and as a diversion and relaxation from the *grand chasse à courre*, these same classes enjoyed *chasse à tir* and

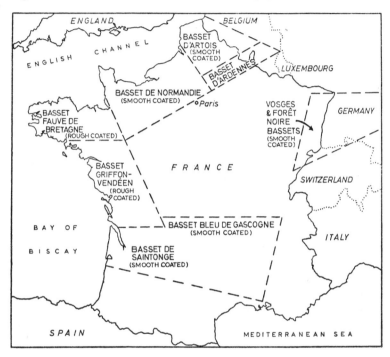

FIG 2 Areas of origin of the Basset breeds.
Allied breeds: Dachshunden—Germany; Niederlaufhunden—
Switzerland; Stovers and Drevers—Scandinavia

the company of the little Bassets. The Revolution saw the collapse of the monarchy and the ruling classes, and with most of the nobility fleeing the country or being sent to the guillotine all hunting came to an abrupt end. The large hunting establishments and estates were disbanded and the hounds, so carefully bred, dispersed. Some breeds were never revived.

With the eventual restoration of the monarchy in the form

of Louis XVIII, the aristocracy gradually re-established and with their return to fortune and favour were able to resume the breeding of hounds and hunting. Some of the lesser-known regional breeds had disappeared altogether, and among the Basset breeds that became extinct were the:

Basset saintongeois
Basset ardennais or *St. Hubert*

and two breeds became exceedingly rare. These were the:

Basset fauve de Bretagne (Fawn Breton Basset)
Basset bleu de Gascogne (Blue Mottled Gascon Basset)

The breeds that were revived and managed to re-establish themselves fairly strongly were the:

Basset d'Artois
Basset de Normandie and
Basset Griffon-Vendéen (Griffon-Vendeen Basset).

At a later period the first two breeds were gradually inter-bred and became known as the *Basset Artésien-Normand* (Artois-Norman Basset).

The surviving Basset breeds continued hunting in the *chasse à tir* order, and eminent authors still regarded them as being the premier hound for the job. M. Elzéar Blaze, author of many French sporting books, says in his *Le Chasseur* (1850): 'The best dog for the *chasse à tir* is without contradiction the *Basset à jambes torses*' and M. Robert, in his *Chiens de Chasse*, says: 'The Basset will hunt all animals, even boar and wolf, but he is especially excellent for the *chasse à tir* of rabbits and hares.'

He continues to say that the construction of the Basset also makes him useful for entering the badger and fox. So it appears that even when the Bassets had become well established as *chasse à tir* dogs they were still occasionally used as terriers, their occupation in the days of du Fouilloux three centuries earlier.

The first French dog show was staged in Paris in 1863 at the *Jardin d'Acclimatation*, and in the sporting dog section Bassets were classified thus:

Bassets of all kinds
Straight-legged short-haired Bassets
,,   ,,   long-   ,,   ,,

Crooked-legged short-haired Bassets
    ,,   ,,   long- ,,   ,,
Baden Bassets, Burgos, St. Domingo,
Illyrian and Hungarian Bassets.

The half-crooked or *demi-torses* Basset is not listed, and it is thought that during this period the *demi-torses* was regarded as the *droites* or straight-legged hound. I am quite unable to give any information about the Baden, Burgos, St. Domingo, Illyrian and Hungarian Bassets. The only clue is, of course, the geographical one, and we can hazard a perhaps wild guess in the case of the Baden Basset: Baden is in southern Germany and this breed is perhaps an offshoot of the early Dachshund. It is possible, of course, that Basset-type breeds were known in these areas and that authorities on dogs indigenous there will perhaps wonder at my ignorance. However, the fact remains that no authoritative work on hounds lists these obscure Basset varieties.

In 1895 Pug, the noted French social commentator, wrote his somewhat satirical *Sports Women* and classified all the field sports and other pastimes suitable for ladies. He especially recommends to ladies the *chasse à tir* with a couple of Bassets. The work is illustrated by a sketch of a fashionably garbed lady complete with gun and two Bassets.

In 1902 the great French authority on hounds and hunting, Count le Couteulx de Canteleu of Etrepagny, published the detailed *Manuel de Vénerie Française*. The work is very comprehensive and detailed on all the French hound breeds, but to my mind is rather sketchy on the Bassets, only one small chapter and illustration being devoted to the whole species of *chiens Bassets*.

Le Couteulx says: 'The Basset is very strong, and perfect for the *chasse à tir*.' On the breeds of Bassets Le Couteulx says that there are many varieties, but mentions only four:

    Basset artésien
      ,, *Griffon-Vendéen*
      ,, *de la Forêt Noire* (Black Forest)
      ,, *des Vosges*

The last two varieties he describes as being small, and black and tan in colour. Despite the fact that no less an authority than Le Couteulx mentions the *Forêt Noire* and *Vosges* breeds, no other French author has recorded them. In colour they are similar to the extinct *Basset d'Ardennes*, but this hound was quite large. Some authorities claim that as one moves eastwards through France the Basset breeds gradually diminish in stature and become darker in colour. Le Couteulx's mention of the two otherwise unknown breeds seems to authenticate this theory. The Vosges are in the extreme east of France, almost bordering Germany, whose boundaries, of course, encompass the *Forêt Noire* or Black Forest. Like the Baden Basset, the *Forêt Noire* hounds could easily have been early Dachshunds. A total lack of detailed text and illustrations prevents us from verifying this.

Beautiful illustrations by Mahler, the noted *animalier*, of the extinct *Basset de Saintonge* and *Basset d'Ardennes* are included in Alain Bourbon's *Nos Bassets Français* (Paris, 1911). However, Bourbon and Verrier recognise the existence of the only breeds to have survived the Revolution, and which I have previously listed. Their works are regarded as the classic books devoted to Bassets, and neither makes any note of the existence of any other Basset.

When dealing with a breed like the Basset, so unique in appearance and obviously of ancient lineage, it would be easy to romanticise and attach to it all sorts of theories concerning its origin. We cannot be absolutely certain that the origins described by Verrier, Pichot and many others are correct, but certainly the majority of Basset fanciers, past and present, feel that this theory is the most probable. Throughout history it has been substantiated by the various facts that I have tabulated, and no other theory of origin can be factually supported in this way.

In the *Livestock Journal*, 1881, an unknown correspondent said, 'I believe that these animals have been, like the mole, provided by nature to do a certain work, which could not be done by those on high straight limbs.' The writer may well be correct in his assumption, but no supporting proof is given. Certainly the small low-set dogs of ancient times existed, and probably were the original terriers, equipped for their work by nature as the writer suggests. However, as I have pointed out, no proof has yet to come to light that the 'distinct' Basset Hound, Artois, Vendeen, Gascon, etc., existed before Verrier and other prominent gentlemen suggest, i.e. about 1500.

Another version of the Basset's origin is rather extreme and improbable. Adherents of this explanation maintain that the Basset, complete with the 'deformed front', was the result of a deliberate attempt to breed such a deformity. In the days of the cruel Forest Laws, implemented by the Saxons and continued by the Normans, all hounds owned by commoners, foresters, etc., were deliberately mutilated by royally authorised game wardens. The reason was to prevent poaching and hunting by commoners in the royal hunting parks and lands. The system of mutilation was barbaric, and entailed 'the cutting-off of pads on the forefeet' and 'the severing of sinews and tendons in the hind legs,' both methods effectively prevented hounds from running down deer or any other game. The commoners therefore set about breeding a hound so 'obviously restricted' by his very build that they would avoid the harsh unnatural handicap meted out by the wardens. The end product of the attempt was the Basset Hound—a slow hound, admittedly, but still quite capable of hunting and killing smaller game.

I will make no attempt to disprove the theory. As I said, the exact course of the Basset's evolution is not certain, but points concerning this latter theory would appear to make it only conjecture.

France prior to 1066 had no laws remotely resembling the English Forest Laws. Therefore this theory would make the 'Basset' an English product, and suggest that the Normans found it after 1066, an 'artificially produced' breed the apparent replica of hounds known in France as early as A.D. 700. Readers must draw their own conclusion, but for me this theory does not ring true.

The succeeding chapter will show that Bassets were known in early Britain, but not until after the Norman invasion of 1066.

2

Early Basset-type and Basset Hounds in Britain

'THERE is this day among us a new kind of dog brought out of France. For we English are marvellous greedy, gaping gluttons after novelties and covetous of things that be seldom, rare and hard to get.' Dr. Johannes Caius, in *Of Englishe Dogges* (1576).

The breed Caius went on to describe was not the Basset but the Blue Mottled Gascon Hound, a most beautiful breed, having, it is thought, the same origin as the Basset, that is to say descent from the St. Hubert hounds. If the Gascon hound was known in Britain in the sixteenth century, why not the Basset? Certainly as a breed 'they be seldom, rare and hard to get' and more of a 'noveltie' than the Gascons. Caius was certainly correct in his summary of the English character concerning livestock—the unusual has always attracted our attention. It therefore seems unlikely that the bizarre and extremely strange-looking Basset should have escaped our attention and not have been introduced until 1866.

The French hound breeds became known in Britain after the invasion in 1066 and the establishment of the Norman monarchy. Since then hunting in Britain has been based on the French pattern of venery, especially the *chasse à courre*, or hunting with a pack of hounds. This sport, popular with the Normans, became equally popular with the succeeding royal houses and British aristocracy. Hound-breeding was given much thought and it was not unusual for hounds to be sent to France to augment packs, and vice versa; these hounds were usually of the *grand chien* order, staghounds, etc., but in 1304 the first Prince of Wales sent to Louis of France 'some of our low-legged hare-hounds from Wales'.

Whether these hounds were Bassets or Beagles it would be hard to say. It is known that a race of short crooked-legged hounds existed in Cornwall in the fifteenth century, and they are thought to have been introduced into that county by Breton wrestlers visiting Cornwall to participate in Celtic wrestling contests. The hounds have been described as 'heavily built and very short-legged, with long ears and deep voices', and colouring: 'brindle or yellowish'.

The colour of the Fawn Breton Basset varies between wheaten and rich tan, and although this variety has a rough (Griffon) coat, the 'Cornish' hounds could easily be the result of crossing with local breeds. The same type of hound is depicted on a carving on a Welsh oak bedstead in Cotehele House at St. Dominicks in Cornwall. The furniture arrived at the house when Katherine, widow of Sir Griffith Ap Rhys, married Sir Piers Edgcumbe in 1532. The Basset-type hounds figuring on the carving are 'low-set, long-eared and crooked-legged', suggesting the basic structure of the Basset Hound. Also depicted on the same carving are the Tudor Arms, English heraldic lions and the French fleur-de-lis, and gentlemen enjoying hawking and hunting.

William Shakespeare wrote *A Midsummer Night's Dream* about 1598, and in the text is the following speech:

> 'My hounds are bred out of the Spartan kind
> So flew'd, so sanded; and their heads are hung
> With ears that sweep away the morning dew;
> Crook-knee'd, and dew-lapt like Thessalian Bulls;
> Slow in pursuit, but matcht in mouth like bells,
> Each under each.'

From the detailed description of the hounds and their style of hunting one would think the Basset had been known to the Bard of Avon. Certainly he was fond of field sports, and some authorities claim that he describes the Southern Hound, a heavy, slow but taller hound than the Basset. The well-known sporting artists Edmund Willis and Philip Reinagle, A.R.A. (1787–1812), both painted the Southern Hound (Willis in 1831), but neither showed it as 'crook-kneed' or 'sanded'—'sanded' means mottled. The Basset, of course, possesses both features.

A book-plate designed in 1793 by Agnes Berry, for Mrs. Damer, daughter of the Hon. Henry Seymour Conway, shows the Damer Arms supported by two crooked-legged dogs. These small dogs tend to resemble those in du Fouilloux's book, especially in head points. The similarity in long ears and decidedly crooked front legs is clear.

Many British families of Norman descent have coats of arms showing Talbot hounds, or St. Huberts, and it would be reasonable to suppose that these same families brought over hounds from France after their settlement in Britain. It is certainly known that the larger French breeds were introduced into Britain at this period and are the forerunners of most English breeds. The Welsh Foxhound and the Otterhound have their French equivalent in the Griffons of Vendee and Nivernais, and the Foxhound is probably the outcome of early crosses of *Saintongeois*, *Franche-Comté*, etc. Caius knew the Gascon Hound in 1576, and with the close proximity of France and the constant interchange of hounds, I cannot believe that the Basset did not figure in the exchanges.

Whatever the answer, it is indisputable that the first mention of the words Basset Hound in British literature appeared in 1866, and it was in the same year that the introduction of pure-bred Bassets and their continued breeding on a scientific basis began.

Regarding the first Bassets, Lord Galway, of Serlby, wrote to Major C. Heseltine (of Walhampton fame):

'In July 1866, I was staying at Royat, Puy de Dôme, France, where I met the Marquis de Tournon and his son, the Comte de Tournon. The latter promised me a pair of Basset Hounds from his pack, which duly arrived in the autumn at Serlby. They were a dog and a bitch and I called them "Basset" and "Belle". They were long, low hounds shaped much like a Dachshund, with crooked forelegs at the knees and with much more bone and longer heads than on Beagles. They were not the dark tan colour of Dachshunds but the colour of Foxhounds with a certain amount of white about them. They had deep heavy tongues more like Foxhounds than Beagles.'

'Sportsman in his *charrette de chasse* going out badger-digging.' Fifteenth-century woodcut from du Fouilloux's *La Vénerie*. Earliest known illustration of Bassets

Mrs. E. L. Grew and some of her Maybush hounds, 1935

Walhampton Arthur, 1925

Walhampton Linguist and Alice, 1922

The hounds 'Basset' and 'Belle' were from the strain built up by Count le Couteulx de Canteleu. This famous sportsman was especially keen on preserving all the old French hound breeds, and with his cousin, Henri de Couteulx de Caumont, had succeeded in saving some from extinction. He had much experience on crossing breeds for new blood and then quickly returning to the type of the rejuvenated breed.

Lord Galway mated Basset and Belle, and in 1867 they produced a litter of five, including a hound called Bellman. However, for some unknown reason the little pack built up by Lord Galway was passed on to Lord Onslow in 1872. Lord Onslow continued breeding the only pack of Bassets in Britain, and there is no evidence to show any public knowledge of the breed. If the presence of these hounds had been known, surely some sporting Press of the day would have commented.

In 1874 Mr. (later Sir) Everett Millais, son of Sir John Millais, P.R.A., the eminent artist, purchased and imported a hound called Model from the *Jardin d'Acclimatation* in Paris. This hound was a tricolour, and was at stud at the *Jardin* with a hound called Fino de Paris. Both hounds were from the Le Couteulx kennels, and Millais was indeed fortunate in having the choice of the two finest Basset dogs in France. Model's vital statistics (compare with later hounds in a subsequent chapter) were at seven and a half years old:

Weight: 46 lb. Height at shoulder: 12 inches. Length from tip of nose to set of tail: 32 inches. Length of tail: 11½ inches. Girth of chest: 25 inches. Of loin: 21 inches. Of head: 17 inches. Of forearm: 6½ inches. Of muzzle at midway: 9½ inches. Length of head from tip of occiput to tip of nose: 9 inches. Length of ears from tip to tip: 19 inches. Height from ground between forefeet: 2¾ inches.

Millais said of Model: 'Rather flat in skull and having badly hung ears, but otherwise as perfect a specimen as I ever hope to see,' and he exhibited him at Wolverhampton in 1875, the first Basset to be publicly shown in Britain. It is due to Millais' perseverance that the breed became established and recognised in this country.

Millais was soon in difficulties due to the lack, or so he

C

thought, of other Bassets in Britain, and in order to breed had to resort to crossing Model with another breed. On the advice of Mr. Lort, a prominent judge, he chose the Beagle; the old-fashioned version of this hound had more points in common with the Basset than its present-day counterpart. The Basset–Beagle cross was apparently successful, and in the second generation produced a winning Basset. Millais said: 'Two generations I found quite sufficient to reduce the Beagle's legs to those of Bassets, plus the racial peculiarities.' He also explained why he had not imported new blood from France; apparently, being very young at the time, it had not occurred to him to do so, and as he possessed a considerable flair for improvisation, he had put this ability to the test.

The Basset-Beagle matings followed this course:

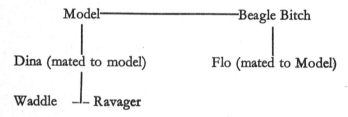

Ravager and Waddle resembled pure-bred Bassets, and both were successfully exhibited, especially Ravager.

Eventually the paths of Lord Onslow and Millais crossed and they were able to combine their breeding of Bassets. In 1877 Onslow imported two hounds from the Le Couteulx kennel, and with this influx of fresh blood Millais discarded his Beagle line and began breeding pure Bassets. Model was put to Onslow's Finette (litter mate of Fino, also owned by Onslow), and the mating produced Proctor and Garenne. The latter, a small tricolour, was given to Millais in lieu of a fee, and Proctor is thought to have been the first lemon and white hound bred in England.

Millais describes the continued breeding:

'Out of six litters Garenne had by her own father Model, I only reared three pups, namely Isabel, Model II and Vesta (Mr. Reg Temperley's). Garenne invariably threw her pups tail first and had difficulty in getting them away. Isabel and Vesta were lemon and whites, and the dog Model II was tricolour.'

Isabel was then sent to Onslow's Fino, and in 1879 produced Bratias, Ulfius, Kathleen, Niniche and Marie.

The year 1880 was a mixed one for Millais; he saw the first Basset class well supported at Wolverhampton, and the favourable reception given to the breed by the public. Unfortunately he was taken ill and, acting on medical advice, went to Australia. His kennel had to be disbanded, and it is also thought that the Onslow hounds were disposed of at that time.

Despite the setbacks due to Millais' partial retirement and Onslow's apparent lack of interest, 1880 was an eventful and important year. In the spring Mr. George Krehl, of Hanover Square, London, and Mr. Louis Clement (the author 'Wildfowler') imported a large and important draft from France. Not all the hounds are known, but details are known of:

Fino de Paris, bred by Le Couteulx and standing at stud in the *Jardin d'Acclimatation*. Tricolour. First brought to Krehl's notice when a report on his success at Brussels show appeared in *The Field*.

Jupiter (1878), bred by Le Couteulx, and known in France as Ch. Bosquet. Tricolour.

Guinevere, bred by Le Couteulx in 1878, and called Gibellote in France. Tricolour.

Pallas, also Le Couteulx-bred, and a tricolour.

Guinevere, and two other hounds in the draft, Théo and Vivien, were all descended from Fino de Paris in the following way:

Fino de Paris, being put to Trouvette and Ravaude, produced from them respectively Mignarde and Fanfaro. He was then put to his daughter Mignarde and produced Finette, who was put to a hound called Termino, and produced Guinevere and Théo, the latter bitch was mated back to Fanfaro and produced Vivien.

In view of their inbreeding to Fino de Paris, it was reasonable to suppose that the three bitches would resemble him in type. They did not, and had inherited the looks of their sire, and in the case of Vivien, of the grandsire, namely Termino. This brought about the existence of two distinct types of Bassets in the early days of the breed: the Fino de Paris type and the Termino. The Fino de Paris hounds took after their prototype and were large and heavy-boned, low to ground and extremely crooked (*torses*) in front; heavily marked tricolour, also lemon and white, and with harsh coat texture.

The Termino type were built on lighter lines, and did not have the substance or bone of the F.D.P. (Fino de Paris); front legs half crooked (*demi-torses*) and usually the head lacked the dignity of the F.D.P.; in colour usually light-marked tricolours or very pale lemon and white; coat short and fine.

Some details of Fino de Paris are known, but almost nothing of Termino, and it can only be supposed that Le Couteulx used him as an outcross to counteract the inbreeding of Fino de Paris.

Millais was not sure if Termino was a Basset! He says:

'What Termino was, or how he was bred, remains an unfathomable mystery, notwithstanding the fact that I have made every enquiry, but it appears to me reasonable to suppose that he was either a large Basset, *à jambes droites*, or one of the smaller *chien courants*, and for this reason the offspring Guinevere and Théo could hardly be called *Bassets à jambes torses*, while Vivien, got by one of Fino de Paris' sons, was correctly described as such.'

The Fino de Paris type attracted more attention and claimed the major awards at most shows, and it was Mr. Krehl who was almost solely responsible for supporting shows, and in his breeding for perpetuating the Fino de Paris type. Among the hounds produced by Fino de Paris were:

Jealousy, Baronne, Violet, Queen Dido, Hebe, all out of Juno.

Bourbon, Bijou and Fino V, all ex Guinevere and Mr. Krehl's Jupiter produced

Franco, Frou-Frou and Diana, all out of Vesta

Nemours, Childeric and Fleur de France, all out of Vivien.

Bourbon was mated to Vivien and produced:

Chopette and d'Augmale and Fino V and Vivien produced Fino VI.

Mr. Louis Clement's imports were bred from, and their progeny included:

Ramée put to Pasqueret produced Ramée Cadet, and the same Ramée, put to Hebe, produced Hebe II, Ramée II, Nichette and Niniche, and out of Finette II (Millais breeding) produced Bergère, Brunette, Loyalty and Sapphire.

In 1882 Mr. Krehl imported Blanchette and Oriflamme from the kennels of M. Louis Lane, of Château de Frangueville near Rouen. M. Lane had a kennel of great renown, equalled only by that of Le Couteulx. He had shown Clochette KCSB 12147 (Fino x Clairette) at the Crystal Palace 1881, and she had won. It is also on record that M. Lane refused an offer of 6,000 francs for a team of four hounds he exhibited at Brussels. In France the 'Lane type' hounds were in greater demand than the 'Le Couteulx' because they were considered to be of purer breeding. Early imports from Le Couteulx had shown the existence of two types within his kennel, namely the Fino de Paris and Termino, and French authors think Beagle blood was responsible. Millais thought possibly another larger *chien courant* breed. It is well known that Le Couteulx and his cousin De Caumont were adept at using other breeds as outcrosses. This seems to establish that the Le Couteulx Basset blood was not entirely pure.

There was no difference in types within the Lane kennels. The hounds were predominantly lemon and white or grey and white, generally bicolour, and a tricolour hound was rare. In build the Lane hounds were heavy, with much bone, and very low to ground, the front legs usually full-crooked (*torses*) or (half-crook) *demi-torses* and with a tendency to knuckle over. The head, to quote M. Verrier, was: 'Splendid, pale orange colour, admirably sculptured, adorned with superb ears, set low, curling and ending in a point.'

Despite their evident quality and purity the Lane hounds failed to gain much support in Britain. It was probably because their uniform colour lacked the glamour of the tricolours, and also their heavy conformation hindered the ability to hunt. It is not known if any pure Lane hounds were bred in Britain; certainly no evidence has come to light.

In 1884 Sir Everett Millais, his health restored, returned to Britain and, much to his surprise, found his old Model alive and well. The old hound had been living with friends of Millais in Yorkshire, and had grown obese. However, on his return to his master, he quickly returned to healthy fitness and was mated to his great-granddaughter Finette II and produced three tricolours—Lady Dolly, Lady Daisy and Kini. In great hopes of Model's evident fertility Millais then mated him to the Lane type, Blanchette, but unfortunately the mating was unsuccessful. It is thought that Model was fifteen or seventeen years old at the time.

With the welcome return of Millais the many Basset devotees felt confident of the breed's future progress, and in order to ensure its welfare the Basset Hound Club was formed in 1884. Among the early members were Millais, Le Couteulx, Lords Onslow and Galway, the Marquis of Coynynghame, Messrs. Krehl, Craven, Muirhead, Kennedy and Ramsay. Others who enrolled shortly after the formation included H.R.H. Princess Alexandra, Mesdames Ellis, Tottie, Lubbock, Walsh and Wimbush, and Messrs. Musson, Heseltine, Owen-Swaffield, Garnett, Jones, Wooton, Taylor, Roberts and Blain.

Needless to say the B.H.C. and the breed prospered under the auspices of such eminent people, and by 1886 the entries at shows had reached record figures. Millais judged the 120 Bassets entered at the Dachshund and Basset Show held at the Aquarium in London.

Gleaning from early records, it can be found that the early Bassets had been purchased by people attracted to them purely by their unique appearance, and the early stages of development showed that emphasis was on the establishment of a show-dog. Fortunately, however, the Basset did not escape the notice of British sportsmen, who were well aware of the hound's great sporting tradition. The *chasse à tir* hunting method did not appeal to British owners, and they therefore adapted the Basset to pack-hunting, and, like Beagles, running hare. In 1886 Mr. Miles B. Kennedy was hunting his pack around Cambridge, and in 1887 Mr. T. Cannon, Jnr., of Dansbury near Stockbridge, imported Cyda, Boulougau and

Ramette as a nucleus for his pack. The following year Major Crocker established a pack at West Brighton.

French sportsmen were sceptical of the success of the Basset's hunting as *chiens à chasse à Courre*, but experience should have taught them that the Basset is most adaptable and not at all perturbed by his quarry or new methods of hunting.

By 1886 the foundations were laid for what was to be one of the period's premier kennels, and the first of a long line to be owned and managed by a lady. Mrs. Ellis of Brettenham Park, Billesden, purchased her first Basset at the Warwick Show, a small tricolour bitch called Venus II, by Ch. Jupiter KCSB 12153 ex Venus, a daughter of Fino de Paris. In 1887 Venus was mated to Mr. Krehl's Fino VI (Fine V ex Vivien) a grandson of Fino de Paris, and she produced Ch. Psyche II KCSB 26074. This hound had a most spectacular show career and became a champion before her second birthday, and also before she was mated to Mr. Muirhead's Ch. Forester, bred by Mr. Craven of Bakewell. This line-breeding to Fino de Paris (Forester KCSB 21677, by Fino VI ex Medore, a granddaughter of Fino de Paris) produced Ch. Bowman, Ch. Paris, Ch. Xena, Napoleon II and Miriam. Repeating this successful mating, Mrs. Ellis produced Zero and Xitta.

Ch. Forester, a tricolour, was obviously a most prepotent sire, and Captain Godfrey Heseltine had very high praise for him: 'Forester is perhaps the finest Basset that ever lived, and the greatest sire.' His litter mates were Fresco, Flora and Merlin. The latter hound was exported to the Melbourne Hunt Club and died in Australia in 1892.

The greatest of Forester's progeny was undoubtedly his son Ch. Paris KCSB 30439, who was out of Ch. Psyche II KCSB 26074. Paris had a great show career and inherited his sire's ability to procreate his type, and he was the sire of the era's most prolific winners, Ch. Queen of the Geisha, ex Fair Star (1895) KCSB 235A, and Ch. Louis le Beau, ex Gravity (1889–97), and Ch. Lurline, a litter mate of Louis. Ch. Queen and Ch. Louis won twenty-one and eighteen K.C. Challenge Certificates respectively. Mrs. Mabel Tottie of Coniston Hall, Bell Busk, Hellifield, Yorkshire, owned Louis, and Mr. Stark owned Queen and Lurline. Queen later passed into the ownership of Mr. Proctor.

The most successful male line of descent can be traced back directly to Mr. Krehl's Fino de Paris; the inbreeding to this fine stallion produced the champions already mentioned plus Isola, and a great many other hounds of high quality. So obvious was Fino de Paris' influence that French visitors to Britain often stated that if they had known the capabilities of Fino de Paris he would not have left the *Jardin d' Acclimatation*.

As it has been clearly shown, the bulk of Britain's Bassets were very much inbred to Fino de Paris. Despite the high-quality hounds resulting from this breeding it was evident to Sir Everett Millais that twenty years of inbreeding was beginning to tell on the breed. New blood would have to be introduced before the state of affairs became too serious. To a certain extent degeneration had begun and previously absent hereditary traits had started to appear. Infertility, difficult whelpings, matings difficult to effect, and a loss of body size and substance were some of the unfortunate faults, but probably the greatest scourge, mental instability, also appeared. One that Millais had bred himself was described as 'a canine idiot' by its owner, Dr. Clifford Allbutt.

In 1892 Millais set about the task of rejuvenating the Basset. He had previous experience of crossing with another hound breed, the Beagle, and he knew that the outside influence could be bred out within a few generations. Greater size was needed, and the only British hound capable of supplying this was the Bloodhound, which also had some common factors with the Basset. Millais said:

'I therefore employed the Bloodhound as the vehicle for importing fresh blood to counteract the commencing degeneration on the part of the Basset, considering that this cross would be of infinitely greater value to us breeders than the importation would be of a number of French Bassets of the same variety, but of inferior type and size. . . . I may state at once that when we imported our Bassets from France, we imported the best that France possessed and notwithstanding degeneration, what we have in England is better than France can now offer us.'

Millais, however, was not the first person to cross Blood-hound and Basset; his friend Mr. Marsden of Leeds had suc-ceeded in producing a littler from such a union a few years previously. Commendable as Mr. Marsden's feat was, Millais considered it a futile mating because, as he said, 'the Blood-hound used was a diminutive weed and rickety', and because of the hereditary nature of this disease Millais did not think the resulting litter a sound enough basis for rebuilding the Basset.

The Bloodhound chosen was Inoculation (Chorister x Artemis), a sound bitch, but by all accounts a moderate speci-men. She was a litter sister of Protection.

The only Basset Millais owned at the time was Nicholas (Ch. Forester x Ch. Psyche II), very much inbred to Fino de Paris. Nicholas was tricolour, with a dark head and light-coloured body, very good legs and feet and an excellent chest. The head of Nicholas lacked some expression but his lip and skull furnishings were good. In fact, comparing him with his sire and dam, he appeals to the modern eye much more.

Millais was of the opinion that the great amount of in-breeding behind Nicholas would break up the Bloodhound influence fairly quickly, but he expected some of the progeny of the alliance would retain the dark Bloodhound colouring and thus be the forerunners of a new colour in the Basset. Results proved both his expectations well founded.

The first litter did in fact contain dark-coloured Basset types, and was also unique in being the first recorded instance of any of the higher mammalia being produced artificially and de-livered artificially. Twelve puppies were born by caesarian section, but unfortunately the bitch died, and, later, five of the puppies. Among the survivors were Ada, Rickey and Cromwell.

The second phase of the operations began with the mating of the half-cross Rickey and Ch. Forester, and the mating of the half-cross Cromwell to Juno IV, a pure Basset. Rickey produced puppies retaining the low Basset body structure and also the variegated tricolour markings. Juno IV's litter also regained the Basset conformation, but they were predomin-antly dark-marked like the Bloodhound. Re-mating on these lines proved that when a half-cross bitch was put to a Basset dog-hound she produced a great proportion of tricolour pups, and seldom dark-marked puppies. Conversely, when half-cross dogs were mated to Basset bitches, the litters always contained a superfluity of black and tan hounds. One such mating in the former category was Napoleon II to the half-cross Bella, which produced a hound of beautiful type called Belladonna, bred by Mrs. Tottie in 1895 and owned by Colonel Heseltine.

The third phase of the programme was the mating of Dulcie (Rickey, by Forester) to Ch. Bowman (Ch. Psyche II, by Forester). A puppy from the resulting litter was then mated to Guignol, a pure Basset. Six pups were born from the union; four were tricolours, one was lemon and white, and one was black and tan, and all were indistinguishable from pure-bred Bassets. Most important and apart from the break-up in colour, all the puppies had an abundance of bone and substance and were comparable to their illustrious ancestors, Fino de Paris, Paris and Forester. Throughout the experiments the latter hound had been in the mind of Millais, as he had wished to build up the new strain on the grand characteristics of Forester. The experimental breeding programme, courageously undertaken, had been an unqualified success and the desired objectives had been gained, as well as a new variation on Basset colour, the black and tan hound.

I doubt if many present-day breeders would ever think of emulating Millais' experiment should a similar situation arise today, and at that time there were those who resorted to more normal methods of obtaining new blood. Despite Millais' low opinion of the French hounds and his disregard of them, some did arrive in Britain in 1895. Mr. George Musson of Liverpool, a prominent member of the B.H.C. and a judge, imported Mastoc, a hound excelling in bone and body substance. M. Puissant of Cambrai sent eleven and a half couple over for sale at one of the British shows, and it is known that the best of these stayed in this country. The breed definitely benefited from the new sources of blood, Bloodhound and French importations, and the size so much desired by British breeders was increased and retained. The Bloodhound contributed most to the size increase, and the influence of that breed is probably the reason why the British Basset is to this day larger than its French counterpart.

The standard of excellence being adhered to at that time was the one drawn up by Krehl and contained the unfortunate specification: 'that the head of the Basset to be ideal should closely resemble that of the Bloodhound'. I say 'unfortunate' because I believe that this specification led British breeders to put too much emphasis on head points, until the head did closely resemble the Bloodhound, and the original noble skull and expression of the Basset become rare. Also, I know of no other breed whose Standard refers to other breeds' points as being desirable.

The Basset Hound Club in 1895 had Millais as secretary, and the club's approved judges were Messrs. Blain of Bromborough, Craven of Bakewell, Garnett of Bolton, Jones of Ipswich, Krehl of London, Musson of Liverpool, Wootton of Oxford, Taylor of Manchester, Roberts of Leeds, Owen-Swaffield of Ilchester and Mrs. Ellis of Billesden.

Showing Bassets was still a more popular pastime than hunting, and entries at shows in the 1895–1900 period averaged fifty. Three packs were hunting: the Walhampton near Lymington, and the Wintershill and the Wolvercote around Bishop's Waltham. The prominent breeders and exhibitors other than those already referred to were Mrs. Walsh, Mrs. Lubbock and Mrs. Tottie. The latter lady, wife of the prominent ornithologist, owned and bred many excellent hounds, including Champions Louis le Beau and Lurline, Napoleon II, Solomon, Sibella KCSB 13C and Dolores. This last hound, by Nicholas ex Gravity, was considered by her owner to be the best bitch she ever bred. Mrs. Tottie was most fortunate in having Gravity (Ch. Forester ex Gruenberg), an excellent brood bitch; she produced more of the period's winners than any other dam. Sibella mated to Ch. Louis le Beau produced Ch. Loo Loo Loo, later purchased by Mr. White of Derby.

Mr. Arthur Croxton-Smith of London was given Witch (Juno IV by Nicholas) by Millais, and she was mated to Ch. Louis le Beau, and produced a fantastic litter containing Champions Welbeck, Wantage and Wensum. Mrs. Tottie

added Wensum to her kennels. Croxton-Smith paid tribute to
Millais' generosity by stating, 'He was a true amateur and never
sold a hound.'

Mrs. Tottie had an interest in the Griffon Vendeen Basset
and owned Champions Tambour and Pervenche, which she
had purchased in 1892 at Cruft's, where they had been sent
from France to be sold. These hounds produced for Mrs.
Tottie Champion Puritan and Priscilla, whelped 6 February
1897. Puritan was of such excellence that he was a champion
by 5 January 1898. Other supporters of this lesser known
(in Britain) variety were Mr. Lawrence of Cambridge and
Mr. Gerrish. Both gentlemen were veteran breeders, and
Mr. Lawrence had great success with Rosebery before his
kennel was wiped out by distemper. The same tragedy ended
Mr. Gerrish's kennels. Mrs. Ellis reckoned the Griffons not as
hardy as the smooth-coated Bassets, and that is perhaps why
they did not attract more breeders. Although this charming
breed will be dealt with in a later chapter, a very brief summary
concerning its introduction into Britain should perhaps be
given here.

As far as can be ascertained by records, the first owners of
Vendeen Bassets in Britain were Dr. Seton and the Rev. J. C.
Macdona of West Kirby, Cheshire. The latter owned the well-
known hound Romano 8807 KCSB. In 1881 Mr. G. Ramsay
of Bray showed his imports Rallie KCSB 12167 and Ramée
KCSB 12168 at Alexandra Palace.

H.R.H. Princess Alexandra was a lover of Bassets, both
roughs and smooths, and kept a prominent kennel at Sandring-
ham. The rough-coated hounds were probably better known
than the Sandringham smooths and they were exhibited often.
Among the best known were Sandringham Vero, Valens,
Valour and Vanity. The smooths included S. Babs, S. Babil,
S. Weaver and S. Warrender (Ch. Waverer ex S. Pamela) and
S. Dido (Tarquin ex Viola).

The Royal Clumber Spaniels, favourites of H.R.H. the
Prince of Wales, were also kennelled at Sandringham, and they
have been blamed for a fault arising in Bassets from time to
time. Occasionally a Basset puppy is born with a long, fine-

textured coat and feathering on legs, tail and ears. They are
definitely not rough coats, the texture of which is very harsh
and wiry. Many present-day breeders think that the faulty coat
is the legacy of a mating, intentional or accidental, between a
Clumber Spaniel and a Basset Hound in the Sandringham
kennels. There is no proof whatsoever to support this theory,
but it is a feasible one. Hounds having this soft, long coat have
been bred from, in attempts to determine the extent of the
influence of the coat texture, and also in attempts to establish
a race of Bassets with this coat. One fact has emerged from
these breedings: on no occasion has a long-coated hound, dog
or bitch, produced its likeness.

Mrs. Walsh, Miss Wimbush and Mrs. Lubbock were staunch
supporters of the breed, and Mrs. Lubbock, of 'Bassets', Farn-
borough, owned two good stud hounds, Lucifer (Wantage
KCSB 99D ex Lucy KCSB 1091F) and Locksley (Ch. Bowman
ex maid Marion). Mrs. Walsh bred Ch. Bowman.

By 1900 the Basset Hound had been in Britain thirty-four
years, and had become very well established, and recognised as
a unique breed of dual-purpose hound. The rough-coated
hounds had never enjoyed public favour, and the smooth-
coated Artois-Norman type had became known to the general
population as the true breed of Basset Hound. As far as the
hound in Britain was concerned, this was not strictly accurate,
because the 'true breed' had been twice adulterated by Beagle
and then Bloodhound stock, and the resulting progeny had
developed on different lines from the breed in France. The
British had drawn up a standard compiled to suit the 'low-
legged Bloodhound' type, and this has been adhered to ever
since, with recent sensible modifications. Although the appearance had been altered, the hunting ability of the Basset remained unchanged, and fortunately the British type retained
all the characteristics and instincts of a true hound.

The British Basset was based on a 'nucleus *par excellence*'; the
early fanciers purchased the very best hounds, and we modern
breeders owe much to their shrewdness and to the great work
of Sir Everett Millais. His only motive for the experiments was
the welfare and improvement of the Basset Hound.

Pedigrees of some of the principal hounds referred to in this chapter. (Where possible I have given colours and Kennel Club Stud Book (KCSB) numbers).

CLOCHETTE ── FINO x CLAIRET
Basset. Lane Type. KCSB 12147.

CH. FORESTER
KCSB 21677. Tricolour
- Fino IV
  - Fino V ── Fino de Pari
  - Vivien
- Medore
  - Ch. Bourbon ── Fino de Pari
  - Cigarette

CH. BOWMAN
CH. PARIS
- Ch. Forester
- Ch. Psyche II

CH. PSYCHE II
KCSB 26074
- Fino VI
- Venus II

CH. GRAVITY
- Ch. Forester
- Gruenberg
  - Bourbon
  - Fama

CHAMPIONS   WANTAGE
            WELBECK
            WENSUM
- Ch. Louis le Beau
- Witch
  - Nicholas
    - Ch. Forester
    - Ch. Psyche II
  - Juno IV

CH. LOUIS LE BEAU
CH. LURLINE
- Ch. Paris
- Ch. Gravity (1889-1897)

CH. QUEEN OF THE GEISHA
Tricolour
- Ch. Paris
- Fair Star. (1895) KCSB 235A.

LOCKSLEY
- Ch. Bowman
  - Ch. Forester
  - Ch. Psyche II
- Maid Marion
  - Ch. Forester
  - Soumise

Pedigree of Nicholas, the hound used by Sir Everett Millais in his series of crossings to improve the Basset Hound.

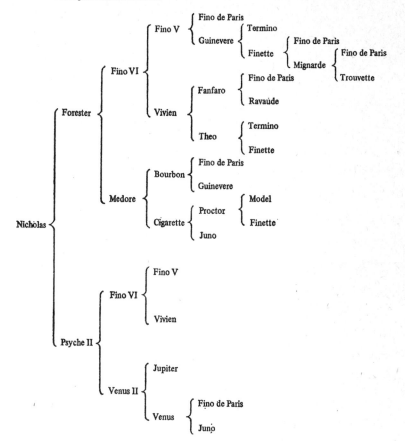

3

The Basset Hound in Britain
Since 1900

FROM the British point of view this is probably the most important chapter in the book, as it outlines the breed's development and the influence of the clubs and certain breeders between the years 1900 and 1966. It is not a difficult task to extend the pedigree of any present-day British hound to the point where it contains the names of many of the hounds mentioned in the first half of this chapter. Many breeds cease to be influenced by any ancestors if they are more than three or four generations back, but not so the Basset, where the present is very much controlled by the past.

By the turn of the century the Basset was in a fairly strong position and was being kept for companionship as well as for exhibition and hunting. Canine authors of the period were high in their praise of the breed, and it was especially recommended for ladies, being so gentle and docile.

In 1900 the Walhampton pack of Godfrey and Geoffrey Heseltine was the only active established pack, but they were joined soon after by Colonel Reynardson of Stamford and Mr. Vincent Eyre of Nuneaton. Two packs were also formed by ladies, the Knowlton by Miss Gladys Peto of Canterbury, and the Chiddingstone by the Misses Denny of Chiddingstone Castle in Kent.

The breed was popular on the show bench and the early exhibitors had a curious habit of putting very high prices on their hounds. Mrs. Tottie had five hounds entered at the 1900 Birmingham National Show priced at £10,000 each! Of course there was never any intention of selling any of the hounds, but for Mr. Croxton-Smith the scheme backfired when his Ch. Wantage (Ch. Louis Le Beau x Witch) was claimed by Mrs.

Thomas Fall

Ch. Monkshood of Reynalton, 1935

Thomas Fall

Ch. Grims Warlock, 1946

Grims Ulema de Barly, 1946

Ch. Grims Willow, 1951 and Ch. Grims Useful, 1950

Tottie at Cruft's for £150. She already owned Wantage's litter sister, Ch. Wensum.

In 1902 the old pillar of the breed, Ch. Louis Le Beau, died aged eleven. He was a direct descendant of the original imports, and as a stud dog had done much for the breed. He had won fourteen C.C.s in his show career.

Another show-bench star, Mr. Proctor's tricolour Ch. Queen of the Geisha '98 (Paris [1889] x Fair Star [1895]) was proving virtually unbeatable, and between 1899 and 1905 she won eighteen C.C.s and set up a record that was to stand for over fifty years. Geisha was quite large (fifty-three pounds) and had a lovely expressive head and long sweep of body. Mrs. Ellis, another breeder, considered her rather stilted in hind-action.

In 1907 Queen Alexandra's Sandringham Dido (Tarquin x Viola) qualified for the championship and went on to win six C.C.s. She was bred by Tarquin's owner, Colonel Annand. Other smooth hounds in the Sandringham kennels at that time were Flora '97 (Zero [1891] x Saracenesca [1894]); Lockey '99 (Locksley [1895] x Saracenesca). Flo (Ch. Wantage '98 x Flora). Medora (1904) (Ch. Loo Loo Loo [1901] x Flo); Loo (1906) (Ch. Loo Loo Loo x Flo); and Zero (1909) (Lockey x Medora). The tricolour bitch Saracenesca (Saracen [1893] '93 x Juniper [1889]) was line-bred to Bourbon (1882) and she proved herself a great force in the Queen's kennel. Locksley (1895) (Bowman [1892] x Maid Marion [1891]) was a big, ugly ungainly dog, but he was an excellent sire and produced many fine hounds.

Mr. W. W. White owned the tricolour Ch. Loo Loo Loo (Louis Le Beau x Sibella) who was bred by Mrs. Tottie, and he had a good show career, winning eight C.C.s. Sir Maurice Bromley-Wilson of Dallam Towers, Milnthorpe, had established a small pack, and he had good success in the show ring with Waverer (1904) (Major x Daisy, both unregistered), whom he had obtained from Mr. Croxton-Smith. Waverer won nine C.C.s between 1908 and 1912 and he was the sire of Queen Alexandra's only home-bred champion, the tricolour Ch. Sandringham Warrender 1910, out of Sandringham Pamela. In 1913 the brothers J. P. and W. Roberts had an excellent year

D

and qualified two hounds, both tricolours, called Melanie (1907) (Ch. Loo Loo Loo x Mirette) and her son Mentor (1910) who was by Waverer. Mirette's pedigree is unknown and some students think she may have been an unregistered French import. She is behind some of the early Walhampton hounds in the following way: when mated to Ch. Loo Loo Loo in 1907 she also produced Mimi, who when mated to Sandringham Zero produced Walhampton Merryman (1911); mated in 1910 to Sandringham Loo she produced Walhampton Lydia.

The Basset Hound Club revised its rules in 1905, and the following amendments were made. The objects of the club were: 'To promote breeding of pure smooth-coated and rough-coated Basset Hounds'. The club's membership was somewhat restricted by a new amendment stating: 'That any respectable person favourable to the object of the club be eligible for membership, except professional dealers. That ladies be eligible for membership.' The worthy members also increased the membership fee to two guineas.

Instead of paying attention to the rules and regulations the B.H.C would have been better occupied by trying to rejuvenate a declining breed. The breed definitely began to deteriorate in quality, stamina and mental health. Mr. Claude Morrison of Chiddingly was one prominent breeder who expressed concern about the state of the breed, and he said, 'The lesson does not seem to have been learned that the Basset needs an outcross every four generations.' Morrison's best-known hounds were Clarion (Ch. Bowman [1892] x Dollie) and Pilgrim (Ch. Locksley [1895] x Maid Marion [1891]).

The secretary of the Basset Hound Club, George Musson, thought the decline of his club and breed was a result of inbreeding. Mrs. Tottie and Mrs. Lubbock, the well-known breeders, regarded the state of the breed with concern, and the latter lady attributed it to the impossibility of buying in fresh stock from France owing to the recent quarantine rule and the breed's lack of improvement in its homeland. Prior to the quarantine regulations French breeders had sent drafts over regularly to be shown and then sold; one of the last to do so was M. Puissant of Mibres le Château.

Mr. Barton, a well-known hound judge of the period, actually tabulated the problems facing Basset Hound breeders. As he saw it the problems were:

1. To preserve true hound characteristics.
2. To prevent loss of bone and substance.
3. To keep the fore-limbs close to the chest wall and to preserve quality of crook.
4. To preserve the massive feet and claws.

To counteract these problems Barton advised breeders to buy from France before it became too late to save the Basset. Hounds were becoming increasingly sterile, and any litters that were born succumbed in alarming numbers to distemper and hardpad. The Heseltines had some bad luck with raising puppies, and two northern kennels, those of the Rev. W. Shields and Miss E. Brown, both of Whittingham, were wiped out.

Unlike most of his contemporaries Godfrey Heseltine did not blame the breed's troubles on inbreeding; he considered that there were plenty of sources of blood but that the deterioration was due to 'lack of knowledge, care, and suitable matching on the part of the breeders of Basset Hounds'. Up to that time the Heseltines had not shown much and their work had been in blending together and upgrading to a high pitch their Walhampton pack. It had a high reputation in the field and the quality of the hounds was well known. They were well qualified to pass judgment and had been amazed at the unsoundness of many show-bench hounds. So incensed were they by the attitude of the Basset Hound Club, which seemed to condone the show-bench hound, that they resigned from the club and shortly afterwards were instrumental in forming the Masters of Basset Hounds Association. Owners of other packs who supported the new club included the Rt. Hon. Dudley Carlton, Lord North, Valentine Fleming, M.P., and Colonel Burns-Hartopp, a former Master of the Quorn Hunt.

The show hound was still being supported by Queen Alexandra and by Mesdames Tottie, Ellis, Wimbush and Messrs. Stark, Kenyon-Fuller, Dalton, Parrot and Woodhouse, who bred Geraldine, a well-known pre-1900 winner.

With the exception of the Queen, no Basset Hound Club 'show-minded' member was allowed to exhibit at M.B.H.A. events. The Queen regularly competed at Banbury and she showed there at the last show held before the outbreak of the First World War. Others who took entries to the same show were Mr. Ivon Jones of Sidcup, who had the Fairworth pack, Mr. Towgood of St. Neots with his Riversfield hounds, Miss D. Ismay of Blandford with her Iwerne Minster entries, and Valentine Fleming, M.P., who had purchased the Greywell Hill pack from Dudley Carlton.

The winner of the 1914 show was Dalby Hall Dorchester (1909), an unregistered hound bred by Dudley Carlton. He was described as 'one of the handsomest Bassets of modern times'. He sired Dreadnought (1912) (x Delicate) who, with Dalby Hall Nimrod (1913), Dallam Towers Saladin and Major Fleming's Chancellor, was one of the best-known M.B.H.A. stallions. Dreadnought sired Walhampton Lively (1918).

Almost all showing and hunting was curtailed during the war years (1914–18), although Queen Alexandra had shown roughs and smooths at Crufts in 1916 under Mr. Croxton-Smith. Lord North continued to hunt his Wroxton Abbey hounds; he virtually kept open house and provided, with his little pack, some welcome recreation for soldiers on leave from the front. The Wroxton Abbey hounds were small and active and full of drive, and they had much of Dorchester's blood in them, as well as Saladin, Chancellor and Walhampton Musket. These sires produced some good Wroxton hounds, including Nobleman and Normandy, Wallflower and Woodman.

Lord North was the secretary and first president of the M.B.H.A. and a true sportsman who hunted with hounds until he was over ninety. His pack was finally disbanded in 1933, most of the hounds going to Scotland.

The working Basset was depleted by the war, but the show hound fared worse and during the years 1914–18 only nine hounds were registered with the Kennel Club. The Basset Hound Club was just hanging on, with the secretary, Mrs. Ellis, doing all she could to save it. The post-war years brought no respite to the show hound; 1920 saw only two registrations, and at that year's Kennel Club Show only a couple of hounds, Melody and Melodious (litter mates by Sandringham Bugler x Rosevern unregistered), were shown by Mr. W. E. Waterhouse of Sutton near Hull.

Queen Alexandra and Godfrey Heseltine showed in 1921; the latter entered three hounds at the Kennel Club Show. For the Basset Hound Club it was the end of the road; the affairs of the club were wound up and, as events had it, lay dormant for a third of a century. The club had not really exercised any influence on the breed or its breeders for about ten years before its demise, and the natural decrease in hounds and showing brought about by the war had only speeded up the ending that was inevitable. Although any breed naturally suffers without guidance from a strong club, nothing is lost if the club is weak and self-centred. The Basset Hound therefore did not really miss the club; in fact the years immediately following the closure were years of activity and importance in the Basset's development.

The Heseltines made a valuable contribution to the breed when they imported a couple of hounds from the French authority M. Léon Verrier of Mont Saint-Aignan. Heseltine and Verrier, who wrote the classic *Les Bassets Français* in 1921, had corresponded and reached the conclusion that an exchange of stock would be beneficial. Heseltine consequently purchased Meteor (1921) (Favourite [1919] x Minervi) and Pampeute (1920) (Farceur [1914] x Gavotte). The two sires, Favourite and Farceur, were litter-brothers and had been bred by M. Mallart of Barly.

Both hounds were very much used by Heseltine and are behind almost every Walhampton champion. In 1923 the Dalby Hall kennel made use of an import called Vanette, about which nothing is known. The new influx of blood did much to cure the legacy of the previous decade, and the Basset, against all odds, entered into a modest renaissance; the registrations in 1924 were more than doubled to twenty, and, what was even more encouraging, some new kennels were founded. Mrs. Foster-Rawlins of Farnham, a prominent Dandie Dinmont Terrier breeder (she bred Ch. Potford Highlander and

Ch. Potford Plunderer), added Bassets to her noted kennel, and purchased Zillah (1921) (Walhampton Gilroy 15 x Walhampton Zea unregistered). She was mated to Major Heseltine's Walhampton Linguist (1921) and her resultant litter contained Ragout (1924). He won a third at Cruft's in 1925 but achieved permanent recognition by being chosen as a model for a ceramic statuette made by the Danish firm of Dahl-Jensen.

There were twenty-three registrations in 1925, and the first Walhampton hound qualified for its championship; this was Walhampton Andrew 20.6.22 (Walhampton Ferryman [1917] x Walhampton Actress unregistered). The pack had achieved great success in the field and had begun to enter the show ring much more. At this point some words about the formation of the Walhampton dynasty may be of interest.

The Heseltines had obtained their first Bassets in 1890 from Captain Peacock, M.F.H., and later the nucleus was augmented by the purchase of nine and a half couple from Mr. T. Cannon, Jnr., of Dansbury, the son of Mornington Cannon of racehorse fame. In 1891 the Heseltines began hunting badger in the New Forest, but in September of the same year they changed to hunting the hare and remained on this quarry until the pack's dispersal in 1933. In the early days the pack was devoted almost solely to hunting, and the only time they showed was in 1895 at Liverpool, when Coquette won her class.

In 1896 Major Ferguson died and the Heseltines took over his pack of fifteen couple. In August of that year Prince Henry of Pless made a present to them of ten couple from his pack in Germany. The Heseltines kept on buying up the disbanding packs, choosing only the best few couple from each to add to their own. One such pack was that of Mr. B. W. Duff-Assheton-Smith of Bangor, North Wales.

For a while, during the Heseltines' service overseas, the pack was in Ireland with the Marquis of Conynghame of Slane, Co. Meath. They were not alone in hunting in Ireland, because two other Basset packs were active; those of Mr. Baylay of Monte, Co. Westmeath and of Major Kemmis of Portarlington, Co. Leix.

The Walhampton pack was kennelled first at Lymington, moving later to Billericay before finally settling at Lutterworth in Leicestershire. Their masters, Geoffrey and Godfrey Heseltine, were great sportsmen, especially the latter, who was a winner of many point-to-point races, and was Master of the Essex Union and Ootacamund Foxhounds. He was also much respected as a judge of hunters, polo ponies and, of course, Bassets. He was found shot dead at his home in August 1932.

The success of Andrew seemed to be the signal for the beginning of the Walhampton's period of show-ring domination, and in 1926 Gratitude 23.6.24 (Walhampton Linguist [1921] x W. Grizel [1921]) qualified for her championship. At that year's Cruft's Show Heseltine, following the custom of former Basset exhibitors, put large prices on his six entries, and W. Arthur and Gratitude were priced at £700 each, W. Arabel £300, W. Lymington £100, W. Grasshopper £150 and W. Grizel £200. There was one difference between Heseltine and his high-pricing predecessors—he actually got the prices he asked, or almost, because in 1929 Lymington was sold to the Maharajah of Alwar for £70.

Miss Ena Adams, daughter of Norman Adams, M.F.H., of Brancaster, founded her kennel of Bassets in 1927. Her father was a well-known hound judge and travelled extensively in France looking for good hounds. He had little time for the show-type Basset and had this to say: 'Nowhere in France did I see the shockingly deformed knock-kneed forelegs and cow-hocked standing under hind-legs to which the show bench of England has reduced our English Basset. What I did see were various packs of the *grand chien de chasse*, and French Masters of Basset Hounds told me that the Basset had been bred down from these hounds, and I feel sure that is so.' Miss Adams bred low-set hounds at the outset, but gradually increased the height of her back to eighteen inches when, of course, they ceased to be Basset Hounds. She bred Amant (Walhampton Lyndhurst [1924] x Walhampton Apricot [1924]), later registered as Brancaster Amant [1926]. He was a popular stallion, being used by the most noted breeders at that time. Miss Adams sold a couple of low-set hounds to Mrs. Nina Elms of Andover and thus established her in the breed. The hounds were Rob Roy 30.12.28 (Dindon x Bounty, both unregistered) and Rosabel 16.1.29 (Amant x Dimity unregistered). Mrs. Elms added to her own prefix and showed the first Reynalton Bassets in 1929. She also owned Wroxton Midshipman (1926) (Wroxton Marmaduke x Dalby Hall Daffodil) who was bred by Lord North.

Mrs. Edith Grew, then of Parkstone, had had Bassets as a child, and in 1928 began to take an active interest in showing. In 1930 she purchased an unregistered brace of Walhamptons, Ambassador 7.5.28 (W. Lymington [1926]) x W. Amber [1927]), a tricolour, but described by Mrs. Grew as being 'mostly tan and white', and Patience 9.2.29 (W. Lingerer [1928] x W. Pardon [1927]). When shown with Walhampton Lynnewood at the 1930 M.B.H.A. show at Banbury, Ambassador and he won the Challenge Prize for the Best Couple of Entered Dog-hounds. Mrs. Grew registered her purchases with the Kennel Club and they had a meteoric rise to their championships in 1931, becoming the first champions in the breed since 1926. In 1931 Mrs. Grew won the 'double' twice, at Brighton and Cruft's, where Ambassador went on to be the Fourth Best-in-Show all breeds.

Patience whelped only one litter, nine puppies to Amir of Reynalton 4.9.29 (Brancaster Amant [1926] x Dignity of Lohaire). Mrs. Grew also owned the heavily mottled tricolour Walhampton Nicknack 22.5.29 (Brancaster Amant x Wal-hampton Ninon [1928]). Ambassador and Patience were fre-quently shown and on almost every occasion beat the many entries of their breeder. Mrs. Grew tried to gain some support for the revival of the Basset Hound Club, and she kept the breed's activities before the public eye by her regular column in the *Dog World*. Her colleague on the *Our Dogs* staff was Mr. Will Hally of Auchterarder and he, too, was constantly beseeching Basset owners to re-form the club.

Miss E. Rumball of Warlingham was another keen sup-porter of the shows and she had the Archdale prefix. Mr. A. P. Fraser had the Of Lohaire hounds, and he owned Dignity and Laval 1.4.27 (Fearless x Lavender) who were bred by Miss

Ena Adams. The latter hound won the C.C. at Richmond in 1933.

In 1932 Heseltine qualified the beautiful Walhampton Lynnewood 22.5.28 (W. Musket [1925] x the unregistered W. Lyric [1923]) and he was the only hound to gain a title in that year. It was a very sad year for the breed with the tragic death of Heseltine at Lutterworth. Some of his pack was auctioned at the L.K.A. show that year and Mr. G. Fearing took Walhampton Abbot, Dipper and Lawless back to the U.S.A. The Dalby Hall pack also exported Dormouse, Vanda and Willow. The results of this auction at a dog show were very disappointing and the sale of the main section of Walhampton hounds was held over for a while.

Mrs. Godfrey Heseltine showed some of her late husband's hounds at Cruft's in 1933, and the pack was actually hunted in the season 1932–3 by Miss Mary Mills. The Cruft's judge, Mr. Harding Cox, awarded the C.C.s to Mrs. Heseltine's Walhampton Grazier 23.4.29 (W. Arthur [1925] x Ch. W. Gratitude [1924]) and Mrs. Grew's tricolour bitch Nicotine 8.1.32. Shortly after this success the rest of the famous pack came under the hammer at the Leicester Hound Sale on 19 May 1933. The response was very poor and the prices paid ridiculously low, averaging only £3. Mrs. Grew paid the day's highest price for Grazier, the sire of Walhampton Nightshade, and Mrs. Elms bought several, including Ch. Lynnewood, Nightshade 28.6.30 (x W. Nicknack), Gravity, Waspish and Gracchus, who had won his class at Cruft's a few months before.

Some of Lord Tredegar's Bassets and Beagles were sold at the same sale.

Mrs. Elms was fortunate to obtain Lynnewood and Nightshade. Heseltine had considered the former the best Basset he had ever bred; he was a heavy-made hound with lots of bone. Nightshade had a lovely head but was not quite as good in front as Lynnewood. She was also fairly heavily mottled on her chest. The couple were mated, and the litter, born 9.12.33, contained Orpheus, Venus, Narcissus and Neptune, and the hare-pied coloured Minerva. By any standards it was a remarkable litter because all except Neptune became champions. Narcissus was owned by Viscountess Chelmsford and qualified for her title in 1938, the last pre-war champion.

Lynnewood was mated to Waspish and the litter contained the winning hound Worthy of Reynalton 9.11.33. Other hounds produced by Mrs. Elms at this time included Digby, Levity, Belladonna and Juno, who was owned by Mrs. Phyllis Salisbury who also owned the Salismore Dandie Dinmont Terriers. Mrs. Salisbury is a niece of Mr. Croxton-Smith, and her daughter, Mrs. Hall Parlby of Sherborne, owns the Huckworthy Bassets today.

Nightshade qualified for her championship in 1933, and in the same year Mrs. Grew mated her parents Grazier and Nick-nack, the litter born 9 October containing Pigeon and Plover, both of whom became champions. Both hounds were very heavily mottled, but it is difficult to say where they inherited the colour, as their ancestry contained not only Walhampton blood but also that of Dalby Hall, Dallam Towers, Wick, Sandringham and the imported French hounds.

Mrs. Elms repeated the Lynnewood-Nightshade mating, which produced a very sound hound who became Ch. Monks-hood of Reynalton, and Nightshades Majesty, Nightshades Myola, and Dulcamera, who was the first hound owned by Miss Peggy Keevil in 1935. The litter brother and sister Orpheus and Venus were mated, this combination producing a beautiful lemon and white hound Velvet, who, before the war cut short her career, won several Reserve C.C.s, and the C.C. at Brighton in 1938.

As well as keeping Bassets at her home, Fyfield Grange near Andover, Mrs. Elms also maintained a large kennel of Beagles and Bloodhounds, the latter being her favourites and having priority. Breeding the large hounds is a skilful occupation, but Mrs. Elms seemed to have no trouble at all in rearing them and Bassets, and the Reynalton hounds were well endowed with massive bone. She had a great love of the lemon and white Bassets and many hounds of that colour today can trace back to the Reynaltons, especially the Trumpeter of Reynalton line. Mrs. Elms made massive entries at shows and an entry of sixty Reynaltons was not unknown. In Bloodhounds she bred Ch. Leo, Marksman, Brigadier and General and the Champion Beagles Bauble and Bellman.

Plover, the hound bred by Mrs. Grew, was owned by Mrs. E. Robinson of Whitstable and he won the C.C. at the 1936 Cruft's Golden Jubilee Show (which attracted an overall entry of 10,650). Plover gained his title in the same year, but his reign was cut short when he was run over by a train shortly afterwards. Three other champions died in 1936, Chs. Patience, Lynnewood and Nightshade.

Maybush Musket 28.8.36 (Draco x Nicotine) was another fine hound whose show career, like Mrs. Elm's Velvet, was curtailed by the outbreak of the Second World War. Bred by Mrs. Grew, he was certainly heading for top honours. In 1937 he won his class at Cruft's under Colonel Geoffrey Heseltine; Mrs. Elms awarded him the C.C. there the following year and also the Special Prize for the darkest-eyed hound, and Mr. Croxton-Smith gave him his second C.C. at Brighton. Strange to say, this prominent tricolour hound was never photographed.

Musket was shown at the 1938 Kennel Club Show, where the Basset judge, the Rt. Hon. Lord Porchester, caused a sensation by withholding both Challenge Certificates despite a high-quality entry including two champions. In bitches the winner 'sans C.C' was Viscountess Chelmsford's Ch. Narcissus of Reynalton, and Miss Keevil's Marquis 1937 (Westerby Luton x Westerby Mermaid) collected the dog honours. Marquis was descended from Walhampton and Brancaster stock. The other breed champion present at this eventful show was Mrs. Grew's Pigeon. The action of Lord Porchester was loudly condemned by the Basset fraternity because his reason for the action was a lack of quantity, not quality. Will Hally, the *Our Dogs* contributor, said at the time: 'If this were the case, Basset Hounds would never win Certificates at all, as last week's total of seven individual exhibits from three kennels was not at all a bad average in this breed. Besides, the award of a Challenge Certificate is based solely on merit and has not even the remotest connection with numbers or the lack of them.'

The following year Mr. Holland Buckley withheld the bitch C.C. and some other awards at the L.K.A. The sole C.C. awarded was won by Debonaire, a dog who had been a consistent winner for his breeder, Miss M. A. Swann of Hayling Island. Her other winning hound Draco, 27.1.35 (Walhampton Grazier x Destinée) was the runner-up. The lowlier dog awards and all bitch class awards were withheld.

Although there is usually more to be said for withholding C.C.s than against it, there does not seem to have been any logic behind the actions of the two eminent judges, and the Basset neither gained nor lost anything by it.

In 1939 my late father purchased a couple of Reynalton hounds from Mrs. Elms, but on the outbreak of war they were sent 'home' to Andover at their breeder's request. She retained stock and actually bred during the war years, and so did Mrs. Grew and Miss Keevil, but all on a small scale. The war also affected the hunting establishments, and the only two Basset packs to survive hostilities were the Scalford Hall of Colonel Colman and the Westerby (succeeding pack to the Walhampton) of Lieutenant-Colonel E. F. S. Morrison. These two packs had absorbed most of the hounds from Mr. Mellor's pack and those of Eastington Park and Willoughby, all disbanded during the war.

Mrs. Grew, owing to ill-health, did not breed after the war, but until her death in January 1963 kept a very active interest in the breed and was a founder member of the revived Basset Hound Club. Her last hound appears to have been Grims Upstart 1950.

Miss Keevil of Inkpen, near Newbury, had established her Grims kennel before the war, and apart from having Marquis and Dulcamera of Reynalton, she owned Walhampton Medway (W. Lightheart x W. Meanwell) sometimes known as Merman (1932), Wick Welcome (Wick Warlike x Walhampton Wary) and Labram (1937) (Westerby Lamport x Wick Welcome). These hounds were the nucleus of what was to become the most influential kennel of the post-war era. In 1940 Marquis and Wick Welcome produced a litter, one of which became Ch. Grims Wishful 14.5.40, and also contained Worship, who when mated to Grims Waspish (Victor of Reynalton x Ch. Grims Wishful) produced Ch. Grims Warlock 26.9.46 and a very useful hound called Wizard. Grims Daisy was mated to Westerby Rennet (Willoughby Roderick x Eastington Park Restless) and she produced the fine Ch. Grims Doughnut and the grand bitch Deidre 11.8.47. Doughnut sired Ch. Grims Waterwagtail 30.4.49 (ex Grims Watercress).

All these champions had been produced from pure British stock (the only remote outcross being the blood of Meteor and Pampeute some twenty years before) which was unfortunately all interrelated and low in numbers. Once again the breed in Britain faced its recurrent danger, inbreeding. Fits were not uncommon, and the undesirable long coat cropped up among litters. Some puppies in a litter by Labram x Dulcamera had the long coat, and Grims Daisy (Medway x Dulcamera) produced long-coated puppies to Labram, Rennet and Victor of Reynalton. About long coats Miss Keevil said, 'Another trouble which I expect we have not seen the last of,' and, of course, since then there have been occasional crops of long-coated hounds to which I will draw attention later.

Once again the obvious answer to the problem was outcross blood, and Miss Keevil was exceedingly fortunate to find and purchase in France a trio of excellent hounds, all Artois-Norman, of course. By far the most important of Miss Keevil's purchases was a magnificent young stallion Ulema De Barly (1946) (Sans Souci De Bourceville x Querelle De Barly), bred and owned by M. Mallart of Barly in the Somme. M. Mallart, one of France's oldest established breeders, had shown Ulema successfully and he was also a prepotent sire. Considering the precarious position of the breed in France after the war, it is surprising, looking in retrospect, that Miss Keevil was able to buy any hounds at all, let alone good ones. On her first visit Miss Keevil also bought a tricolour bitch Cornemuse De Blendecques (Tayau x Vistule) (1946) from M. Paul Leduc of Blendecques, Pas de Calais. This bitch is sometimes shown in pedigrees as Ulema Cornemuse.

Miss Keevil paid a second visit to France and purchased a tricolour dog, Aiglon Des Mariettes (1951) (Taiaut de la Chee

x Soupirante de Bourceville), bred by Mme Raulin of Cher-
mizy, in Aisne.

All three imports had come from old-established breeders in
northern France, the traditional home of the Artois Norman
breed. Ulema, a noted sire in France, was an immediate success
in England, and in his first litter out of Grims Wallflower (G.
Worship x G. Waspish) he produced the bitch Ch. Grims
Useful 9.7.50. Grims Waterlily, a daughter of Ch. Grims
Doughnut, had an excellent litter to him which contained the
Champions Grims Wideawake and Grims Willow, both tricolour, born 1.11.51. Three years later Ulema sired the well-
known tricolour litter brothers Ch. Grims Westward and Ch.
Grims Whirlwind 5.5.54.

Apart from siring some hounds whose influence is still felt
and who won many major awards, Ulema himself was no mean
performer in the hunting field and show ring and he won one
C.C. and a Best-of-Breed at Cruft's in 1951 when there were
no C.C.s allocated.

Although Aiglon's litter mates Agile, Azur and Anatole had
great influence as sires on the Continent, he never achieved the
same power in Britain, as he was always overshadowed by the
great Ulema. Nevertheless he did assist in the rejuvenation of
the breed, which was perhaps more important than the production of champions. Among the useful hounds he sired were
Grims Minx and Major, and Caress of Kimblewick, bred by
Mr. Allen of Aylesbury.

Cornemuse was a lovely hound with well corkscrewed ears.
Being a bitch she could not have the immediate effect the two
males had on British hounds. She did produce some notable
winners, including Grims Caprice, Celeste, Carefree, Best-of-
Breed winner Grims Chanteuse and the two C.C. winning
Grims William.

The French hounds brought into the British breed their zest
and unparalleled soundness, and did much to transform the
image of the Basset from that of 'an old slow-plodding hound'
to that of a workmanlike, balanced dog.

In supporting shows Miss Keevil had been, since the war,
almost alone, although Mrs. Elms still showed occasionally,

and with Miss Keevil registered a few hounds that kept Bassets figuring modestly in the Kennel Club records. It really cannot be over-emphasised to new breeders today that but for the work of Miss Keevil the breed would have come disastrously close to extinction in the post-war period. As I have said, she showed wherever possible, and hunted the Grims hounds in the Craven, Vine and Tedworth hunt country.

In 1953 Mrs. Angela Hodson, a Bloodhound breeder of Maidenhead, founded her Rossingham kennel with Grims Willow (later champion) and bred her first litter in the same year, using Ch. Grims Warlock. Mrs. Hodson retained the tricolour bitch Rossingham Anxious 1.7.53, and my father and I purchased the hare-pied Amber (qualified for her title in 1957 with Anxious). Two fine dog puppies, both bicolours, were Autocrat, owned by Mr. and Mrs. Shelley of the St. Wolstan Bullmastiffs in Huntingdonshire, and Ambassador, who was sold to Mrs. Pellow-Walton of Cornwall. This large hound later passed into the ownership of Mr. Douglas Appleton, then of Baldock, Herts, with whom he won two C.C.s and twenty-one Reserve C.C.s. Let nobody say competition was easy in those days.

All these Rossingham hounds were large, long-bodied, with excellent bone, sound legs, and unexaggerated but very expressive skulls. The French hounds, although smaller than their British counterparts, did not have the effect of reducing size, and their progeny was all well-sized and boned. Ch. Grims Whirlwind was fifty-six pounds in weight.

In 1953 the registrations actually dropped to twenty (the lowest since 1949), but there were encouraging signs of increasing activity, and Miss Keevil and Mrs. Hodson were instrumental in gathering support for a new Basset Hound Club. They were successful, and in May 1954 the B.H.C. was formed and obtained Kennel Club recognition. The following were founder members: Mr. E. Allen of the Kimblewick hounds, Aylesbury, Mr. and Mrs. C. H. Baynes of the Breightmet Hounds, East Hendred, F. Beckwith of Allercoats, Dr. Beer of Thame, Miss Brown of Lowestoft, Mrs. Candy of Duresly, Mrs. Cane of Newbury, Mrs. Canton of Stroud, Lord and Lady Chelmsford, D. Egremont of Andover, Mrs. Edith Grew of Maybush fame, D. Harrison-Sleap of London, Miss Hind of Ewell, Mrs. Hodson of the Rossinghom Hounds, Mrs. Hurst of Stockport, Mr. G. Johnston, Snr., G. I. Johnston, Jnr., of the Sykemoor Hounds, Miss Keevil of Grims fame, Sir Jocelyn Lucas, M.P., of Ilmer, A. G. McDonald of the Wickwell Hounds, J. G. Martyn of Chagford, G. Mossman of Luton, Mrs. Scott-Plummer of Galashiels, Miss D. Still of Newport Pagnell, Mrs. Tarry of Croom, Eire, Mrs. Walker of Thringstone who had the Peldartor St. Bernard Kennels, and Mr. L. R. Woolner of Cotlands and the West Lodge Hounds.

Mrs. Hodson was the club's first secretary, and its formation seemed to herald a new era for the Basset. The breed began to emerge from the shadows in a way that no founder member ever imagined. If anyone had said in 1954 that in ten years the breed would show an annual registration of four figures, the speaker would have been classified insane. The handful that supported shows were delighted if Bassets had a paying entry, and even more delighted if the judges knew what breed they were judging. Specialist judges were rare and it was not unusual to be approached by the judge and asked what sort of hound one was showing! It was fortunate, however, that such experienced all-round judges as Mr. Bill Siggers, and the late Messrs. Leo Wilson, Tom Corbett, Tom Scott, Jimmy Garrow, Lord Northesk and Dr. Aubrey Ireland were available to pass judgment on the emerging breed. All judged the breed in the early fifties, and almost unanimously chose the large long-bodied hounds with plenty of substance.

One difficulty facing the early exhibitors was the problem of qualifying champions owing to the fact that so few sets of C.C.s were issued. Only four sets were available in 1954 (five sets were allocated, but Cruft's was cancelled owing to an electricians' strike) and four sets in 1955 at Cruft's, Glasgow SKC, Cheltenham and Birmingham. The registrations in 1954 were sixty, and in 1955 eighty-one. The principal exhibitors at this time were Miss Keevil, Mrs. Hodson, Mrs. Jagger, Mrs. Rawle, Mr. Dakin, Mr. Mossman and my father. Mrs. Jagger of Shrewsbury had the Fochno Hounds, Mrs. Rawle of Allerford had the Barnspark Hounds, and Mr. Dakin, M.R.C.V.S., owned the Brockhampton pack. Mr. George Mossman had no prefix.

In 1954, almost as if to display that pure British hounds and old-time breeders could still produce the goods, Mrs. Elms qualified Ch. Songster of Reynalton 1.1.48 (Sovereign of Reynalton x Miranda of Reynalton). He won his final C.C. at Blackpool under Viscount Chelmsford and was the last Reynalton hound to be shown.

Ch. Rossingham Amber was retired from the show ring and was mated to Mrs. Jagger's old Reynalton dog, Trumpeter (1948), a lemon and white litter mate of Ch. Songster. The resulting litter of nine was his only one. All the puppies were lemon and white, and the most prominent were Sykemoor Garnet 19.7.55, who won two C.C.s in 1957, Gossip and Gadabout, who were bought by Mrs. Jagger, and Gravity, Grateful and Gaiety. Two puppies in the litter, a dog and a bitch, had long hair, and as an ancestor they had Victor of Reynalton (G.G. Sire) who was responsible for some long-haired pups bred by Miss Keevil.

Gossip went later to Mrs. Lorton of Northfield and was mated to Ch. Grims Whirlwind, and produced a beautiful brace of mottled hounds, Ch. Fochno Trinket and Ch. Fochno Trooper 29.4.57, and an orthodox tricolour Sykemoor Jealousy. These prefixes denote that the hounds were bought by Mrs. Jagger and my father.

Mrs. Jagger owned Ch. Grims Whirlwind, and in the show ring he was a constant rival of his litter mate Ch. Grims Westward, owned by Miss Keevil. When they finally retired from the ring Whirlwind had nine C.C.s to his credit and Westward had five. These figures may seem paltry now (when there are about twenty sets of C.C.s per annum) but it was no mean feat in the earlier half of the fifties. Miss Keevil showed another fine dog-hound at the same time, a very attractively marked tricolour Grims Emblem (Envoy x Ch. Grims Water-wagtail). He won two C.C.s in 1956 and a number of reserve C.C.s. He was also one of the last remaining dog-hounds of

E

virtually pure English descent, and had no French blood in him
at all. With Westward and Whirlwind he completed a trio of
very influential Grims sires. In all they sired ten champions.
These were:

by Emblem:

    Ch. Grims Vapid (1956) x Ch. Grims Useful.

    Ch. Kelperland Baneful (1959) x Kelperland Amanda.

by Whirlwind:

    Ch. Fochno Trinket (1957) x Sykemoor Gossip.

    Ch. Fochno Trooper (1957) x Sykemoor Gossip.

    Ch. Sykemoor Aimwell (1959) x Ch. Rossingham Amber.

by Westward:

    Ch. Barnspark Rakish (1957) x Ch. Grims Gracious.

    Ch. Brockhampton Solomon (1956) x Grims Minx.

    Ch. Barnspark Vanity (1959) x Ch. Grims Vapid.

    Ch. Mareseni Breightmet Wessex (1959) x Grims Vanish.

    Ch. Appeline Rochester (1961) x Solemn Melody.

The breed has recovered from some lowly positions and these
recoveries are due in no small way to the sires and the dominance of these three stallions in the fifties.

Emblem produced Ch. Grims Vapid, who, in turn, produced Ch. Barnspark Vanity 23.4.59. Of Whirlwind's three
champion offspring, Ch. Fochno Trooper produced the great
dog of the 1960s Ch. Fredwell Varon Vandal 21.11.60 (x
Rollick of Fredwell). Vandal has since produced many champions (they are listed in Appendix C) and Ch. Sykemoor
Aimwell 3.6.59, who emulated his sire by also producing three
champions (Ch. Sungarth Phoebe, Ch. Hooksway Cheeky
Checkmate and Ch. Wingjays Fanciful). Westward sired Ch.
Mariseni Breightmet Wessex, who sired Ch. Fredwell Ideal.

During this period the Basset Hound Club was developing.
Mrs. Rawle took over as secretary from Mrs. Hodson in 1957.
In the same year Miss Mary Povey issued the club's first newsletter, and Mr. Dakin edited the club's year book, which was
sent out to the seventy-two members. The Earl of Northesk
was the president, Mr. Lionel Woolner chairman, Dr. S. Beer
vice-chairman, and the treasurer was Mrs. C. H. Baynes. The
committee consisted of Miss Keevil, George Mossman, Robert

Townson, M.R.C.V.S., Gerald Dakin, M.R.C.V.S., Alex McDonald and myself.

The activities of the club's working branch were abandoned for the season 1956–7 because of petrol rationing.

Mr. Dakin was a keen supporter of the working branch and was responsible for the few meets that were held in the north, and Mrs. Jagger organised some meets in Shropshire.

Mr. and Mrs. Townson of Bray had the Kelperland Bloodhounds (they bred Ch. Scarcity of Kelperland) and obtained the young tricolour dog Rossingham Badger 20.2.55 (Ch. Grims Doughnut x Ch. Grims Willow). Badger was a massive hound with exceptionally heavy bone and a noble head. He quickly gained his title, and at Windsor Show in 1958 he was Best Hound, and Best Opposite Six in Show, a remarkable achievement and the highest award ever attained by a Basset in this country. As a stud dog, he sired two champions, both tricolours, Ch. Mariseni Rarnee 12.4.58 (x Barnspark Rustic) and Ch. Kelperland Artful 11.11.57 (x Rossingham Amorous). Artful's litter sister Amanda, also tricolour, was the dam of the Townson's second home-bred champion, the tricolour Kelperland Baneful 7.6.59 (by Grims Emblem).

In 1960 some long-haired puppies were bred by Mr. and Mrs. Townson, but I have no details of their breeding. When judging an exemption show in 1961 Mr. Townson was confronted by a 'long-haired' Basset whose breeding was Bockleton Comic out of Nobello (Bockleton Comic x Fochno Graceful).

Badger's litter mates included Brocade, who won a C.C. at Birmingham in 1955 before being exported to India, where she went Best-in-Show at Calcutta in 1959. Mr. Bassett, of Washington, U.S.A., purchased Barrister, a bicoloured hound who proved to be a fine sire in America.

The most ardent supporters of shows were the owners of the Grims, Fochno, Sykemoor, Rossingham, Kelperland and Barnspark kennels. Mrs. Rawle of Allerford, Somerset, owned the latter, whose nucleus was Ch. Grims Vapid 19.6.56 a lemon and white, and Ch. Grims Gracious 18.7.54 (Ch. Grims Wideawake x Grims Garrulous), a tricolour. Gracious was the dam of a couple of champions, the tricolour dog Rakish 7.7.57 (by Ch. Grims Westward) and the tricolour dog Clarion 5.11.60 (by Ch. Breightmet Chimer), and Vapid was the dam of Ch. Barnspark Vanity (23.4.59 by Ch. Grims Westward), a tricolour owned by Mr. Brian Ghent of the famous Thornville Clumber Spaniel kennels.

Other keen supporters were Lieutenant-Colonel Biss of Weybridge, who owned Ch. Rossingham Cosy 7.8.56 (Ch. Grims Doughnut x Ch. Rossingham Anxious) and Mr. W. W. Wells of Dipton who owned the lemon and white Ch. Jamestown Generous 22.7.55 (Rossingham Ambassador x Grims Gainful). Mr. John Evans of Arkley owned a kennel of Bulldogs and Bassets and was interested in the working Basset as well as the show type, and did much unseen work for the West Lodge Harehounds and the B.H.C. working branch. He bred Ch. Stalwart Debbie 2.6.59 (Grims Varlet x Stalwart Thoughtful), a tricolour who was later exported to Italy. He also produced the useful hounds Stalwart Anna and Blazer.

Although the oldest Scottish kennel is that of Mrs. S. Goldie of Milton of Campsie, whose Kierhill Hounds have Cotlands, Grims and Reynalton backgrounds, the pleasure of owning the first Scottish champion fell to Mrs. McArthur-Onslow and her daughter Mrs. Kewley of Lochmaben. They owned and campaigned Barnspark Rakish to his title in 1959. He was a dark tricolour. Mrs. McArthur-Onslow and Mrs. Kewley are descendants of the Earl of Onslow, who had much to do with the Basset in the very early days.

The stock of all the older kennels and the new was all closely related, and things were fast approaching the danger-point of British Basset life, inbreeding and restriction of choice. In 1957 the Basset Hound Club had decided to look for a suitable outcross stallion and it was thought an American hound would be beneficial. Miss Keevil and Mrs. Jagger were allotted the task of finding a hound, and in their endeavours to do so they wrote to dozens of American breeders. Many did not reply, and it seemed obvious that few were prepared to sell winning adult hounds, so it was decided to try for a youngster instead. This brought results, and at the 1959 A.G.M. it was reported that the club, using its own and some subscribed funds, had purchased a tricolour dog-puggy, Lyn Mar Acres Dauntless 14.8.58 (Lyn Mar Acres Demarch x Lyn Mar Acres Black Magic), for two hundred and fifty dollars from Mrs. Lynwood Walton of Mount Holly, New Jersey, a leading American breeder. He arrived in Britain on March 25th and was released from quarantine in September 1959, and with club assent was kennelled with Miss Keevil. He was the property of the Basset Hound Club and for the use of members' bitches only.

While the negotiations were going on for the American hound, I decided to buy and import a young dog from France. The *Société Centrale Canine* and M. Jean Rothéa, president of the *Club du Basset Artésien-Normand*, both strongly recommended me to try to obtain a hound from the de L'Ombrée pack of Pierre Leparoux of Combrée, Maine et Loire. On this advice I purchased a tricolour dog puppy Hercule de L'Ombrée 6.7.58 (Danic Dit Danois x Gazelle de L'Ombrée). He was released from quarantine in July 1959. Hercule was never shown much; he was a typical Artois-Norman, and as such did not appeal to the bulk of British judges. He went to stud almost immediately on his release, and his first litter was out of Sykemoor Gravity. I was not concerned about Hercule's show record—he was imported solely to provide new blood and because I thought it essential that the British Basset should not lose 'accord' with its forerunner.

In her description of Dauntless, Mrs. Walton said, 'Tricolour, good bone, very sound, good in shoulder, both feet go dead ahead, very low-set ears, good head and bite and has good rear and topline. He is a terrific mover and I sincerely hope you will show him to his English championship.' Unfortunately Mrs. Walton's hopes never materialised, because when Dauntless was shown he did not gain the favour of British judges. He also drew unfavourable criticism from some breeders, which culminated in the B.H.C. selling him to Miss Keevil (who I don't think ever showed him). As many members had subscribed to a fund to buy Dauntless, the B.H.C. refunded donations to those who wished it.

The B.H.C. deserve high praise for having recognised the danger to the breed and for doing something positive about it. The only mistake was in showing Dauntless at a time when so few specialists were officiating. His importation was for the primary purpose of providing new blood, and in doing this he has since fully justified the faith of the B.H.C. and, together with his offspring, has contributed to the breed more than mere show wins.

In 1960 Mrs. McArthur-Onslow and Mrs. Kewley purchased the dark tricoloured American Champion Bold Turpin of Black Heath (12.7.57 Santana Hounslow Highwayman x Santanas Kate Hardcastle). Mrs. Babson of Batavia, Illinois, at that time a prominent exhibitor in the U.S.A., had always nursed the ambition of breeding a hound capable of gaining status in Europe and America. Turpin fulfilled this ambition and in his new owner's hands became a Champion in Britain, and thus became the first American and British champion Basset and the first import to become a champion. At the Scottish K.C. Show in 1962 Turpin teamed with Sykemoor Dingle (Hercule de L'Ombrée x Ch. Rossingham Amber) and won Best Brace in the show, amply proving that the American, British and French stock is fully capable of being blended unobtrusively.

Only one champion qualified in 1960, the beautifully mottled Fochno Trooper. He had passed from Mrs. Jagger's ownership to Mr. Dakin's. While with Mrs. Jagger his career had been overshadowed by that of his illustrious sister Ch. Fochno Trinket, also mottled, who won nine C.C.s. As a Brace the pair were invincible and I do not think they were ever defeated in this section.

In the same year Miss Keevil judged at a championship show, at the L.K.A., where she awarded the C.C.s to Ch. Fochno Trooper and Stalwart Anna. The country's most experienced breeder had always refrained from judging and has, in fact, never judged since the L.K.A. 1960.

Before the fifties were out, Mr. Dakin qualified his dark tricolour Ch. Brockhampton Solomon 8.8.56 (Ch. Grims Westward x Grims Minx) and Mrs. P. Warren of Holland-on-

Sea made her tricolour Mariseni Rarnee into a champion. Mrs. Wells of Little Gaddeston had added Bassets to her well-known gundog kennels and her Fredwell Hounds were just beginning to enter the ring, and two Sykemoor Hounds formed the nucleus of a new Scottish kennel for Mrs. McKnight of Cleland.

Mrs. Prior of West Dean had had the breed for some time and her Sungarth hounds had success in the late 1950s, but in 1961 she made her bought-in red and white hound Sykemoor Aimwell 3.6.59 (Ch. Grims Whirlwind x Ch. Rossingham Amber) into a champion, and I qualified the tricolour bitch Sykemoor Wiza 5.6.58 (Sykemoor Garnet x Sykemoor Jealousy) in the same year.

There were, as there are today, a great many different types of hounds being shown. When one considers that the breed seems to defy standardising and that the influence of three new outcross sires was showing it is not really surprising that this should be so. Unusual colours had cropped up, the mottles and red and white, and the long-coated puppies had appeared. Kinky-tailed puppies plagued Millais and were known, fortunately rarely appearing, in early 1960 litters. However, all these points and others yet unwitnessed will, I am sure, appear again.

In the sixties the Championship Show entries, Kennel Club registrations and Basset Hound Club membership increased dramatically, and on the show bench Bassets were often the strongest represented hound breed. About the upsurge in registrations, Mr. Binney, the secretary of the Kennel Club, said, 'I cannot think of anything comparable.' In 1959 the registrations were 237, and in 1964 no fewer than 1,529 hounds were recorded. In short, the Basset had almost overnight become the boom breed and ripe for commercialising. The Basset was 'in'. Advertising agencies used the sorrowful expression of the breed to promote sales of everything from room-heaters to shoes, records to mineral water. Hounds appeared on TV and a brewery opened a new public house called 'The Basset Hound' in Cheshire. In the *Daily Mail* the strip cartoon hound Fred Basset captivated old and young alike, and was syndicated throughout the world.

In the 1900s the great Sarah Bernhardt had some of Verrier's hounds as pets until her footman rebelled against carrying them up and down about five flights of stairs. However, her modern show-business counterparts have no such problems, and Brigitte Bardot and Dany Robin keep Bassets as companions, and so do Dirk Bogarde, Rex Harrison and Russ Conway.

Naturally, all the publicity the breed received resulted in a great demand for Bassets, and there is no doubt many people had hounds simply to breed from and cater for this demand. In the main, the established breeders did not make any gain from the boom, and they certainly had no wish to. More and more joined the ranks of the older breeders, and some fine kennels were founded within this decade, and some notable hounds produced.

A tricolour hound born in 1960 became famous when, after a great show career, he had gained twenty-three C.C.s, thus establishing a new record for the breed. This was Ch. Fredwell Varon Vandal 21.11.60 (Ch. Fochno Trooper x Rollick of Fredwell) bred by Mr. Evan Roberts of the Varon kennels, Kettering, and owned and campaigned by Mrs. Joan Wells-Meacham of Little Gaddesden. Vandal won his Certificates under different judges, and met with the fullest approval of M. Jean Rothéa, President of the *Club de Basset Artésien-Normand*, when he judged at Dumfries Ch. Show in 1963; Captain Verwey of Holland also awarded him the Birmingham C.C. in 1964. The champion offspring of Vandal are listed in Appendix C.

With this great hound at the helm, Mrs. Wells-Meacham's Fredwell kennel became one of the most powerful, and she bred the first Basset hound dog to win the Kennel Club Junior Warrant. This was the tricolour Fredwell Maestro 2.7.62 (Barlindal Nebbish x Gaiety of Fredwell). The very useful tricolour dog Ch. Fredwell Ideal 1.12.61 (Ch. Mariseni Breightmet Wessex x Fredwell Rennet) qualified for his title at the Basset Hound Club's Championship Show in 1965, which had an entry of one hundred and seventeen hounds.

Mrs. Rawle relinquished the job as secretary of the B.H.C.,

and Mrs. Seiffert of Oxted took over in 1962. She founded her Maycombe Kennel in 1959 with the tricolour bitch Syke-moor Modesty, and since then Mrs. Seiffert has owned several champions, including Ch. Chantinghall Jemima of Maycombe 13.11.62 (Grims Lager x Mariseni Goodness Gracious) and the lemon and white Ch. Chantinghall Kitebrook Barley 19.6.63 (Ch. Breightmet Chimer x Kitebrook Lilliesleaf Helen).

The dog Barlindal Nebbish already mentioned was a tri-colour imported from Canada in 1962, and shown for the first time at Windsor by Miss Latham. His breeding was Ch. Mon Ami Two Spots of Barlindal x Striding Flash of Barlindal. In the few litters he sired he proved himself more than adequate and would, I am sure, have proved an asset to the breed, but unfortunately for some unknown reason he disappeared from the scene.

The blood of both American hounds was behind the lemon and white bitch Ch. Dreymin Appeline Coral 8.9.61 (Grims Lager x Appeline Dawn) who was the breed's first Junior Warrant winner in 1962. Owned by Mrs. Minto of Edenbridge, she was bred by Mr. and Mrs. Appleton. Lyn-Mar Acres Dauntless produced his first champion, Ch. Pointgrey Suss's Folly 13.11.62 (x Julie of Aldbury) who was owned by Mrs. Benge-Abbot of Esher, who also had another tricolour dog champion in her kennel, Ch. Barnspark Clarion 5.11.60 (Ch. Breightmet Chimer x Ch. Grims Gracious). Folly, a heavy mottled dog, was unfortunately killed.

The French influence of Hercule de L'Ombrée was also evident in Britain, although most of his progeny went abroad. His tricolour son Sykemoor Gilpin (x Ch. Sykemoor Wiza) won two C.C.s and qualified for the Junior Warrant with Ch. Sykemoor Emma 16.5.62 (Fochno Trumpeter x Sykemoor Jealousy). Trumpeter and Jealousy are the same way bred, by Ch. Grims Whirlwind x Sykemoor Gossip.

Other young hounds who also qualified for the Junior Warrant included Fredwell Model and Perfect, Kitebrook Actor and Barley, Wingjays Phantom, and Avenwood Dulcis and Chantinghall Ancestor.

In 1964 Peardrop Princess, a tricolour owned by Mrs.

Symonds, died while whelping nineteen puppies. This must be the record for a Basset litter, but not all survived. In a 1961 litter Princess had produced Ch. Hooksway Cheeky Checkmate 8.10.61 (by Ch. Sykemoor Aimwell), a tricolour who was owned by Mrs. Thompson of Portsmouth.

Most of the older breeders remained active in the breed, although some curtailed showing activities. Miss Keevil had purchased Ch. Fochno Trooper when Mr. Dakin retired from showing. She also owned Ch. Breightmet Chimer 15.3.58 (Grims Charlie x Grims Vanish), a tricolour dog who has had much influence on the hounds of the sixties. He produced innumerable C.C. winners and champions, Avenwood Dulcis 4.4.63 (x Wingjays Beautiful), Barnspark Clarion, Kitebrook Barley, Grims Fochno Charming 3.5.63 (x Ch. Fochno Trinket) and Wingjays Ptolemy 13.7.64 (x Ch. Sungarth Phoebe).

Ch. Avenwood Dulcis, a lemon and white hound bred by Mrs. Ashton of Warminster, was a champion before her first birthday, and from the same kennel has come Ch. Mapleroyal Avenwood Atalanta 18.4.64, also a lemon and white, owned by Mrs. Stewart of Rugby.

Mrs. Rowett-Johns founded her kennel in the sixties and has produced a predominantly lemon and white and red and white hound line descending from Ch. Sykemoor Aimwell or Ch. Sungarth Phoebe 30.9.60 (x Aesops Able), both bicolours. Apart from Ch. Wingjays Ptolemy she has also produced Ch. Wingjays Fanciful 22.11.61 (Ch. Sykemoor Aimwell x Sungarth Jasmine), a chestnut and white dog, and the tricolour Ch. Wingjays, Fabulous 22.10.63 (Ch. Fredwell Varon Vandal x Ch. Sungarth Phoebe).

In 1965 the Basset Hound Club of Scotland was formed. Its first secretary was Mrs. McKnight of Cleland, whose brainchild the club was. She had established her Chantinghall kennel in 1959. By the mid-1960s she had built up a strong pack, and has produced Ch. Chantinghall Jemima of Maycombe, a tricolour with French and American ancestry, Ch. Chantinghall Harmony 15.9.63 (Chantinghall Cognac x Mariseni Goodness Gracious) and the tricolour dog Ch.

Chantinghall Ancestor 24.6.64 (Ch. Pointgrey Suss's Folly x Ch. Chantinghall Harmony).

Mrs. Goldie, the oldest established Scottish breeder, was a founder member of the club and so was Miss Macmillan (now Mrs. Moncur) of Dunlop, who has had success with Bassets in the Obedience section as well as the show ring. After Mrs. McKnight emigrated to Canada in the late 1960's, Mrs. Moncur's Balleroy kennel became the most prominent in Scotland, and she bred the Red and White hound Ch. Balleroy Chestnut 24.3.67 (Ch. Chantinghall Ancestor x Chantinghall Beatrice). Shortly after the formation of the Scottish club, the Irish fanciers founded the Basset Hound Club of Ireland with Mr. Butler of Dublin as the first secretary. Mrs. McGuirk of Enniskerry, owner of the Van Kuypers kennel, was also a founder member; so were Mr. Stronner of Dublin and Mr. and Mrs. C. Mitchel of Monkstown.

In Ulster Mr. and Mrs. Bridgham of Bangor have done much to popularise the Basset, and they have often travelled over to the mainland to show their Ballymaconnel hounds. Their tri-colour dog Ballymaconnel Forester (Ch. Chantinghall Ancestor x Ballymaconnel Boule de Suif) is an Irish and British Champion.

Within the framework of the Basset Hound Club several area branches have been set up, and these should do much to further the aims of the club in their respective regions. With club membership nearing one thousand some decentralisation was required and the branch secretaries are able to organise social events, shows and walks, and to play host to the Basset Hound Club pack during the season.

The policy of the B.H.C. since its revival in 1953 has been most praiseworthy, and it has certainly played a major role in establishing the breed on the bench and in the field. The club also gave many specialist judges the chance of experience by guaranteed classifications of many Open shows; without guarantees many societies just would not entertain Basset Hound classes, especially prior to 1963. Now Open shows are well supported and the breed entry at Championship shows frequently exceeds three figures.

I hope that in the event of a decline in the breed's popularity, the existence of three clubs in Britain will not prove an embarrassment to Bassets. Harmony must be the theme, and the welfare of the breed must be the sole consideration of all the clubs.

In 1965 Mrs. Seiffert, the B.H.C. secretary, wrote: 'Perhaps in our very strenuous efforts to breed sounder hounds (feet are much improved generally) in the last few years, we may have underplayed heads a little. If we can consistently breed Bassets with quality heads (without the broadness of skull that detracts so much from the well-bred look) plus unexaggerated fronts we may perhaps at last escape from the dreadful adjective "quaint" which has haunted the breed far too long.' Here I must beg to differ with my friend. The Basset, if it is to remain a Basset, must at all costs be retained with all the curious little points and the long, low structure that have, since its innovation in the fifteenth century, attracted much attention. 'Quaint' is a kind word to use, and much better than some used by those who are ignorant of the role a Basset can play in hunting today.

The breed must retain its individuality, and any tendency to breeding it along a semi-Beagle framework must be vigorously curtailed. In the mid-sixties it did appear that the 'mini-Basset' type was becoming the accepted type by some breeders and judges, but happily this phase passed and by the end of the decade the correct type of Basset—with some size, substance and length—became predominant.

In this chapter I have tried to set out the breed's development during the last seventy years as accurately as possible, and to emphasise the high and low spots of this development, and the parts played by breeders and the B.H.C. Reviews of every individual kennel would be impossible, and I have naturally concentrated on the kennels of the 1939–60 period because, as far as the modern Basset is concerned, these are the kennels that are the foundation of the breed as it is today. Some are still active and together with more recently established kennels are continuing to play their part in the future development of this fascinating breed.

4

Standards and Breeds

A BREED'S Standard of Excellence is a concise and detailed word-picture, compiled by a breed society to describe as clearly as possible the ideal specimen of that particular breed. Because of its form and method of tabulating the desired virtues and the undesirable faults, the standard is used by breeders and judges as a guide in their efforts to produce and find the perfect representative of the breed. Almost all pure-bred and officially recognised breeds have a standard which is officially sanctioned by the governing bodies, i.e. the Kennel Clubs.

Three standards apply to the Basset Hound, and they are:

1. The British Standard, compiled by the Basset Hound Club, and recognised by the Kennel Club. This standard applies to Bassets in Britain, the Commonwealth countries and Scandinavia.

2. The American Standard, compiled by The Basset Hound Club of America, Inc., and recognised by the American K.C. This standard is followed in North, Central and South America.

3. The French Standard, compiled by the *Club du Basset Artésien-Normand*, recognised by the *Société Central Canine* and followed by France and most other European countries.

The breed chiefly dealt with in this book is the smooth-coated Basset, the descendant of the Artois and Norman Bassets. However, three other breeds of Bassets exist in France and these are briefly described at the end of this chapter. Naturally they have their own standards, but as the breeds have played little part in the development of our own Bassets it is not thought necessary to reproduce their standards in full.

None of the three standards given is the original. At various times they have all been changed and revised, and the present

British and American standards are fairly recent. In a breed so ancient as the Basset, which has been scientifically bred for so long, some change in type is inevitable, and in order to meet the changes the standards must be revised to avoid becoming outdated and perhaps out of touch with the hound they should describe.

It was also inevitable that the Basset would develop differently in Britain and the U.S.A.; adherence to the original French standard would be impossible, hence the need for different standards. Basically speaking, the three standards, although differing in many ways, describe the 'low-set' hound. The main difference is found in the size of the Basset required: the Americans prefer the heaviest type, the British show a preference for a substantial hound of medium size, and the French look for a finer-made agile Basset.

I do not want to over-emphasise the differences in the three standards, because they have not had any adverse effect on the import and export of hounds and have certainly not affected the mutual benefit that each national type derives from the outcross the other types provide. It would have been a tragedy for the breed everywhere if the national types had varied so much that each proved to be unacceptable to the others, breeders and judges. The extremes of each type must be guarded against and efforts to breed a balanced hound maintained.

One method of avoiding the extremes of each type would be for representatives of the national clubs to meet occasionally and discuss the standards and keep each other informed of any impending changes. The breed societies, as guardians of the breed, have a duty, and the preservation of the essential characteristics is of prime importance. I think the Basset Hound Club and its contemporaries in the U.S.A. and France realise this.

The Basset Hound is not easy to breed and does not conform easily to the standard. The combination of essential breed type and soundness is difficult to achieve, and uniformity of type is equally hard to attain. At Championship Shows one can see a large class of Beagles all looking more or less identical, but the same cannot be said of Bassets. It is my opinion that the unique conformation of the Basset prevents this; its body structure is so abnormal that it defies attempts to perfect it. What other reason can there be? Basset breeders are no less skilled than breeders of other breeds. Continuity of type is markedly absent in the Basset. One breeder can build up a recognisable strain for a few generations and then it disappears; one stallion-hound can stamp his likeness on a few successive generations and then his type disappears, despite inbreeding in an attempt to perpetuate it.

Every breeder has in the mind's eye a mental picture of the type of hound he feels is the ideal, and it is very seldom that two people agree on what actually does constitute this elusive ideal Basset. One reason for the differences of opinion is the question of priorities, that is to say, what particular feature or points of the hound should be given most importance? Some think heads, others soundness, others body points, and on it goes. In an attempt to place these points in some order of importance the old standard for Bassets (and other breeds used the same method) had a scale and each feature of the breed was allocated a percentage of points, the whole totalling one hundred.

The scale of points for Bassets was:

(1)	Head, skull, eyes, muzzle and flews	15	(14)
(2)	Ears	15	(10)
(3)	Neck, dewlap, chest and shoulders	10	(18)
(4)	Forelegs and feet	15	(18)
(5)	Back, loins, quarters	10	(18)
(6)	Stern	5	(5)
(7)	Coat and skin	10	(5)
(8)	Colour and markings	15	(5)
(9)	Basset character and symmetry	5	(7)
		100	100

This scale was a sore point with some early breeders, and especially the hunting people, and in 1898 Captain Godfrey Heseltine, co-founder of the Walhampton pack, drew up his own standard and scale of points and distributed it to his puppy-walkers. The allocation thought correct by Heseltine is given in brackets alongside the official scale, and it will immediately be noticed that whereas the club scale places emphasis on head points, and also attaches great importance to colour and markings, the Heseltine scale allocates most points to the body and limbs of the hound.

Even today the standards do not please everyone, and because of the differing interpretations of breeders and judges there will always be great differences of opinion. Knowledge of all three standards is beneficial and can only mean a greater understanding of the Basset Hound, and an attempt by all breeders to work to an amalgamation of them is sensible. It is my opinion that the very best hounds of Britain, France and the U.S.A. can conform reasonably well to each other's standard, and the illustrations of the modern Bassets have been chosen in an attempt to illustrate this. They also serve to demonstrate a very important feature of any good hound, balance and symmetry, and an abundance of breed type. The whole hound must present a balanced outlook, and no single feature should predominate or outweigh the others. A Basset can possess every essential point needed, but if these do not blend together pleasingly then the whole hound is spoiled.

THE KENNEL CLUB BASSET HOUND STANDARD

General Characteristics. A short-legged hound of considerable substance, well balanced and full of quality. Action is most important. A smooth free action with forelegs reaching well forward and hind legs showing powerful thrust and the hound moving true both front and rear. Hocks and stifles must not be stiff in movement, nor must any toes be dragged.

Head and Skull. Domed, with some stop and the occipital bone prominent; of medium width at the brow and tapering slightly to the muzzle; the general appearance of the foreface is lean but not snipy. The top of the muzzle nearly parallel with the line from stop to occiput and not much longer than

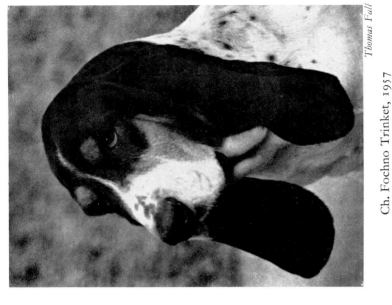

Thomas Fall

Ch. Fochno Trinket, 1957

Sport & General

Ch. Sykemoor Aimwell, 1959

Ch. Sykemoor Emma, 1962

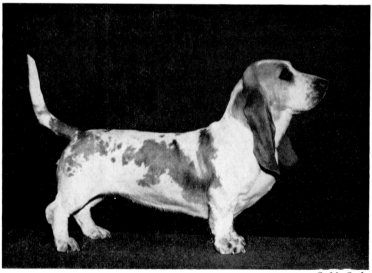

C. M. Cooke

Ch. Chantinghall Kitebrook Barley, 1963

the head from stop to occiput. There may be a moderate amount of wrinkle at the brows and beside the eyes and in any event the skin of the head should be so loose as to wrinkle noticeably when drawn forward or when the head is lowered. The flews of the upper lip overlap the lower substantially.

Nose. Entirely black, except in light-coloured hounds, when it may be brown or liver. Large, with well-opened nostrils, and may protrude a little beyond the lips.

Eyes. Brown, but may shade to hazel in light-coloured hounds, neither prominent nor too deep set. The expression is calm and serious and the red of the lower lid appears, though not excessively.

Ears. Set on low but not excessively so and never above the line of the eye; very long, reaching at least to the end of a muzzle of correct length, narrow throughout their length and curling well inwards; very supple, fine and velvety in texture.

Mouth. The teeth level with a scissors bite although if they meet edge to edge it is not a fault.

Neck. Muscular and fairly long with pronounced dewlap but not exaggerated.

Forequarters. Shoulder-blades well laid back and shoulders not heavy. Forelegs short, powerful and with great bone, the elbows turned neither out nor in but fitting easily against the side. The knees at least slightly crooked inwards but not to so great an extent as to prevent free action or to result in legs touching each other when standing or in action. Knuckling-over is a bad fault. There may be wrinkles of skin between knee and foot.

Body. The breast-bone slightly prominent but the chest not narrow or unduly deep; the ribs well rounded and sprung and carried well back. The back rather broad, level, and with withers and quarters of approximately the same height, though the loins may arch slightly. The back from withers to the inset of the quarters not unduly long.

Hindquarters. Full of muscle and standing out well, giving an almost spherical effect when viewing the hound from the rear. Stifles well bent. The hocks as low to the ground as possible and slightly bent under the hound but not turned in or out.

F

They should be placed just under the body when standing naturally. One or two wrinkles of skin may appear between hock and foot and at the rear of the joint a slight pouch resulting from the looseness of the skin.

Feet. Massive well knuckled-up and padded. The forefeet may point straight ahead or be turned slightly outwards but in every case the hound must stand perfectly true, the weight being borne equally by toes with pads together so that the feet would leave the imprint of a large hound and no unpadded areas in contact with the ground.

Tail. Well set-on, rather long, strong at the base and tapering with a moderate amount of coarse hair underneath. When the hound is moving the stern is carried well up and curves gently sabre-fashion over the back but is never curling or gay.

Coat. Smooth, short and close without being too fine.

Colour. Generally black, white and tan or lemon and white, but any recognised hound colour is acceptable.

Height. Thirteen to fifteen inches.

Faults. Any departure from the above standard is a fault, but the following should particularly be penalised:

(a) Unsoundness of legs or feet.

(b) Faulty mouth.

(c) Lack of balance (i.e. undue exaggeration of any point).

(d) Lack of typical Basset appearance and expression.

THE AMERICAN BASSET HOUND STANDARD, 1964

General Appearance. The Basset Hound possesses in marked degree those characteristics which equip it admirably to follow a trail over and through difficult terrain. It is a short-legged dog, heavier in bone, size considered, than any other breed of dog, and while its movement is deliberate, it is in no sense clumsy. In temperament it is mild, never sharp or timid.

Head. The head is large and well proportioned. Its length from occiput to muzzle is greater than the width at the brow. In overall appearance the head is of medium width. The skull is well domed, showing a pronounced occipital protuberance.

A broad flat skull is a fault. The length from nose to stop is approximately the length from stop to occiput. The sides are flat and free from cheek bumps. Viewed in profile the top lines of the muzzle and skull are straight and lie in parallel planes, with a moderately defined stop. The skin over the whole of the head is loose, falling in distinct wrinkles over the brow when the head is lowered. A dry head and tight skin are faults.

The muzzle is deep, heavy, and free from snipiness. The nose is darkly pigmented, preferably black, with large open nostrils. A deep liver-coloured nose conforming to the colouring of the head is permissible but not desirable.

The teeth are large, sound and regular, meeting in either a scissors or even bite. A bite either undershot or overshot is a serious fault.

The lips are darkly pigmented and are pendulous, falling squarely in front and towards the back in loose hanging flews. The dewlap is very pronounced. The neck is powerful, of good length, and well arched.

The eyes are soft, sad and slightly sunken, showing a prominent haw, and in colour are brown, dark brown preferred. A somewhat lighter-coloured eye conforming to the general colouring of the dog is acceptable but not desirable. Very light or protruding eyes are faults.

The ears are extremely long, low-set and, when drawn forward, fold well over the end of the nose. They are velvety in texture, hanging in loose folds with the ends curling slightly inward. They are set far back on the head at the base of the skull, and in repose appear to be set on the neck. A high set or flat ear is a serious fault.

Forequarters. The chest is deep and full with pronounced sternum showing clearly in front of the legs.

The shoulders and elbows are set close against the sides of the chest. The distance from the deepest point of the chest to the ground, whilst it must be adequate to allow free movement when working in the field, is not to be more than one-third of the total height of the withers of an adult Basset. The shoulders are well laid back and powerful. Steepness in shoulder, fiddle fronts, and elbows that are out, are serious faults.

The forelegs are short, powerful, heavy in bone, with wrinkled skin. Knuckling over of the front legs is a disqualification.

The paw is massive, very heavy with tough heavy pads, well rounded and with both feet inclined equally a trifle forward balancing the width of the shoulders. Feet down in pastern are a serious fault. The toes are neither pinched together nor splayed, with the weight of the forepart of the body borne evenly on each. The dewclaws may be removed.

Body. The rib structure is long, smooth and extends well back. The ribs are well sprung, allowing adequate room for heart and lungs. Flatsidedness and flanged ribs are faults. The top-line is straight, level and free from any tendency to sag or roach, which are faults.

Hindquarters. The hindquarters are very full and well rounded and are approximately equal to the shoulders in width. They must not appear slack or light in relation to the overall depth of the body. The dog stands firmly on its hind legs, showing a well-let-down stifle with no tendency towards a crouching stance. Viewed from behind the hind legs are parallel, with the hocks turning neither in nor out. Cowhocks or bowed legs are serious faults. The hind feet point straight ahead. Steep, poorly angulated hindquarters are a serious fault. The dewclaws, if any, may be removed.

Tail. The tail is not to be docked, and is set in continuation of the spine with but slight curvature, and carried gaily in hound fashion. The hair on the underside of the tail is coarse.

Size. The height should not exceed fourteen inches. Height over fifteen inches at the highest point of the shoulder-blades is a disqualification.

Gait. The Basset Hound moves in a smooth, powerful and effortless manner. Being a scenting dog with short legs, it holds its nose low to the ground. Its gait is absolutely true with perfect co-ordination between the front and hind legs, and it moves in a straight line with hind feet following in line with the front feet, the hocks well bent with no stiffness of action. The front legs do not paddle, weave, or overlap and the elbows must lie close to the body. Going away the hind legs are parallel.

Coat. The coat is hard, smooth and short, with sufficient density to be of use in all weathers. The skin is loose and elastic. A distinctly long coat is a disqualification.

Colour. Any recognised hound colour is acceptable and the distribution of colour and markings is of no importance.

Disqualifications. Height of more than fifteen inches at the highest point of the shoulder-blades. Knuckled-over front legs. Distinctly long coat.

Standard drawn up by the Committee of the B.H.C. of America and officially recognised by the A.K.C. in early 1964.

In 1968 this standard was adopted as the official standard for Basset Hounds in countries under the jurisdiction of the *Fédération Cynologique Internationale.*

THE FRENCH BASSET
(ARTOIS-NORMAN) STANDARD

General Appearance. A long dog, longer than his size calls for. Standing firm, well balanced and well made. Clearly indicating his great ancestry.

Head. Domed, medium width. The cheeks not formed by muscles as in the Bulldog, but only of skin which makes one or two folds on them. Overall the head must have a fleshless appearance.

Nose. Black and wide and coming a little over the lips.

Nostrils. Full and wide.

Skull. The stop marked but without exaggeration. The occipital bone prominent.

Eye. Large, dark, and with a calm serious expression. The red of the lower eyelid may show.

Foreface. Of average length, slightly convex before the nose.

Ears. Set as low as possible, never above the line of the eye. Supple, very fine and delicate in texture. Narrow when coming from the skull, curling well inwards, corkscrew fashion, very long and ends well pointed.

Neck. Fairly long, with dewlap but not exaggerated.

Forelegs. Short, heavy-boned. Crook or half-crook (or less than half-crook provided there is a principal of crook suffi-ciently visible), but never with a pastern displaced in front. The front of the forelegs presents several folds of skin often under the articulation of the first joint.

Shoulders. Round, strong and short. Well muscled.

Feet. Placed vertically, but with the toes turned out without deformity. The feet of the Basset must leave the imprint in soft earth of a much larger hound.

Chest. Breast-bone prominent. Chest expanding downwards a moderate way, but wide and round.

Ribs. Rounded. Compensating for their lack of depth by their rotundity.

Back. Wide and well supported. Straight and level.

Loin. Slightly tucked up.

Flank. Full and extending downwards.

Hindquarters. A little aslant and giving a slight dip to the rump. Thighs well developed and muscled. Should form with the rump in a spherical mass.

Hocks. Slightly bent and strong. Often the sights of one or two folds of skin. A slight projection of skin on the calcaneum.

Stern. Well attached. Long, strong and getting thinner pro-gressively. Carried sabre-fashion but never curled over the back. It is absolutely forbidden to trim the stern of the dog for show.

Gait. Calm and free.

Size. Ten and a half to fourteen and a half inches.

Coat. Close, not too fine. Waterproof.

Colour. Tricolour or orange and white. The tricolour dogs marked with tan heads, black backs and tan extremities. White tips preferred but not essential.

Faults. Flat or wide forehead. Flat, thick or high-set ears. Forelegs touching or knuckled. Flat ribs and feet. Toes splayed. Closed hocks.

Disqualifications. Undershot. Straight legs. Any flecking on the white marks which give a blue mottled effect.

Compiled by the *Club du Basset Artésien-Normand*, and recognised by the S.C.C. and the *Société de Vénerie*.

Before the analysis of the standards I must admit to a passion for the preservation of the smaller points so essential to a good hound. I say 'smaller points' because many people obviously pay little regard to them—all that matter to some are head and skull points. Those I have in mind include ear texture and the inward curl, wrinkling on the front legs, fine elastic body skin, kind eye and expression. At the risk of being called a 'faddist' I will continue.

The first definition covers much ground, and much that is hard to define comes under the heading 'General Appearance'. How can one define type and character! Quality is obviously the key factor, and overall balance is equally essential. All the points must balance and 'undue exaggeration of any point' is a fault. All the points are given in the standard in detail and the hound should possess the desired points plus character. It is character that puts animation into the hound. The French Standard states that the Basset should 'clearly indicate his great ancestry', and usually the strange-looking hound, with mild manners and kind disposition, gives an aura of antiquity, a feeling of not really belonging to the twentieth century.

The head of any breed usually claims most attention from breeders and judges, and many consider it to be the most important feature. The Basset head and skull is very noble and it is doubtful if any other breed of hound possesses such a wonderful headpiece. One can fully understand the emphasis

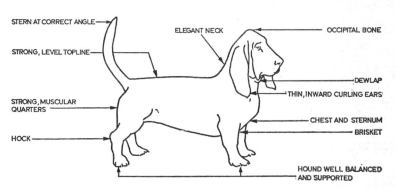

FIG 3   Points of the Basset Hound

placed on the skull. The correct and original skull is a replica of the heads of the Basset's 'parent' races, the *chiens de grand chasse*, Normans, Artois, Gascons, etc., and the early British breeders knew this, so I fail to understand why they chose to base the head on that of the Bloodhound. In the words of the old standard, the head 'to be ideal should closely resemble that of a Bloodhound'. Granted there are similarities, but usually the Bloodhound skull is narrower and carries much more wrinkle than the Basset's. Because of the Bloodhound reference in the standard, undue emphasis was placed on narrow heads with masses of wrinkle, and the proper Basset head as depicted in Bourbon's *Nos Bassets Français* (1911) and Verrier's *Les Bassets Français* (1921) virtually disappeared, probably because it was considered too plain.

The modern standards do not call for narrow or wrinkled heads; all three specify that skulls should be of 'medium width'. The French Standard does not even mention the word 'wrinkle', and the British and American versions ask for a 'moderate amount' to be noticeable only when drawn forward. No hard-and-fast rule could be laid down about the width of skull; obviously a large dog-hound needs a stronger skull than a very sweet and smaller-made female, and it is therefore a question of the head being in proportion to the body.

FIG 4   Correct inward curling ears, prominent occipital bone and dewlap

Incorrect flat skull, ears lacking inward curl, round-ended ears

Viewed from the front the outline of the head should resemble an elongated 'V' or wedge shape, tapering from the
nose to the rear of the skull, and the deep side of the skull
should be devoid of any cheek-bumps or muscle, and the whole
skull has a fleshless appearance. Looking from the side the
head should be of an approximately oblong outline. The flews
should be deep, hanging down under the nose and coming
over the bottom jaw, and continuing back, gradually deepen-
ing to blend with the loose skin under the neck to form the
dewlap, the two pouches of skin on the neck. A dry neck is a
fault. The topline of the skull should be formed of a line from
nose to stop, then a moderately defined stop, and then a line
from stop to the occipital bone. The two lines run parallel and
are roughly the same length. Some hounds have a Roman
nose caused by the topline of the muzzle sloping towards the
nose. A dish-faced look caused by the same line sloping from
the nose into too deep a stop is a bad fault.

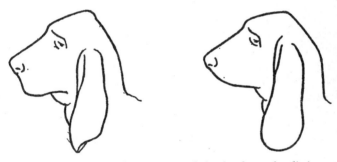

Fig 5   Correct ear placement, good depth of muzzle, distinct
occipital bone
Incorrect, high-set ears, round-ended and lacking inward curl.
Snipy muzzle and indistinct occipital bone

The occipital bone, or peak bone, should be prominent, and
the old French Standard called this feature *la bosse de chasse* (the
bump of hunting).
The whole skull should be strong, within the context of the

standard, and a snipy muzzle and Greyhound outline are inexcusable.

A dark eye is essential and the maxim 'the darker the better' should apply. Light-coloured hounds are allowed a lighter shade of eye, but really light or yellow eyes are serious faults even in the palest of hounds. The eye should not be prominent, and the British and American Standards call for a moderate amount of haw; excessive haw should be avoided as it can lead to eye disorders. Most French hounds are devoid of haw and their standard does not specifically call for it to be present. The nose should be large, well formed and dark-coloured. Light-coloured hounds are allowed paler noses and most lemon and white hounds have brown noses. The spotted nose should be discouraged.

The French Standard is most explicit about earage and the texture of the ears, and most Artois-Normans excel on this point. The British Standard wisely follows the French version, and calls for fine-textured ears that curl well inwards cork-screw style. The end of the ear should be pointed rather than rounded. Some length of ear is necessary but excessive ear span is not really called for, and the standards only specify that the ears should come past the end of the nose when drawn forward.

An essential feature of the correct inward curling ear is texture, and this must be very fine and when felt between finger and thumb should be no thicker than four pages of this book. The ear is set low on the skull and almost appears as though it comes from the neck and not the head; it curls inwards and very often when one views it from the front one can see the twists of the 'corkscrew' as it were. The point-ended ear can be spotted at birth, and is the shape of a tiny 'V'.

Thick and flat-hanging ears are ugly and are usually rounded at the bottom, and can spoil the appearance of an otherwise good head. British and French breeders criticise the ears of American hounds for lack of corkscrew, but it must be re-membered that their standard says 'ends curling slightly inwards'.

Most breed standards call for a good mouth—there are

exceptions but basically the scissors bite or level mouth is demanded. This type is considered correct in the Basset, and the upper set of dentures just overlap and fit closely to the lower set. Also permissible is the edge-to-edge mouth, where the upper dentures rest on the lower set. The old breed standard did not condemn the overshot mouth (upper teeth and jaw protruding over the lower) but called the formation the *bec de lièvre* (hare-lip) and many early hounds including some of the Le Couteulx strain had this type of mouth. Needless to say it is considered a grave fault today, and so is the undershot mouth (lower teeth and jaw protruding below the upper). It is probably due to the acceptance of the *bec de lièvre* that the breed is still plagued with incorrect mouths, although the fault seems to be diminishing.

I personally would not severely penalise a hound with one or two misplaced teeth. By comparison with many large breeds the Basset has small teeth and they are probably easily twisted by bones and so on.

A good head featuring all the desirable points can be further complemented by being set on a good neck. A short, thick, heavy-looking neck can not only detract from the head, but it also upsets the balance of the hound. Considering its importance the standards seem to be undemanding—they all call for a strong, lengthy neck with some dewlap underneath, but only the American Standard asks for the neck to be 'arched', an important addition. The arched neck sets the head at a correct downward-looking angle. A muscle on the neck should be easily felt by running one's hands down from the base of the skull to the shoulder, and naturally this gives strength to the neck. Length is desired for balance; the bulk of the Basset's weight is in the forepart of the body, and a short stuffy neck would only add to the overloaded look and spoil the balanced outline. I do not subscribe to the theory that length of neck is required to enable the hound to lower the head when scenting. To all French breeders and many of their British counterparts, a Basset which has to lower its nose to the ground is lacking in olfactory powers.

A beautiful head and elegant neck are certainly important to the hound, but of equal importance and most essential are correct body structure and sound shoulders, limbs and feet. The motivation power must be good if the Basset is to perform its legitimate function. Near perfection is attainable in skull points, but to achieve this in body and limbs is not so easy. One glance at the elongated body and the short, crooked front legs tells us why. It is, let us face it, an abnormal conformation, and to breed anything so unnaturally formed must present difficulties, and a challenge.

I have said that most of the bodyweight is concentrated in the front, and in view of the stress this places on the short forelegs it is small wonder that they are often unsound. The cause of poor feet, knuckled fronts and out at elbows can usually be found at the shoulder. When the shoulder is well laid back and forms a right angle with the humerus, and the humerus and radius and shoulder equal each other in length, the front will be correct; the forelegs will support the heaviest part of the hound and the deepest point of the chest will be immediately between the front legs. If, however, the humerus is shorter than the radius and the shoulder, the legs are automatically brought forward, and therefore the bulk of body-weight is behind, not between, the legs, causing the knees to knuckle forward, the elbows to come out and the pasterns to bend, making a very deformed and incorrect front assembly.

The Basset is a heavy-bodied hound and the weight must be

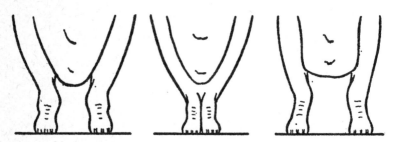

FIG 6   Correct frontal view showing chest well supported by
an even front
Incorrect front. Narrow-chested, legs and feet close-fitting
Incorrect front. Chest too wide, unsupported by the legs

supported not only on sound front legs but also on substantially boned legs. Not only must the legs look substantial, but when encircled by the hand they must be firm and solid, with good strong bone from shoulder to foot. Poor, weak bone is unsightly and gives a hound a poverty-stricken look.

The description I like best for the shape of the crooked front is a 'Queen Anne' front, denoting close similarities between Basset legs and those on Queen Anne period furniture. Sir Everett Millais considered some crook essential if the chest had to be well supported, and the British and French Standards, recognising this need, ask for crook-knees, the half-crook or *demi-torse* front being preferred. The American Standard is unspecific in that crook is not mentioned, a grave omission in my opinion.

The feet, front and rear, must be well shaped, deep-padded, with short, hard nails, providing a proportioned ending to the massive-boned legs. Dewclaws may be removed or retained, depending on the custom of the breeder. I see no harm in their retention. Needless to say the hound should always be up on his toes and never down in the pasterns.

Balancing the front and sharing equally in supporting the

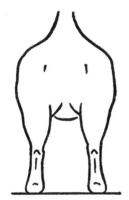 

FIG 7   Correct rear view, showing well-rounded quarters, rear legs even, fully supporting the hound

Incorrect rear view, showing narrow, unmuscular quarters and cow hocks

long heavy body are the hindquarters. Good heavy bone is hard to obtain in the hind legs, but if possible it should be in proportion to the front. American breeders must be given credit for producing hounds excelling in hindquarters. Viewed from the rear the muscles of the thighs should be so firm and prominent that they form a spherical mass; these thighs were described in the early standard as being as 'round as an apple'. The French hounds have firmly muscled quarters and a peculiar little curlicue formation of hair on each hip joint. Looking from the side, the hindquarters should be deep and wide through the thigh. The legs are short from hock to foot, the hocks being well down and well bent with the pouch of loose skin on each one.

The legs should be straight and true, in stance and movement, and any tendency towards cow-hocks or bowed hocks should be penalised. When standing naturally the hind feet come well under the body, but any similarity to a crouching stance is to be avoided. In common with all the other body points the hindquarters should be strongly made and capable of providing a very forceful hind action. The height of the hound at the quarters should be the same as the height at the shoulders.

FIG 8   Correct angulation of the hind legs, showing good bend of stifle and low-set hocks
Incorrect angulation of the hind legs. Hock is high. Steep stifle causes wrong topline

At the outset of the discussion on body points I said the actual body of the Basset should be 'a long dog', and it is given this definition in the French Standard. The overall body structure should be oblong-shaped and on no account should a Basset be short-backed or cobby. There is a compromise, and I am not defending the exaggerated 'crocodile type', but equally bad, if not worse, are the short-backed hounds, and I think that when confronted by a too long hound and a too short hound one should favour the former.

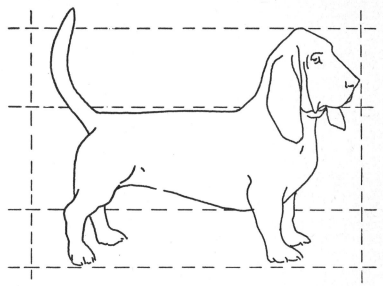

FIG 9   How the Basset Hound should fit into the oblong shape

Giving additional length to the body is the prominent sternum or breast-bone, and this should protrude in front of the forelegs. It is sometimes called the hook-bone—one should be able to hook a finger or thumb in the protruding bone, and it should always be readily visible. From the sternum, the chest should curve down to its deepest point, the brisket, which should be immediately between the front legs and supported seemingly in the crook of the knees. Apart from being deep in the brisket, the chest should also be well rounded, and behind the shoulder and in the barrel of the body the ribs should be well sprung and rounded. When sounding the rib-case with the hands it should be deep, round, and free from flange-ended ribs—a deformity at the bottom of the ribs and usually present in flat-sided hounds. Some tucking-up under the loins is usual, but the rib-case should be deep enough throughout, and the back rib deep enough to prevent any lack of depth through the loins.

The topline from shoulder to quarters should be long and level, with no tendency to dip or roach. The British Standard permits some curve over the quarters, but this must always slope down to the base of the tail and thus even out the topline. A dip behind the shoulder usually denotes some flaw in the front. The back should be wide and as strong as an oak beam, and well covered with good firm muscle.

Just as the neck helps to balance the forepart, the tail should perform the same function in the rear. It should be of good length, strong and thick at the base, tapering slightly towards the end but continuing strong and thick. When moving, the tail should be held 'sabre-fashion', and I interpret this to mean a gentle curve up and out from the body. Except when excited the hound should not carry the tail curved over his back. A thin, spindly and curly tail is hideous, and a very unsightly fault. Some differences exist in the standards regarding exhibitors holding the stern up when posing their hounds in the show ring. The French Standard absolutely forbids the practice, but British and American exhibitors usually form the hound's stern, and it appears to be the practice in the U.S.A. to hold the tail in a tight curve over the back.

Over the whole body the coat and skin should be healthy, and supple and elastic to feel. One should be able to draw the skin from the body at any point, and not just about the neck where it is always loosest. The coat should be shiny and glowing with health and it must be of such a texture that it can withstand damp and cold. Naturally texture and coat density vary from country to country because of differing climatic conditions.

One attraction of the breed is the multitude of colour schemes, the classic tricolours, the variegated tricolours, and

Thomas Fall

Fredwell Maestro, 1963

Ch. Brackenacre Annabella, 1964

English Basset, Westerby Sabre, 1956

Artésien-Normand Basset, Int. Ch. Maja, 1963

the mass of varying shades of bicolours. All are beautiful. A good hound cannot be a bad colour, and quite wisely colour is not assessed by judges. It is all a matter of fancy, and any colour is acceptable because no officially approved colours are given with the 'recognised hound colour' definition. The old books tell of Bassets coming in all colours and this is how it should be today. The Artois-Norman Standard defines desirable colours, but in France this is essential because of the presence of three other closely related Basset breeds. The French regard orange and white as the oldest colour combination, but the tricolour is most common. For an example of the orthodox colouring see the photograph of Ulema de Barly.

We have now completed the analysis of all the Basset's points, but one important factor remains, movement. Naturally if the hound is constructed properly to the definitions of the standards, correct movement should follow automatically, but I have stressed the absence of perfection in the Basset and in view of this some variation in movement is inevitable. The Basset must move in a way which denotes strength, and therefore, although free and unerratic, the movement must be forceful and thrusting. The forelegs should reach well out and straight ahead, and avoid any tendency to weave or paddle. The hind legs should bend well at the hock, permitting the foot to come well under the body, and thrust back powerfully as befits a well-muscled hound. Both fore and hind legs should have room between them, and closeness or a narrow action is not desired, neither is a short choppy stride. The stride must be even, in a controlled 1.2.3.4. gait, and there should be no similarity between Basset action and that of a short-coupled Terrier.

Many judges describe the Basset as having a 'rolling gait', but I think the movement of the loose skin on the mobile body can create the illusion of a roll. In action the tail should be up, and also if possible the head. However, many hounds, intrigued by show-ring scents, hold the head low and judges should make allowances for this, as they should for young, novice hounds who, because of inexperience, carry tail and head low, and who sometimes because of immaturity are not so steady in movement as a mature hound.

G

Recalling that Basset means 'low-set', the height limit, regardless of which standard they conform to, should be fifteen inches. Most hounds come well under this limit, and in weight and height the dog-hounds usually exceed the females.

Some measurements of old hounds may be interesting and provide comparisons with the measurements given in the previous chapter: In his book *Les Races de Chien* (1897) Count de Bylandt gives measurements and weights for:

1. Le Couteulx Type: height $8\frac{1}{2}$–$12\frac{1}{2}$ in.; weight 39–48 lb.
2. Lane Type: „ $11\frac{3}{4}$–$13\frac{3}{4}$ in.;   „   44–53 lb.

All three standards, in conclusion, give a list of the more serious faults, and in the U.S.A. and France the faults that mean disqualification are: U.S.A, over fifteen inches in height, knuckled front, and long coat; France, undershot mouth, straight legs and blue mottled markings—this latter point is to avoid encroachment on the Blue Mottled Gascon.

It is all too easy when discussing the standards to fall into a habit of fault-finding, and a breed as difficult as the Basset abets one in this. The breeder must be continually on the lookout for serious faults and take necessary steps to eliminate them; they cannot be overlooked. Vigilance must be exercised, but faults must not become an obsession, as every single specimen has them and always will have. Therefore I think one would be better occupied searching for the virtues that every hound has, and trying to increase and perpetuate them.

The standard must remain the sole guide, and the application of the national standard must be paramount; however, a good knowledge of the other two versions cannot be anything but beneficial, and they can be a great help to the breeder who is, or should be, constantly desiring to improve the Basset Hound.

The Artois-Norman Basset. I have said that the Artois-Norman is very much a hunting dog. Breeders place much emphasis on the hunting qualities of their hounds and breeding plans are arranged to improve on these qualities. The old, slow-hunting, heavy Basset has gone, and the modern Artois-Norman presents a much lighter and racier outline than its ancestors, the Artois or Norman breeds.

A really good hound is very elegant. This is a description

that does not fit many Bassets, but it ideally describes the Artois-Norman. It is much finer throughout than the British or American hound, and much more agile and sharp-witted. The skull is long and the muzzle tends to be Roman shaped, but the head is absolutely fleshless. The skin is very fine-textured and elastic, but it does not wrinkle much on the head, and consequently when compared with British and American Basset heads the Artois-Norman is often incorrectly called plain-headed. The eye is dark and very bright and expressive, but the red of the lower eyelid seldom shows. The French breeders have considered the retention of the low-set fine texture and corkscrew curling ears as of paramount importance, and on this point the French hounds excel. The heavy, flat-hanging and round-ended ear is markedly absent from French hounds.

The standard says the Artois-Norman is 'a long dog' and he must stand '*bien planté, bien assemblé*'—'well made and standing true'. Take a glance at the photograph of Ulema de Barly and observe how well he demonstrates these features. The neck is long and elegant and the lengthy topline is level throughout its length; most hounds stand true on the soundest of legs and feet. The foot tends to be elongated rather than round, but the tendency to a hare foot is a virtue.

Lack of depth in the brisket gives the illusion of a higher Basset than the British hound, but in fact most good Artois-Normans measure less than their British counterparts. Excessive depth of chest is not encouraged as it would impede speed.

The French love even colouring in a pack and to meet this desire most breeders have concentrated on the very dark tricolour. The standard sets out the most acceptable form of colouring, but any combination is allowed, although unofficially the breeders are not fond of hounds having a predominantly white body. The common colouring is the whole tan head, no white blaze, black back and sides, with tan shoulders and quarters, and white only on the feet and tail-tip and chest. In effect the colour is that of the old Norman hound. The lovely bright orange and white of the Artois breed is now seldom seen; breeders do nothing to encourage it and it is in danger of disappearing altogether. Having owned an Artois-Norman for many years and been in close contact with many more, I can vouch for the pleasantness of their character and sweet temperament. They are constantly happy, sterns up and very mobile, and they are on the move all day investigating this and that. They are undaunted by anything or anybody and need no encouragement to hunt. Should one fault a breed as over-exuberant, because Artois-Normans are, or should one be indulgent to this trait? I think the latter, because in a primarily hard-working breed some eagerness and virility are desirable.

Kennelled up, the breed can be noisy, probably because of boredom. They thrive on work and in the field are fast, diligent workers with good voice and more patience than the other Basset breeds. Their lightness and agility is a help, of course, and it takes a severe obstacle to stop them. Most are hunted on hare and rabbit but occasionally some owners hunt deer and fox.

The Artois-Norman coat and fine skin are no match for the British climate, and I found my Hercule had no resistance at all to the cold and damp winter weather.

The breed is second in popularity in France and holds its ground well. The hard core of breeders and the *Club du Basset Artésien-Normand* see to this. I do not think for one moment that any of these people would like to see the breed reach the kind of popularity it has in Britain; they are at the moment proud of the great improvement that has taken place in modern Artois-Norman type and they would naturally like to maintain quality and hunting prowess and ignore quantity.

There remain three distinctive French Basset breeds, the Blue Mottled Gascon, the Fawn Breton and the Griffon-Vendeen.

The Blue Mottled Gascon Basset. Although this very beautiful breed survived the Revolution in all its forms—*Grand Chien, Briquet* and *Basset*—it has never been numerically strong since. Its close relative, the Saintonge hound, disappeared and it is very likely that it became integrated with the Gascon. In the large *Grand Chien* this did happen, and the breed consequently developed is now known as the Gascon-Saintongeois.

As its name suggests the Gascon breed originated in the old province of Gascony in south-west France. From 1150 to 1450 Gascony was under British rule and it is thought that hounds taken back to Britain were the forerunners of the old Southern Hound, whose nearest descendants are now the Holcombe Harriers.

The chief characteristic of the Gascon is the most wonderful colouring, and words cannot really do its beauty justice. The head is black, with tan marks over the eyes, on the cheeks and inside the ears. The muzzle is usually blue-mottled. The body is basically blue-mottled, blue-black flecks on a white base, and the large black patches should not predominate. The feet and legs are tan-mottled and tan is usually found on the thigh joints. All the colours, black, blue-black, and white and tan, should be vivid and not washy.

There is also a puce or plum-mottled colour, giving a deep wine-red splashed effect, but this colouring is exceptionally rare.

The Gascon Bassets are smaller than the Artois-Normans and do not possess that breed's enthusiasm for life. The Gascons I have seen were, without exception, rather shy and very sensitive. If these traits have always been common it probably explains their lack of popularity. Like the Artois-Normans they are long-bodied, and in correspondence the skull is very long and lean and the muzzle lengthy and more sharply defined than the normal Basset profile. The ears are ultra-fine and curl well inwards in the corkscrew style. The breed has a tendency to light eyes and a really dark eye is rare. Unfortunately substance and heavy bone are rare too, and good strong hounds are an exception. However, despite the drawback of not having substance the Gascons do not lack hunting ability, and they are very sagacious hunters with probably the best nose and voice of all the Basset breeds. They are especially good on hare and rabbit, and can hunt ground that is difficult from the scent-holding point of view.

The breed today is in a precarious position, although the *Briquet* and *Petit Bleu* are fairly popular.

The Fawn Breton Basset. At one time the whole range of

Breton hounds seems to have been very popular, but now the only remaining version is the *Basset*, and even it is exceedingly scarce. The breed is very old and thought to be the forerunner of the *Griffon-Vendéen* and *Griffon-Nivernais* hounds. All the rough-coated breeds have much in common, structurally and temperamentally, and may well have shared the same origin. Geographically, too, they all originated on the west coast of France in the old province of Brittany.

The culture of the people of Brittany and the people of Cornwall and Wales has always been similar and there has always been lively interchange. It seems reasonable to suppose that the 'low-set fawn-coloured hound, with deep voice and long ears' found in Cornwall about a century ago is a descendant of the Fawn Breton Hound.

The breed had not been popular for some time and was in grave danger of extinction when a club was formed in an attempt to re-establish it. The little Breton hound is now in the process of a slow regeneration. However, because of the scarcity of good hounds the great problem facing the race today is the effect of continued inbreeding.

The two chief causes for the decline of the Fawn Breton are temperament and colour.

The little hounds, smallest of the four breeds, are notoriously difficult to manage, and for amateur huntsmen one couple is considered ample. The Breton is very excitable, fiery and generally quarrelsome. A characteristic of the breed is the very quick gait and the stern carried well over the back, things usually associated with a sharp temper. Despite their lack of size Fawn Bretons are tireless and fearless hunters, and although chiefly used on small game they have no second thoughts about pursuing wolf or the wild boar.

In a world constantly demanding more glamour, the monotony of the Breton's colouring is a decided drawback. The colour is basically fawn and the ideal is a wholly coloured fawn hound, the fawn being an even shade and white markings absent. The colouring can, however, vary from very dark russet fawn to a pale wheaten shade or fawn with a grey-grizzled back. White markings are discouraged. Because of the colour and the speed of the Breton it could be mistaken for game and shot at.

The Griffon-Vendeen Basset. The Department of Vendée in western France has always been a traditional stronghold of hunting and a cradle of hound-breeding. That tradition is proudly maintained today and the smaller Vendeen hounds very vigorously preserved. Before 1900 the large *Grand Chien* of the same race seems to have been popular and many packs were hunted. However, possibly because of the expense of keeping numbers of large hounds it is now virtually extinct. Incidentally, the Vendeen was also found in the smooth-coated version.

Today the Griffon-Vendeen is very popular. It is certainly the most numerous of all the French hounds and in the *Briquet*, *Grand* and *Petit Basset* has many admirers.

The *Briquet* is a medium-sized hound, very useful as a worker, standing fifty centimetres. The *Basset* version is sub-divided into two types, the *Basset grande taille*, or large Basset, standing around forty centimetres, and the *Basset petite taille*, or small Basset, standing under thirty-eight centimetres.

In all types the accent is on soundness and working ability, and it is largely due to the Vendeen's great aptitude for hunting that it is now the most popular hound in France. Some very knowledgeable hound-breeders have been connected with the Vendeen, and their influence on the breed in the early days set a high standard of quality, apparent today.

The coat and texture of the hair are very important points, and the standard states that the coat should be 'thick, harsh and tough. Never long, silky or woolly, fringes not too abundant'. Clearly a very workmanlike and protective coat is desired. The hair is hard and crisp to feel and has a good undercoat. It is not unlike the coat of a really good Dandie Dinmont Terrier.

The colouring of the Vendeen varies and is conveniently divided into three groups by the breed club: unicoloured hounds, grey or grizzled, but self fawn not encouraged; bi-coloured hounds, hounds coloured in a combination of orange, black, gold, grey, tan, with white; tricoloured hounds, hounds coloured in a triple combination of colours, usually black, tan and white or grey, tan and white.

The light bicoloured hounds have always been the most popular and at one period the intensive breeding of bicolours began to produce albino puppies. The same undesirable feature was found in the large *porcelain* hounds, which are delicately coloured. The condition seems to have been remedied by the infusion of dark-coloured well-pigmented hounds, but the continued preference for bicoloured Vendeens and inbreeding of this colour combination seems to be inadvisable.

There is nothing sober about the Vendeen and the description 'reposeful, sad, full of sorrowful expression' which is given to the smooth-coated breeds would not apply to the Griffons. They have great dignity but their whole carriage is geared to activity; the head is characteristically held high, the expression is very alert and the hounds find it difficult to stand still for long. They seem to be poised in constant readiness for work. This attitude, coupled with the short back and straight legs, seems to veer more to the terrier than to the hound and Mr. Muir, one of the few British breeders to own a pack of Griffons, has said that their style of hunting is not hound-like but more in the style of terriers.

Every hound authority, ancient and modern, agrees that the Vendeen is a very admirable little hound and I would humbly concur: the breed is attractive and full of character. Its effervescent nature and independence is perhaps its only fault. I am convinced that, now the breed has been reintroduced into Britain, it stands every chance of becoming firmly established and will be a welcome addition to the Hound group. This prophecy seems to ignore the record of past vicissitudes of Vendeens in Britain, but today I think that most Basset fanciers have a clearer picture of the Vendeen and that they are no longer such an unknown quantity because of coverage in recent books such as Appleton's *The Basset Hound Handbook*, Braun's *The Complete Basset Hound*, and previous editions of this one. Most important too is the Kennel Club's decision to register them as Bassets Griffon-Vendeen and not as Basset Hounds (rough-coated) which was the case in the past and which caused much confusion.

5

The Basset in Other Countries

THE Basset has clearly demonstrated on many previous occasions a most adaptable character, and it is probably this trait which has contributed most to the present position it holds as one of the world's best-known hound breeds. The breed seems unaffected by climate; it thrives in the cold northern lands and is equally at home in Australia and the East and West African heat and humidity. This chapter will show, too, the Basset hunting jackal and leopard in South Africa, a far cry from the more normal modern quarry, the hare.

The Basset Hound proper, be it American or British type, claims the biggest following, and the largest assembly of breeders is found in the U.S.A., Britain and Australia, with rapidly growing support in South Africa and New Zealand.

The surveys of the Basset in other countries must unfortunately be only an outline.

Australia. Owing to ill-health Sir Everett Millais had to leave England in 1880 and go to Australia, where he stayed for four years. During that time he was in contact with Australian hound-breeders, and later he was responsible for sending them the first Bassets ever to go to Australia. Between 1890 and 1893 he organised the selection and export of several hounds on behalf of Messrs. J. C. Anderson, J. McLaughlin and A. Harvey, and with the nucleus draft these gentlemen formed the Melbourne Hunt Club and had the hounds at Surrey Hills, Victoria.

Sir Everett Millais gave Ch. Merlin to the Australians, and at the same time Mrs. Stokes presented them with Chilworth, who was described as 'a magnificent young dog'. Six bitches were chosen from the kennels of Mrs. Stokes, Mrs. Ellis, Mr. Krehl, Mr. Matchem and the Rev. Jackson, and these were Diana II by Fino VI, Venus II, Amazon by Comus x Busybody, Jessamy by Jocelyn x Justine, and Chloe II and her daughter Viva, both by Bourbon. The large draft was followed by Wanda and Levity, imported by Mr. Anderson and Mr. McLaughlin.

The nucleus was representative of the finest blood in England, and the Melbourne Hunt Club was indeed fortunate in having the patronage of Millais. A small band of enthusiasts hunted the hounds and the first Basset was exhibited at the Melbourne Royal in 1891. Unfortunately the enthusiasm of the few Basset devotees was not infectious; the breed failed to gain any further support and was virtually unknown outside the Melbourne area.

An intention to import pure French stock is revealed in a letter from Millais to McLaughlin when he states, 'buy only from western France, the breed in the east of France degenerates almost to a Dachshund'. The intention seems to have remained unfulfilled because there is no trace of any French Bassets having entered Australia.

A total lack of interest seems to have been the only reason for the breed's eclipse. It appears to have died out in the early 1900s. It was not reintroduced until 1957, when Mr. Spira of Turra-Murra and Mr. McInolty of Baulkham Hill commissioned the late all-round judge, Mr. Macdonald Daly, to select a couple from the Grims kennel of Miss Keevil. By 1959 the breed had become firmly re-established, especially in New South Wales, and although there was a lack of larger kennels numbers were well maintained by many fanciers who kept only one or two hounds. The ancestry of every Australian hound was pure English and therefore rather restricted in the range of bloodlines, and the Australian hounds were as susceptible as the English to deterioration due to continued inbreeding. In Britain recent importations of French and American hounds had been made, and Mr. Spira very quickly and wisely obtained some of this fresh blood by importing two hounds, direct descendants of the French and American hounds. In 1960 he purchased Fochno Lavendar, a very dark tricoloured daughter of Lyn-Mar-Acres Dauntless from his first English litter, out of Fochno Cherry and bred by Mrs. Jagger. In the same year he bought a very dark tricoloured dog-puggy, Sykemoor Dauphin, out of the third litter sired by my French import Hercule de l'Ombrée and out of Ch. Rossingham Amber.

The two hounds have had an unprecedented influence on the Australian Basset and the modern type is a direct result of this. The home-produced hounds have had high praise from visiting British, American and New Zealand judges, and there seems to be no doubt that the overall quality of the Basset Hound in Australia is as high as anywhere else in the world. The Basset Hound Club of New South Wales is very active and the Australian breeders wisely continue the policy of buying good hounds from Britain, which ensures that no isolated national type of 'Australian Basset' is ever likely to appear.

The first Basset in Tasmania made its appearance in 1960, but the breed has gained few admirers in the succeeding years. In 1964 only sixteen hounds were recorded. All are descendants of Australian hounds.

New Zealand. In 1889 Lord Onslow was appointed Governor-General of New Zealand. He was so annoyed by the strict Australasian quarantine laws that he refused to take any hounds out with him. Because of this New Zealand missed the early opportunity of an introduction to Basset Hounds.

It was not until 1960 that the breed first appeared. Mr. Janee of Woodlands Park imported a draft from Victoria. They were Longview Mandy (Fochno Chestnut x Calumet Camille), Longview Loyalty and later Calumet Camille in whelp to Australian Ch. Blandville Bugler. Her resultant litter of eight was the first to be born in New Zealand.

The breed slowly gathered support, especially in the Auckland area of the North Island, and in 1962 the Basset Hound Club of New Zealand was formed.

Seventy-four breeds are recognised by the New Zealand K.C., and the Basset Hound, with twenty-seven registrations in 1965, occupied thirty-ninth position of popularity. The breed is very fortunate in having a prominent hound judge as one of its champions, and Miss Gorrie has done much to provide guidance for the Bassets during its initial settlement in New Zealand.

Africa. It is known that a farmer in the Transvaal had Bassets in 1924, and another had hounds in Cape Province in 1932. The hounds they had are reputed to have come from South-West Africa, where some German settlers had Bassets of a type described as 'shorter-eared and broader-headed than today's Bassets, but still a useful little hound'. The same settlers are also known to have had hounds resembling Griffon-Vendeen Bassets.

In South Africa today all the Bassets are descended from stock sent out from Britain. The original resurrection and establishment of the breed can be traced back to the importation of four hounds between 1957 and 1959. It is not surprising, considering the close relationship of the original imports with top-ranking British hounds, that their progeny should be of a very high standard and identical in type with the older type of British hound.

The newly formed Basset Hound Club of South Africa should ensure that the breed gains strength and is promoted as a dual-purpose hound. Mrs. Newby-Fraser, Mrs. Evans and Mrs. Fletcher are founder members of the club and are ably supported by Mr. Clark of Lyttelton who has the Maitland hounds, Mrs. Eales of Pretoria with her Hatherleigh stock, and Mr. Behrman, Mrs. Scott, and Mr. De Ridder.

The breed has a definite future as a hound proper. The Department of Nature Conservation in Cape Province have used Bassets for hunting jackal but found the breed unsuitable as it was too prone to injuries to the feet and cuts on the ears. Fortunately the department has not lost faith in Bassets and have two hounds in the process of being trained for tracking lynx and leopard.

In Rhodesia Mr. and Mrs. Whittaker have a kennel founded on South African stock. The breed seems to have no difficulty in getting acclimatised and British breeders have sent stock to Kenya, Zambia, Ghana, Nigeria and Sierra Leone in addition to the countries already mentioned.

France. It is, of course, generally conceded that the Artois-

Norman Basset is the ancestor of the Basset Hound, though it may not have found the universal acceptance of the latter. Some of the French history of the Basset has been traced in Chapter 1, and in Chapter 4 I have given the standard and a description of the Artois-Norman as well as briefly describing the other three existing French Basset breeds and their present standing in France. Many more Artois-Normans are now being exported than formerly, but the other three native breeds are not found in any quantity outside France and the Low Countries.

Scandinavia. Danish-born Queen Alexandra was a great lover of the Basset Hound and had a renowned kennel in Britain. There is no evidence pointing to the existence of the breed in her native land at that time, although French and British hounds illustrate early Danish canine books.

In 1959 and 1960 Mrs. Ries and her daughter, of Holte, began to found their Reisbo kennel with several imports from Britain. Indefatigably the Rieses campaigned their hounds all over Scandinavia. Sykemoor Blossom qualified for her Int. Ch. title and became immortalised when the Royal Copenhagen Porcelain Company used her as a model for a statuette. A precedent for this had been set many years earlier when another equally famous firm, Dahl-Jensen, had made a similar model of Potford Ragout, one of Mrs. Foster-Rawlin's hounds.

The Basset slowly progressed and attracted the attention of a few more admirers. The nucleus of the breed in Denmark is the same as the present-day hound in Britain, a composite of British, French and American types. It was probably for this reason that the Danish Kennel Club, contrary to Continental custom, adopted the British breed standard. Two very prominent Kennel Club members, Mr. Parkild and Dr. Krasilnikoff, have given much guidance and assistance to Danish Basset fanciers, and it is largely because of their influence and the perseverance of Mrs. and Miss Ries that the breed is a regular exhibit at Danish shows.

Danish-bred hounds are, for some unknown reason, invariably Blue Mottled, and Riesbo Ajax and Agathe are two prominent winners who have carried this colouring.

The pioneer of the breed in Sweden is Police Sergeant Petersen of Odeshog, and his Astors hounds have been known since the early 1950s. The British breed standard is followed in Sweden, too, but in the 1950s some concern was expressed about the dangers of crossing Bassets with the low-set native hounds in the *Drever* and *Stover* groups. Fortunately this drastic course was averted and the pure Basset continued. Further imports of British stock implemented a somewhat weakening breed.

The breed is making progress, albeit slow, in Norway and Finland, and a club for Basset Hounds and Bassets Artois-Normands has recently been formed in the latter country. In both countries most of the present stock has been imported from Britain and France.

Belgium. The Basset was known in Belgium from its very birth. Du Foulloux mentions the Flanders type and the *Basset d'Ardennes* was common to France and Belgium. However, for some reason the breeds of Bassets did not retain their popularity in Belgium as they did in France.

Some years ago Mr. Gerald Dakin, M.R.C.V.S., exported Brockhampton Admiral to the Royal Belgian Household, but despite this revival of royal patronage for Bassets they remain rather low in numbers.

Holland. The breed was first recorded in Holland in 1895 but did not gain much support. Even today the Basset is not numerically strong, but the bloodlines of the Dutch hounds are interesting and remarkable because of their purity.

The oldest kennel is the du Toutounier, founded before 1939 by Mrs. Gondrexon Ives-Browne of Rhenen. She has recently been joined by Miss Martin of Harfsen and Mr. Phillipens of Amby.

Like very many other Continental kennels, that of Mrs. Gondrexon Ives-Browne had to disband in 1939 and was not re-established until after the war. Three hounds were imported, Agile and Anatole des Mariettes and Arabelle de L'Ombrée, all from France. It was the intention to reproduce the older stamp of Artois-Norman that had been lost in the war years, and all Mrs. Gondrexon Ives-Browne's hounds were inbred to the early de Jaulzy, de Barly and des Mariettes hounds of the 1930s that had the desired substance.

Mrs. Gondrexon Ives-Browne wanted to regain the substance without resorting to introducing outcross Basset Hound blood. It was a question of inbreeding with an already intensively inbred group of hounds.

Several Basset Hounds have been imported into Holland from Britain, and are shown as such in classes separated from the Artois-Normans. Two standards are therefore applied.

The United States of America. One glance at Appendix A will clearly show the extent of the Basset Hound's popularity in America; without a doubt there are many more hounds there than anywhere else in the world. The statistics also demonstrate that the present state of popularity has been reached in a very short time. In this respect the breed's development in the U.S.A. has been similar to that in Britain. In both countries it was first officially recorded in the late nineteenth century but failed to attract much attention and, after several periods of alternating activity and inactivity, finally emerged as a very popular breed in the 1950s.

Although the first official registrations of Bassets were made in 1885, the breed was certainly known in America before that date. George Washington was a well-known hound-lover and sportsman. His diary reveals that he had Bassets, and it is thought that he came to know the breed when Lafayette and his followers introduced him to the curious little hound.

In 1883 Mr. George Krehl, the well-known British breeder, exported Nemours 1883 (Jupiter x Vivien) and by 1886 he was a champion. Jupiter was also the sire of some other early imports. Lord Aylesford, a Texas cattle-baron, had a little pack for hunting hares and it contained a couple by the well-known English dog. Mr. Gilbert of Connecticut also had a hound Canace, by Jupiter.

The first hounds to be recorded with the American Kennel Club in 1885 were Bouncer (Major x Venus), a tricolour owned by Mr. Campbell of Pennsylvania and bred by Mr. Dorsey of Maryland, and Countess (Nero x Lotta), owned by Mr. Seitner of Ohio and bred in Germany by Mr. Krecht.

The breed did not attract much attention and outside the little groups of admirers was virtually unknown. A real turning-point came in the 1920s, when several prominent Eastern gentlemen became attracted to Bassets almost simultaneously, and with no expense spared imported outstanding hounds from leading European packs. I must be forgiven for harking back to similarities with English development, but in this case the same thing happened—men of means buying the very best stock. Had not the insistence been on quality, the Basset Hound in both countries might have been very different today.

Among those who imported hounds in the 1920s and 1930s were Mr. Gerald Livingstone of Huntingdon, Long Island, who founded his Kilsyth pack in 1921; Mr. Erastus Tefft, a New York stockbroker, who founded the Staridge kennel; Mr. Lewis Thompson of Rochester, Mr. Sloan, Mrs. Consuela Ford and Mr. Carl E. Smith of Xenia, Ohio. Mr. Smith, now aged eighty-three, is still very active in the breed, and his hounds have had a decided influence on the American Basset.

The importers purchased French and English stock, and the Walhampton pack was heavily drafted upon. Major Heseltine exported many prominent hounds at very large prices. The highest recorded figure, according to Lieutenant-Colonel E. Morrison, was £500, but Tefft is said to have paid £1,000 for Lavenham Pippin and £350 for Leader.

In 1933 Dr. Rosslyn Bruce sold Walhampton Nicety 1930 (W. Grazier x W. Nicknack [1929]), a litter sister of Ch. Walhampton Nightshade, to Mr. Lewis Thompson, along with Amir of Reynalton (Brancaster Amant x Dignity of Lohaire). Lieutenant-Colonel Morrison, the present custodian of the Walhampton records, stated in a letter to me that the Heseltines had two types of hound, the hunting hound and the show hound, and it was the latter type that was sold to America.

The Dalby Hall was another pack from which the Americans drew nucleus stock, and the owner, Colonel Burns-Hartopp, exported Dalby Hall Drifter, Dormouse Vanda, Willow and a well-known stallion, Diligence 1924. Diligence had sired some Walhampton hounds including Wafer 1925.

Mr. Erastus Tefft imported a couple of English hounds called Leader 1922 (Gallant x Daffodil) and Lavenham Pippin 1922 (Parkmore Gameboy x Pampeute).

As well as purchasing hounds from major English kennels, the Americans also bought many French hounds. Mr. Livingstone's first hound was French, although not very good quality. He had some unfortunate dealings with an unscrupulous French dog-dealer which delayed his plans for forming a first-class pack, but eventually he did import a fine hound, Brano (Meteor de Fremont x Ravaude), from M. Baillet of Rouen.

Some American hounds contain in their ancestry a couple of hounds called Old Deck and Dolly M. They are said to be descended from stock that came from Russia. Apart from that, little is known of them except that they were the forerunners of a very hardy hunting strain.

Because of some disagreement with the French Kennel Club (S.C.C.) the American Kennel Club would not accept the registration of the French imports until several years after, and Mr. Tefft and Mr. Carl Smith were obliged to register stock with the United Kennel Club and the American Field of Chicago. It was not until the formation of the Basset Hound Club of America that the A.K.C. accepted the registrations of the hounds they had previously refused to recognise. It is for this reason that several gaps and omissions of prominent imports and early hounds exist in the A.K.C. records.

Despite these 'political' discords the early importers used the hounds a great deal and they are to be found in the pedigrees of almost every American hound today. Since the middle 1930s very few European Bassets have been imported. Therefore the influence they once had has waned and the breed has developed differently in the U.S.A. The deeper, heavy-chested and somewhat shorter-coupled hound has emerged, and today there are some considerable differences between the American, British and French types. To meet these changes, a standard applying only to the American was drawn up and adopted by the A.K.C.

In 1930, after the death of Mr. Tefft, Mr. Carl Smith took over all that remained of the Staridge pack, and on behalf of Mrs. Tefft sold many of the hounds and purchased the re-

H

mainder himself. A good price was difficult to obtain in the Depression years and most of Tefft's hounds went for very low ones.

The two hounds with Russian ancestry, Old Deck and Dolly M., produced Smith's Major D.

Mr. Leslie S. Kelly, of New Alexandria, Pennsylvania, whose stock is descended from Smith's hounds, always wanted completely red hounds, and bred a great many Bassets with this colouring. To perpetuate the colour in his stock, Mr. Kelly inbred and selected only red and white and lemon and white hounds to breed from.

In the early days of his kennel Mr. Kelly used his own name as a prefix (this is a custom peculiar to the American Basset world; even today many prominent breeders use their name as a prefix). Later Mr. Kelly changed his kennel's name to Belbay and he also used the prefix Neleighs.

A prominent influence in the transition between Kelly's and Belbay was a hound called Butzs Ch. Yankee Boy (Kelly's Ch. Chief Hareman x Kelly's Jet Girl).

The Belbay hounds were noted for their gay temperaments and showmanship, and they had great success in the ring. If Smith had worked in the background, fusing all the various bloodlines and making the American Basset, then Kelly brought the American Basset into the sphere of the shows. The European hound was very much in the background, and the formation of the Basset Hound Club of America in 1936 heralded the start of the systematic perpetuation of the wholly American hound.

The breed is widespread in the United States, with the greatest density of breeders in the eastern coast states, California and the Ohio, Illinois, Pennsylvania complex. There are hundreds of kennels all worthy of honourable mention, but it is impossible for me to deal with them here. The most comprehensive and exhaustive study of the local American Basset scene is to be found in Mrs. Mercedes Braun's *The Complete Basset Hound* (New York, 1965).

In such a huge country it is not surprising that some differences in type should exist between hounds in the east and those in the west, although today the differences are being evened out. It is by no means unique for a Californian breeder to send a bitch for mating to a dog on the east coast; the emergence of fast jet-travel has made this possible. Despite this evening-out of breed-type, there is still a considerable difference between show-bench hounds and those bred specifically for hunting and field-trial work.

The average weight of the American show hound, according to a survey conducted in 1964–5 by Mr. Ben Harris, was: Male, 61·02 lb.; Female, 52·86 lb., and the comparable average weight of the field trial hound was: Male, 46·88 lb.; Female, 39·87 lb. From these stark figures it is obvious that the two groups of breeders have a wide difference of opinion as to what constitutes a Basset Hound.

One American hound has qualified for a dual championship title, and there are many hounds in Britain and a great many more in France that successfully combine show-ring success and hunting ability. In the face of this there does not seem to be a need for such a wide difference between the two groups in America.

The American Standard generally describes a hound rather more substantially constructed than the European hounds, and it is obvious that it cannot ideally accommodate lightweight and heavyweight hounds. Excess can be carried either way: the ultra-light, racy and verging on the lightweight Artois-Norman type, which is now being discarded by the French in favour of a more middleweight hound, or, on the other hand, the really heavy and deep-chested hound incapable of performing the Basset's legitimate role. The latter type verges on the 'show-bench curiosity' type that European breeders, and fortunately many Americans, work so hard to avoid. The photographs I have chosen to illustrate the American Basset Hound have been specially selected to show the existing type of hound without exaggeration—one that is capable of pleasing even the most pro-British or pro-French type fancier.

Bassets in the U.S.A. come in all the usual array of hound colours and the tricolours and bicolours are the same as elsewhere. There are, however, two colour schemes that are unique to the American Basset, the red and the black and tan. Both are reminiscent of the extinct Ardennes Basset. They are very attractive and the American breeders are to be envied for being able to produce them. The Belbay and Smith's hounds were strong in red colour properties, and the owner of the former, Mr. Kelly, was one of the first to attempt colour-breeding in the Basset. By inbreeding and selection he succeeded, and almost every Belbay hound is heavily marked with red.

Why these colours should be the virtual monopoly of the American hound it is difficult to say. They could be throw-backs to the Ardennes hounds or to the ancient orange and white Artois Bassets. If this assumption is correct, why do the colours not appear more often in British stock? After all, they have more French background than the American hounds. The colours are not found in France today, and this is probably due to the almost total insistence on breeding orthodox tricolours.

Quantity should never be a substitute for quality. Fortunately for the American Basset, although it is very numerous the number of high-quality hounds is also vast. The pioneer breeders of the American-type Basset are held in high esteem and their skill in formulating the type is legend.

Traditionalists in Europe may shudder at the wide use of Bassets in obedience and competitive field trials, at the employment of handlers and at the disregard of the old hound names. This diverse usage has allowed many more people to keep a Basset and to discover the vast amount of enjoyment there is to be had from it.

6

The Working Basset

MANY working breeds that become popular do so at the expense of their legitimate purpose, and the popularity they enjoy is purely because of their visual appeal. This is most marked in the terrier group, where only a minute proportion does any work at all. Fortunately a good number of gundog and hound breeds are still used for shooting and hunting as well as being bred for show. However, in all working breeds today the number of dogs being shown far outnumbers the dogs being worked. This is precisely the position with Bassets, and I doubt if the trend will ever be reversed, but it is a fact that more people, including ardent show-bench fanciers, are showing an interest in the Basset's working capabilities. The calibre of these is well known and has been for centuries, and to let such outstanding and versatile qualities stagnate for want of interest on the part of Basset breeders would be a sin.

There is not really such a wide division between the show-minded group and the hunting group. The latter must realise that not everyone is equipped to hunt; time and suitable country are not always available. Because some do not hunt their hounds they should not be labelled unsympathetic to the Basset's true purpose. Most are only too well aware of the great debt owing to the few who have maintained packs through very difficult periods, and it is true to say that those who cannot hunt hounds still try to breed them sound enough to do so if given the chance.

The Basset Hound Club today has a very enlightened policy towards the utility side of the breed and regards the maintenance of working ability as just as important as the quality of the show points. The policy is not to differentiate between the two: the Basset Hound should be handsome *and* useful. Soon after the club's foundation attempts were made to organise a club pack; unfortunately little information is available other than the record of a meet held at Bishopstone, near Aylesbury, in 1885, when the pack came under the control of a Mr. Etherwood. However, it appears that in succeeding years the attention of the club was devoted to the show hound, much to the disgust of the many members who kept packs. In 1908 there were thirty-nine packs and the owners included many prominent Basset personalities, the Heseltines of Walhampton fame, Sir Maurice Bromley-Wilson of Dallam Tower, Milnthorpe, and Lords North and Dorchester.

Great controversy raged between the show-minded breeders, who, backed by the B.H.C., continued to breed a type which the rival faction contended was too unsound to perform in the field. The split gradually widened and was accompanied by some bitterness, and it is not surprising that, in view of the illustrious names in the pro-hunting-type camp, the term 'class distinction' cropped up. Miss Ena Adams, co-owner of the Brancaster pack, later wrote about the Basset Hound Club: 'It had done a good job in popularising the breed, but like all show-clubs had started to insist on peculiarities of type, which caused the animal to lose its natural hunting ability. It is still argued by show-bench enthusiasts that the crippled Basset Hound of the show type is the right kind to hunt, as he is purposely evolved so that the sick, the lame and the blind can run with him and enjoy a day's hunting.'

Miss Adams need not have censored anyone for insisting on peculiarities when she herself had a pack of 'Bassets' standing eighteen inches at the shoulder! There were faults on both sides and a total absence of compromise. The B.H.C. judges continually gave awards to unsound hounds whose only virtue was the head, and yet the secretary of the B.H.C., Mr. Musson, is on record as saying that he was satisfied with type at that time.

The split was bound to come, and finally the admirers of the working hound washed their hands of the B.H.C. and formed the Masters of Basset Hounds Association in 1911. The principal founder members were the Heseltine brothers, Lords

North, Dorchester and Tredegar, Sir Maurice Bromley-Wilson and Colonel Burns-Hartopp. The new society opened a Stud Book and organised its own shows, which were held at Rugby and Banbury. One of the M.B.H.A. rules was that no member should exhibit at any show other than those organised by the society. The breakaway and the effects of this rule were catastrophic for the B.H.C. and Kennel Club registrations, for between them the founders of the M.B.H.A. had more hounds than anyone else. In thirteen years (1911–24) only fifty-seven hounds were registered at the K.C. Granted, World War I (1914–18) affected hound-breeding, but the principal reason for the appalling figures was the boycott by the M.B.H.A. The final low was reached in 1921 when the Basset Hound Club closed its books. Pride and personal prejudice had been satisfied, and the only sufferer was the Basset Hound.

The show hound and hunting hound lost much ground, and both sides lost even more, when the famous Walhampton pack, founded in 1891 by Major Godfrey Heseltine, was sold in 1932 after the death of the owner. The hounds were widely dispersed to British, French and American breeders for very low prices, and among those who bought hounds were Mrs. Nina Elms (Reynalton), Mrs. Edith Grew (Maybush) and M. Jean Rothéa of France.

Lieutenant-Colonel Eric Morrison had whipped-in for Heseltine for many years, and he eventually reformed the depleted pack and changed the name to Westerby, the reason being that Walhampton was being used as a prefix for Mr. Christopher Heseltine's gundogs. Lieutenant-Colonel Morrison re-formed the old pack on Harehound lines by introducing other hound breeds to the pure Basset. In 1959 he wrote to me saying: 'I am responsible chiefly for the dreadful crime of crossing the Basset with other hound breeds. I would like you to know that I did this solely to keep the breed alive, as in the middle thirties it was in danger of becoming extinct.' The statement concerning the breed in the thirties is correct, and not many hounds were being shown or hunted.

The period of inactivity was brightened by the foundation of Miss Keevil's kennel in 1935. She had cared for Mrs. Foster-

Rawlin's Potford hounds when they were kennelled at Bell-mead, and eventually purchased her first hound, Dulcamara of Reynalton, from Mrs. Elms. From the beginning Miss Keevil was interested in the work of the Basset and on the advice of Major Wade, Master of the Wick and Districk pack (founded 1925), she contacted Lieutenant-Colonel Morrison and added some early Westerby hounds to her Grims kennel.

With the development of the Grims kennel a simile can be drawn with the Walhampton pack. Both were intended to combine the original Basset type without losing the ability to hunt, and both kennels in their time have produced hounds that have had great influence on the breed, not only in Britain but also overseas. Miss Keevil fortunately managed to keep some hounds during the war and had a small nucleus in her possession when hostilities ended. Imports from France introduced valuable and urgently needed new blood, and the breed in Britain was again relatively safe but very low in numbers; Miss Keevil's was the only kennel of any size remaining.

Interest in the breed grew and eventually in 1954 the Basset Hound Club was re-formed, principally by the efforts of Miss Keevil and Mrs. Hodson of the Rossingham kennels. From the beginning the 'new' club set out to foster co-operation between those interested in showing and those whose pleasure was in hunting. Mrs. Hodson wrote in 1957: 'We want to breed Bassets that retain the old characteristics but who are active and sound enough to hunt, in other words hunting hounds that can win on the bench, and bench hounds that can hunt in the field. I think the future of Bassets is bright, there is definitely an effort being made to breed sound, active Bassets of the correct type.' Thus right from the start the revived B.H.C. made sure that the situation that had caused the schism many years earlier did not arise again.

Apart from Miss Keevil, other early members of the B.H.C. who had interests in the working hound were Mr. Lionel Woolner, Mr. Allen, who had the Kimblewick Hounds, Mr. George Mossman of Luton, and Major Jones-Stamp of Langholm, who had the Craigcleuch Hounds.

The early committee organised a series of drag hunts, and

these proved quite successful in opening up new activities to many Basset owners who would otherwise have been unable to work their hounds at all. The drag was usually a sheep's paunch or a hare, and a trail was laid for the pack to follow. Some northern members used the aniseed drag which is used for the hound trails in the northern counties. Miss Keevil and Mr. Allen both allowed members to take hounds along to their kennels and meets in order to gain experience and to get them used to hunting in a pack. In time, with the growth of the B.H.C., a working branch was formed to encourage and organise on a still wider scale the working of Basset Hounds. The club chairman, Mr. Alex McDonald, committee member Mr. John Evans, and, of course, Miss Keevil, were instrumental in setting up the new branch of the expanding club.

Today the working branch is a large and energetic section of the B.H.C., very active during the season from September to March. Before the season starts it holds walks and the occasional drag.

The 'walks' are informal affairs, with members taking along hounds mainly to get them used to strange pack companions and the commands of the officials. Preliminary drags are also staged to give the novice hounds an idea of a hunt and the discipline they will encounter on the hunt proper.

The officials not only take great pains to ensure that the hounds are fitted for the season; they also give talks and lectures on hunting etiquette and procedure to the newer members of the working branch.

In the late 1960's the Basset Hound Club decided to organise and run its own pack of Bassets and, with gifts of stock from club-members and the progeny from that nucleus, soon established a worthy pack of hounds with a hard-working and keen brand of followers. The pack is kennelled at Arkley near Barnet in Hertfordshire; the Huntsman is John Evans. As is to be expected, the pack hunt the European hare during the season.

For some years now the B.H.C. pack officials have worn a uniform, dark fawn jacket with mustard collar.

The B.H.C. award Working Certificates and these are keenly sought by hound owners. Unlike the French clubs, the B.H.C.

has no scale of points or set of requirements for judging a hound's ability in the field, but basic essentials are that the hound, as a member of the pack, must identify and hold a line, give mouth at the appropriate times and hunt steadily for two hours. There is no British equivalent for the American title Field Trial Champion.

The smooth running and organising of the working branch has contributed much to its popularity, and for many years the secretary responsible was Mrs. Joan Cherrett, who with Mr. Gerard Kemp devoted much time to the venture. The post is now held by Miss Jane Blois. The working branch is an essential and most necessary feature of the Basset Hound Club, and the fact that many formerly inexperienced hounds are now competent workers shows that although hunting prowess may become latent, it never quite disappears.

Because my experience of the Basset Hound in the field is virtually nil, I have called upon Mr. Lionel Woolner, m.h., to discuss this important and fascinating side of the breed. Mr. Woolner was a founder member of the B.H.C. and is now president and his kennel prefix is Cotlands. He was also a founder member of the re-formed Masters of Basset Hounds Association, and as Master of the West Lodge Harehounds is well equipped to deal with the Basset's style in hunting the hare. He is a 'hound man' from top to toe, with a particular interest in the French breeds. His contribution will be found in the following chapter.

In recent years some of the other Basset Hound clubs have realised the importance of keeping the breed's ability alive and have formed working branches very much on the British pattern. The Basset Hound Club of New Zealand have organised walks and meets and are progressing well in the field. The Basset Hound Club of New South Wales have a hunting committee and tracking committee. All four French Basset Hound societies regard the maintenance of hunting ability as the most important purpose of their existence. This is not surprising when one considers that the Basset in France is first and foremost a working hound and showing definitely of secondary importance.

The great popularity of the Basset in America as a show dog and companion often hides the fact that it is a very popular utility dog, being used in packs, field trials, and in obedience and tracking work.

There are eight packs of Bassets registered with the National Beagle Club, the governing body for hare-hunting packs in the U.S.A. The packs are almost wholly centred on the Eastern States, and it seems to be a curious fact that as one moves westward in America the interest in hunting diminishes. The packs, which hunt cottontail rabbit and imported European hare, are the Tewkesbury Foot, founded in 1951 and hunting in New Jersey, and the Stockford, formed in the thirties, by Mr. and Mrs. Bissell and hunting in Pennsylvania. Two other Pennsylvania-based packs are the Coldstream, founded in 1962, and the Skycastle, established in 1949. The Ashland, founded 1960, and the Somerset, formed a year earlier, hunt in Virginia, and the State of Maryland is represented by the Timberidge, formed in 1947. Hunting in the Mid-West are the Bridlespur Hounds founded in 1958.

The American packs all consist of pure hounds, and some were founded on Lyn-Mar Acres hounds from the prominent show kennel of Mrs. Lynwood Walton. Some packs, including the Stockford and Tewkesbury, have imported hounds from the Grims, Walhampton and Sykemoor kennels in England, and also from the Eastington Park and Westerby Packs.

Since 1937 the B.H.C. of America has encouraged the working and hunting of the breed, and in that year they held their first field trial. Today this sport has a wide following and is considered an integral part of the club's affairs. There is no equivalent in Europe to the field trials for hounds, but there is some resemblance to gundog trials in that the competing dogs run in pairs and the competition is decided on a knock-out basis.

The trials are usually held on land loaned to the Basset Hound societies by the Beagle clubs. The ground is owned and stocked with game by the regional Beagle clubs, and very often there is a clubhouse on the land too.

A line of beaters sets out over the ground, and when a rabbit is flushed the first pair of hounds is brought up to the spot and slipped on the line of the rabbit. The hounds must hunt the indicated line only, and in this respect the field trial differs from the normal procedure of a hunt, in which the hounds must find and flush the game themselves. The trialling hounds are judged by two judges, and although the handlers may follow their hounds they are not permitted to assist them in any way unless indicated by the judge.

No scale of points for evaluating the hounds' skill exists, but it stands to reason that the chief requirement is the ability to remain steady on one line. The title of Field Trial Champion is gained by amassing points calculated on the number of hounds competing in the trials. Since the inauguration of B.H.C.-sponsored trials in 1937, just over one hundred hounds have qualified for the title, but it was not until very recently that the first dual champion (show and field) qualified.

Some difference exists between the American show hounds and their field trialling counterparts, and these were clearly shown in the results of a survey by Mr. Ben Harris previously mentioned. The main difference was one of size and weight, the working hounds being considerably lighter. It is always regrettable when two types are found within a breed, but the fact that the first dual champion has been qualified surely shows that the position is improving.

If field trials for Bassets are unique to the U.S.A., so, too, is the interest in obedience and tracking. I think the reason for the lack of interest in obedience in Europe is that most breeders consider that the Basset is a traditional hound, and that to subject the breed to the rigid discipline and standardised form of obedience would mean that it would lose a degree of the initiative and self-reliance that are important points in a true hunting hound. This is only a theoretical argument because there is no way of knowing that this would be the case—there is almost no interest in obedience in Britain and none at all in France.

Tracking is a different matter, and is, of course, a by-product of hunting—the hound is still using the nose and hunting line. Bloodhounds are the traditional hounds for tracking, but the Basset is certainly as well equipped to hunt 'the clean boot'.

Both obedience and tracking are popular in California, and the B.H.C. of Southern California is especially keen on furthering the two 'sports'. Mr. Bodle, chairman of the club's Obedience Committee, says, 'A new understanding of the Basset's mentality is spreading through the canine world . . . but as with a gifted child, seldom is his potential reached if little is demanded of him. If no demands are made, a Basset may become a dull and sedentary animal.' Most show hound owners are guilty in that they demand nothing of their dogs except beauty, and it is surely a good thing that in recent years more and more owners are seeking an outlet for their Basset's hidden talent.

Some people who have attended training classes in the British Isles have been told abruptly by the organiser that 'all Bassets are untrainable'. This is, of course, nonsense, as is vividly demonstrated by the success of American hounds and the less spectacular progress of some British ones. No doubt if some hounds in pet homes had the benefit of even rudimentary training there would be less talk of difficult and problem hounds.

It is obvious that a hound so kept should be trained and held under firmer control than a kennelled hound, which has at least some freedom in the kennel yards. To train for obedience a hound which is really kept for hunting and show can be a mistake. One British breeder who discovered this was Mrs. Fulford-Dobson of Laleham-on-Thames. She found that after a number of training classes her hound Stalwart Heedful (Lyn Mar Acres Dauntless x Stalwart Anna) became difficult to handle and always wanted to adopt the 'sit' position taught in obedience. When hunting with the B.H.C. working branch pack, it became apparent that Heedful was 'hunting the pack' and making no attempt to figure out the line for himself. He had been quite a useful pack hound before obedience training.

This experience does seem to lend weight to the theory held by the majority of British hound breeders, which is that any form of obedience training must eventually result in a loss of initiative in the working hound. In a pack this would be most unfortunate and the hounds would constantly be seeking verification for their action from their owners.

Of course, not everyone has the facilities at hand or the inclination to hunt their Bassets, and the same applies to exhibiting. Vast numbers of people are content with the companionship of a Basset, and it is obviously this large group which would derive most from obedience training. The participation of lots of Bassets in obedience classes certainly does not present an acceptable picture to the majority of Basset lovers in Britain, and it is doubtful if this will ever be the case. However, no fancier likes to have a favourite breed labelled 'untrainable', and nobody would deny credit to the Americans and the few British stalwarts who have, with great skill, so soundly demolished that widely held belief.

7

The Hunting Basset

By LIONEL WOOLNER, M.H.

THE hunting of the hare with Basset Hounds, the hunt staff and field being on foot, may, in the absence of a better word, be fairly referred to as 'beagling', but it differs in some respects from the same sport as carried on with Beagles.

It must be remembered that the Basset Hound, as evolved in France, was intended for use, a couple or two at a time, as canine beaters to drive game to the guns and not for hunting 'at force', without the assistance of man and his weapons. The requirements of a hound for this purpose were that it should have a really good nose for scenting his quarry and a powerful voice, so that the accompanying guns would know where it was working. Also it should be slow-moving. The point about this last requirement is that game seem to have a pretty good idea of the strength and pace of the canine enemy. Pursued by a large pack at speed and in full cry the game will remove itself speedily from the area, probably offering the guns no chance of a shot. On the other hand, if aware that the pursuit consists only of one or two slow hounds, the game will move gently forward in front of them. If a hare is followed in this way it will frequently be seen only a field or two ahead, giving the guns plenty of time to position themselves for a shot.

The Basset Hound having been specially bred for this purpose as a heavy, slow-moving hound, it is not surprising that its use for hare-hunting 'at force' involves certain disadvantages arising almost entirely from its unsuitable conformation. Fortunately such disadvantages are, at any rate to some extent, offset by the Basset's magnificent working qualities, which explains why many hunting enthusiasts in this country have found it possible to hunt hare successfully with Bassets.

I have so far in this chapter referred simply to 'the Basset Hound' although, as explained earlier, there are still four entirely distinct breeds of Bassets in France. What we in this country call 'the Basset Hound' is, in effect, the Artois-Norman Basset as it has evolved over here in the past hundred years. Two of the other French breeds, the Gascon and the Fawn Breton, were seriously depleted as a result of the two world wars, and although once more on the increase through the efforts of their breed societies, are still so relatively few in numbers, even in France, that we need hardly consider them as hunting hounds. However, the fourth breed, the Griffon-Vendeen Basset, is now used in France in even greater numbers than the Artois-Norman, although hunting the hare 'at force' is still very much the exception in that country.

The only substantial introduction of the Griffon-Vendeen Basset into this country, at any rate in modern times, was made by Major Rupert Buchanan-Jardine, who in 1938 imported five hounds and bred up a pure pack (the Castle Milk) from them. They were later crossed with Harrier and Beagle blood and all the crossbred Basset packs to which I shall refer later have a substantial proportion of this Griffon blood in their ancestry. As the Griffon hunts in a different style from the Artois-Norman, what follows should be taken as referring to the later breed, and at the end of this chapter the differences in the Griffon style will be briefly indicated.

To come now to a comparison between the Basset and the Beagle as a hound for foot-hunting: in the first place the Beagle is a good deal more lightly built and a much more active hound. This activity will display itself not only in sheer speed over the ground, particularly when running in view or on a breast-high scent, but in the ability to twist and turn more easily and therefore to cover ground more quickly when working at the checks. It will also enable the Beagle to negotiate more speedily obstacles which would delay the more heavily built Basset. Indeed, in a country of high walls or banks Bassets would be well-nigh useless as they would require considerable manual assistance over the obstacles. The lifting of several couple of fifty-pound hounds over a succession of

Stephen Klein

American Ch. Richardson's Hello Dolly, 1964

Frasie

American Ch. Luella of Linden and Ch. Moore's Dominance

Griffon Vendéen Basset (Petit Taille), Petit Prince de la
Levraudiere, 1966

Artésien-Normand Bassets Int. Ch. Daguet de l'Ombrée, Azur des
Mariettes and Arlette des Mariettes

stone walls is not a pastime that commends itself to the average whipper-in!

In a hilly or plough country, too, the Basset is at a disadvantage. He has so much additional weight to carry—the average beagle weighs only twenty-five pounds—and his build simply does not lend itself to speeding up hills or skipping lightly over the ploughs. It is not, as many people suppose, the crookedness of the forelegs which is the primary cause of the Basset's lack of speed, but the heavy, loaded shoulders to be found in so many hounds and the consequent lack of stride and scope. Of course, if the forelegs should be knuckled-over as well as crooked, the hound will be quite unsound and incapable of moving freely. Even when the Basset finds the type of country really too much for him his determination and stamina will get him there in the end: he is a great trier and never gives up.

It is an expensive business to keep hounds these days, and it has to be admitted that the Basset, which, apart from his short legs, has the general bulk of a full-sized staghound, will require a good deal more food than the Beagle. He will also require more kennel-space and more room in the van or trailer which carries him to the meet.

It must not be supposed, however, that the advantages all lie with the Beagle. Quite apart from the undesirability of 'o'ermatching' the hare, as Somerville calls it, a great deal of the pleasure of hunting is lost if the hare is hunted with hounds which, from the outset, press her so hard by sheer speed that she has no opportunity to play the many tricks the unravelling of which by the hounds is the principle delight of hare-hunting. Further, sheer speed can easily degenerate into flashi-ness and over-running, faults of which the Artois-Norman Basset, at least, can never be accused.

The Basset's principal love is undoubtedly the scent rather than the actual killing of the quarry, whereas the reverse is, I think, true in the case of the Beagle. Hounds in a Basset pack like to own and speak to the line individually, which will cause them to run rather more strung-out than Beagles: in column rather than in line abreast. This, in my view, is by no means a

I

bad thing. It is customarily said that all hounds should 'carry a good head' and should run as close together as possible 'so that a sheet would cover them'. I have never seen any argument advanced to support this view except that 'it looks well', which is hardly an adequate justification. In fact if a pack of, say, fifteen couple is running in a group, quite a large proportion of the hounds will be running wide of the comparatively narrow scent-line. Except perhaps on a really good scenting day they are not carrying the scent but are being 'lifted' by the leading and centre hounds running on the line.

If a pack hunting in this way is examined it will be seen that many hounds are running and speaking with their heads up. At a check these hounds will have to lower their noses and feel for the scent again in the same manner as if they had been lifted by their huntsman. There will in consequence be some delay before the entire pack is again operating usefully.

On the other hand, with the Basset style of hunting, each hound is carrying the scent all the time and, coming up at a check, one or two of the following hounds will frequently be able to carry the line on uninterruptedly in the changed direction before the leading hounds have had time to cast themselves.

I am not, of course, advocating that hounds should run strung-out over more than, say, a hundred yards, nor indeed do Bassets run in this way. If individual hounds do sometimes lag and seem unwilling to force their way back into the hunt it is usually because they lack the speed to do so. On a good scenting day Bassets, with their low-scenting ability, will be running almost as fast as their conformation permits, and accordingly if a hound is left in covert or kale or otherwise thrown out it will not have the surplus speed to overtake its fellows.

Only recently I had the opportunity of seeing a Beagle pack and Basset pack in action in similar country and on successive days. At a check the entire Beagle pack could be seen swinging and making their cast very rapidly almost as one hound, moving and working together over the ground almost yard by yard but very fast. On the other hand, in the same circumstances the Bassets fanned out and worked as individuals in different but adjoining areas until the voice of one hound or, perhaps, violent feathering indicated that the line had been re-found. The reason for such a difference in the style of working at a check stems from what has been said about the respective styles of the two breeds when running on the line. The Beagle, running close to his comrades who have the scent, but not himself owning the line, swings with them as they begin their cast: the Basset, running the line individually, makes his own cast, working from where he last had the scent in the direction which his nose or instinct suggests as best.

There may not be much difference in the results of the two styles of making a cast. If the Beagles are not quartering simultaneously all the ground round the point of check, they make their cast more rapidly and are all on the spot to confirm the line as soon as it is re-found. When a single Basset hits off the line the others must rally to him to confirm the good news before the hunt can really be said to be up again.

Although when drawing and casting they like to work individually, Bassets are not what is generally known as independent hounds. As soon as it is apparent that the line has been hit off they will at once abandon their own casting and rally to the cry. And what a cry to which to rally! Somerville talks of 'the harmonious thunder of the field', and no breed of hound can lay better claim to this expression than the Basset. The clamour of a Basset pack running in full cry, perhaps in covert along a valley side, has no equal in the whole of hunting.

The Beagle has never been noted for its voice, and in many packs this seems to have degenerated over recent years. As with Foxhounds and Harriers, many hounds run with little more than an intermittent whimper. A good cry is surely one of the great pleasures of the hunting field, and the heavy sonorous note of the Basset can be heard over a great distance. Some people think that the cry of the Artois-Norman Basset is perhaps even a little too deep for real excitement. He is, as the French say, a *cogneur*, a producer of heavy, individual notes, as distinct from the long-drawn-out cry of the *hurleur* (howler) which is represented by the Gascon and some others of the

French breeds. There is, too, a real value in a good cry because, particularly in close country, it helps to keep the pack together and enables hounds temporarily thrown out to find their way back to the pack without loss of time or the necessity for any intervention by a whipper-in. A Basset pack is very seldom other than 'all-on'.

As regards scenting ability it is generally accepted that the Basset is a very low-scenting hound indeed, which on a really bad scenting day enables him to make something of a line and show sport when no other breed of hound could do so. On an average or good scenting day Beagles can probably carry the line as well and faster than Bassets.

At the end of a hunt Bassets are slow to take advantage and are not quick and determined when their hare is fresh-found towards the end of the run. They are not good 'killers', perhaps because they have been used for generations as beaters and it was not their function to kill.

They are handy and disciplined as a pack and little work on the part of whippers-in is necessary. They have very sensitive natures and are inclined to be whip-shy. A firm rate is usually all that is required by way of correction, and if more is needed a gentle swing of the whip without any cracking or physical contact will certainly do the trick.

From what has been said about the physical limitations but fine working qualities of the Basset it may now be clear why certain Masters of Hounds have thought it sensible to try to produce by crossbreeding a hound which would have the first-class nose, voice and other working qualities of the Basset, but would be housed in a more active frame. Such hounds, it was thought, would be successful in country which would be quite unsuited to the pure hound. There seems no reason why, by selection over what would probably be a longish period, a really active, lightweight, pure Basset should not have been evolved capable of coping with all types of country, but so far as I know no pack has been bred on these lines. Such hounds would, of course, be a long way removed from the Kennel Club Standard for the breed.

Results of the present crossbreeding of Bassets—the so-called 'English' Bassets—appear to have justified the hopes of the Masters concerned, and about ten packs are now using hounds bred from crosses made from the Artois-Norman Basset on the one side and Griffon-Vendeen Basset, Harrier and a little Beagle blood on the other. Such hounds are now being hunted successfully in such testing country as the heavy ploughs of East Anglia and the mountains of Wales. As time goes on they are increasingly breeding true to the desired type, and this may soon be regarded as reasonably fixed.

To the purist in this country all crossbreeding of hounds is anathema. In France, however, where our hounds and methods of hunting originated, the improvement and fixing of working qualities by combining the best points of different breeds is quite usual. The four Basset breeds, not being primarily used in France for hunting 'at force', have been kept completely pure, but almost all packs of *grands chiens* used for hunting stag, roe, boar and fox are now of mixed blood and are frankly described as *anglo-poitevins-saintongeois, bâtards de Haut Poitou, Harriers Somerset-Griffon Vendéen*, etc.

Turning now to the Griffon-Vendeen Basset, we find a hound which looks quite different and hunts in a different style. Its wiry, almost shaggy coat is impervious to thorns and brambles. Its head and ears are quite undistinguished when compared with the Artois-Norman hound and its voice, although good by general hound standards, is also not really comparable. The Griffon is not, of course, simply a rough-coated variety of the Artois-Norman hound, but is the Basset version of quite a different French breed of great antiquity. It is therefore not surprising that its qualities of temperament and work are quite different and, if the truth be told, the Griffon, in its pure form, is not an ideal hound with which to hunt the hare. Tremendously fond of hunting, he is, as the French say, *trop chasseur* and even what we would call riotous. His reputation and that of his staghound ancestors was that of a hound which would hunt any game that jumped up in front of him: he was even difficult to break from hunting farm stock. His great dash and bravery made him ideal as a hunter of the wolf and boar, straight-running beasts far different from the twisting roe-deer and hare. The Griffon's stamina is also distinctly suspect and he tends to burn himself out early in the day.

It is indeed a pity that so many of the Griffon's qualities unfit him for hare-hunting, because as far as conformation goes he is well suited. Much more lightly built than the Artois-Norman, his shoulders are clean and well sloped. The forelegs can be either straight or slightly crooked but, as I have said, the crook does little to hinder a hound's activity. Even if it is undesirable to use the Griffon for hare-hunting in his pure state, he has a great deal to offer as an element in the crossbred hound. His nose and voice are very adequate and his great love of hunting and consequent drive can be a valuable element in matings with hounds perhaps too fond of the scent to press on with it fast enough.

So there we have the Basset Hound, with its good and bad points, as a hound with which to hunt the hare on foot, and even when one has put them all in the scales on either side there is yet one more thing to say for the Basset. There is undeniably a colour and panache about hunting with Bassets which one does not find with the Beagle or, if I may be allowed to say so, with the Harrier or even the Foxhound. The domed head; the wise, judicial expression; the bright, tricoloured livery; the glorious voice: perhaps it is that with their aid we recapture something of the music and pageantry of hunting as it was carried on in the Middle Ages.

8

The Character and Future of the Basset Hound

THE American Standard is the only one that attempts to throw some light on the character of the hound it describes. It states: 'In temperament it is mild, never sharp or timid.' The definition is perfectly correct: the Basset is a mild hound, but that is only one side of the breed's fascinating character. To define all the aspects would be impossible, but I think that with due allowance for its brevity the American insistence in writing this into the official standard is very praiseworthy and could be emulated by the British and French breed societies. Some guidance regarding the desirable temperament should be given. It is all very well to describe how an animal should look, but failing to state how it should conduct itself is a grave omission.

The original of the smooth-coated breeds in the U.S.A. and Britain and elsewhere is the Artois-Norman, but as I have stated the look and character of the national types now vary considerably. The pure British hounds do not have the vitality and verve of the Artois-Norman and are generally much more sedate. The best adjectives one could use for the Basset Hound would be docile, gentle, kind and patient, with a rather sobre outlook on life. How much the Bloodhound outcross affected the character of the British Basset is hard to define, but I should be inclined to think that the Bloodhound cross had a sobering influence. I am not saying that the British hounds are incapable of gaiety—they can, of course, be quite jolly hounds —but by comparison with the French hounds they do lack sparkle.

However, the character of the Basset Hound is commendable, and any vice in the real sense is fortunately absent. In any pack hound a sound temperament is essential, and the Basset has the character and temperament for pack life. It enjoys company, and I have said before that it is cruelty to kennel a Basset alone. Leading a healthy, active life in the correct environment, the Basset Hound, I would think, has one of the canine world's most even and enjoyable dispositions. It is when the environment and treatment are wrong that cases of malevolent hounds crop up.

The breed really jumped into prominence overnight, and from near obscurity the Basset was suddenly found appearing in TV and newspaper advertisements that never failed to exploit the sorrowful expression. It was inevitable that many people should buy a Basset just because of the 'look' and because it was the fashionable breed, and it was equally obvious that many new Basset owners were ignorant of the breed's requirements, physical and mental.

Every Basset Hound breeder has had experience of the owner with 'difficult' and 'problem' hounds, and all know that the cause is closely connected with the Basset boom and the almost total inability of an ancient working breed to adapt itself to twentieth-century living. The Basset is not a suitable dog for a flat, and it is not a breed for owners who wish to have their dog at a word! Unfortunately many people think the Basset can fill the requirements, and it is not surprising when the hound rebels and becomes short-tempered, dirty and destructive and is classified as a rogue.

The most common mistake made by new owners is their refusal to discipline and reprimand a small puppy. Granted, the Basset youngster is a beguiling creature, and the temptation to let him get away with misdemeanours is great, but it must be overcome if hound and owner are to live amicably together. Sharp words, or at the most a good firm slap, are all that are required to check or scold a puppy. All lessons are best learned when young, and although the Basset requires a little more patience than most breeds, he will eventually learn the lesson.

The Basset is not the quickest-witted breed of dog, although individual hounds would belie this fact. Usually the hound will not respond immediately to orders and commands, and he should not really be expected to because the inherent instinct is to figure everything out for himself. Impatience, harsh words or ill-treatment will achieve nothing, and some leeway must be allowed because the Basset will always respond as quickly as it wants to, and not as quickly as one wants it to.

Slow thinking and a mournful expression must not be confused with shortage of brains; any hound having the versatility, diligence and scenting powers of the Basset is no fool. At his 'present-day' legitimate work, the Basset is unequalled; no other hound is better fitted to slow, sure hunting. I say 'present-day' work because the occupation of the breed has varied with time, and the Basset has worked as gundog and terrier, as well as a hound used to hunt a variety of game. Its diminutive stature has not impeded it from fulfilling many functions, and one could well add adaptability, and determination to please its owners as well as itself, to the more usual list of attributes.

Bassets can make excellent companions, but only if the upbringing is on the right lines and they have the space and exercise needed to keep body and mind healthy and active. They are very docile and extremely patient with children. If a hound is introduced to a home with children, then they, the children, must be taught to observe a few rules. They must be taught to respect the feeding and sleeping times of the hound or puppies and not to haul them about or pick puppies up incorrectly; and I think puppies should have at least one period per day when they can be out of sight and sound of everyone in the household.

Bitch-hounds share their affections more than a dog-hound and because of this probably make a better family pet. They have a very sweet nature and even when kennelled *en masse* seldom quarrel. As dams they are excellent, produce lots of milk and tend their puppies really well. It is rare to lose puppies because of the dam's carelessless or neglect; most puppy mortality occurs when they are swept behind or below the dam by her very low-hanging udder.

In their young days dog-puppies are probably more affectionate than the bitches, but it is usual to find the affection being concentrated wholeheartedly on one person, and in later life they do become very much 'one-man dogs'. They will do anything for the person they really like, but will try to play up to others, and consequently need a little more discipline and closer control than females. After beginning stud work some males become very overbearing and would, if not checked, pick fights with other dogs in the kennel. If, however, they are checked, there is nothing to prevent several stud hounds living peacefully together, and this is the case in several prominent kennels.

The full extent of the Basset character is difficult to assess and define clearly, because it is not a surface character but rather one of depth. Consequently one is always discovering new sides to it, and often finding out that one has underestimated the Basset.

Nothing emphasises the fact that the French Basset varieties are different breeds so much as the temperamental differences, and the styles of hunting which Mr. Lionel Wooner has touched upon. The Griffon-Vendeen is needle-sharp in action and thought, and like the Fawn Breton can be difficult to manage. Artois-Normans are very gay and lively but extremely kind and universal with their affection, whereas the beautiful Blue-Mottled Gascons are very shy and sensitive and very, very seldom reveal their character to strangers.

Throughout the ages Basset breeders have been able to change the occupation of their hounds with the changing phases and fashions of field sports, and one would have thought that a breed so versatile would always have been popular. This has not been the case: the breed has had many dismal periods as well as bright spots. To forecast the future of a breed so inconsistent in the past is a rather precarious undertaking, and one has just to read some of the older canine books to see how many authorities have done so, only to be proved wrong in the succeeding years.

The American Mr. Will Judy voiced very strong words in 1936 when he said: 'The decadence of this breed is logical and in its gradual trend towards oblivion, fanciers of today should learn a serious lesson. The custom requires that the chest be not more than two inches from the ground, that the chest be more expansive than the Bulldog's, that the feet be crooked and apparently a mass of joints, and that the skull be peaked like that of a Bloodhound with the same dignity of expression. How dignity could be maintained on a very long-bodied dog of this nature is irony. [M. Hubert Desamy, speaking about Artois-Norman Bassets, said the selfsame thing—Author.] A monstrosity or other unnatural bodily proportion obtained by man's selective breeding demands the penalty of low vitality, lessened usefulness and eventual oblivion. And the Basset Hound, slowest of all hunting dogs, is suffering this fate.'

The unusual conformation of the Basset does make it liable to become a show-bench curiosity without any purpose other than being ornamental. It has happened in the past when the breeders concentrated on head points and neglected to ensure that the body and limbs remained sound. This policy led to the breed entering a period of unpopularity because it was of little use as a worker. Today there is great determination to produce a balanced dual-purpose hound, and breeders and hunting-minded people have the full support of the breed societies in the maintenance of this type. There is no threat of any break-away group of show or hunting people forming a separate club. There is no need, because the present clubs encourage all aspects of Basset ownership, showing, hunting or just plain companionship, and the exhibitor, breeder and hunter are treated equally.

To judge by the registrations of Bassets in Britain and the U.S.A. (see Appendix), the breed certainly appears to be in a very healthy position, but sheer weight of numbers is not the most important feature of a breed's progress—quantity is never a match for quality. Most serious breeders in Britain view the registration figures with misgiving and would hate to see any further encroachment of purely commercial interests. The peak for registrations seems to be approaching—for the last few years the numbers have begun to settle and even out.

The greatest danger facing the breed as a whole is the con-tinuing policy of retaining the three different standards, and the problem is how to prevent a further widening of the gap between the various national types. All three types have been crossed together successfully, proving that each type has a need for the other, which in a breed as unique as the Basset is not so surprising. A great service would be rendered to the breed if representatives of the world's clubs could get together with a view to the production of a universally accepted standard. As the position is now, there is nothing to prevent the Australian, New Zealand or South African Basset Hound clubs framing their own standard should they so desire.

With the club's present insistence on a dual-purpose role for the breed, I doubt if Bassets will ever descend to the lows of past days, and therefore it is reasonably safe to suppose that the Basset Hound proper has a long-term future. So, too, has the Artois-Norman. The Griffon-Vendeen has a massive following in France and the breed's welfare is looked after by a very progressive club; there is no sign of any decline in its popularity, and if it were re-introduced into Britain or introduced into the U.S.A., I think it would prove very acceptable to Basset exhibitors and hunters.

For two breeds, the Fawn Breton and Blue-Mottled Gascon, the future does not seem to hold much hope for continued survival. At the moment the little spark of interest has been revitalised, and for the Fawn Breton a great attempt is being made to save the breed, but the problem is obtaining new blood, and it is the same for the Blue-Mottled Gascon. The probable solution would be an introduction of Griffon-Vendeen and Artois-Norman, and a long-term programme of selection until finally all trace of the outcross had been eradicated. There is a precedent for this solution in both breeds, as the method of using outcross stock was used in the past when the breed's position was somewhat uncertain.

It would be a tragedy if two ancient hound breeds had to disappear and not only the Basset species, but the whole hound group, would be poorer for the loss.

9
Founding a Kennel

THERE are some factors which must be considered before deciding to found a kennel of Basset Hounds. It is no good deciding hurriedly and setting out to purchase stock without weighing up the pros and cons of one's venture.

The environment and surroundings naturally regulate the eventual size of a kennel. Bassets are large hounds and some space for ample housing and accommodation is a necessity. It therefore stands to reason that kennels situated in a thinly populated rural area are more suitable than kennels in a large town. Apart from the question of accommodation the reactions of neighbours must be taken into account; not all people are keen dog-lovers, and it is always advisable to find out the local Town or Urban Council's attitude to a kennel. Kennels are rateable, unfortunately, although most local authorities are reasonable in their assessment.

Most modern kennels are numerically modest affairs: the number of hounds kept per average breeder in Britain is ten or twelve. Some larger kennels do exist in all the main breeding centres—one can readily bring to mind the Grims hounds owned by Miss Keevil of Newbury and the *de L'Ombrée* pack of M. Leparoux in France, and in the U.S.A. Mrs. Walton of New Jersey has the Lyn Mar Acres Hounds. The breed benefits from the stock produced by such old-established and large kennels. In a way a large kennel can be likened to the 'hub' and the smaller kennels, whose stock is usually descended from the large influential kennel, to the 'spokes'.

The hound must not become a burden, and the keeping, breeding, showing or hunting of Bassets must first and foremost be a pleasure and a recreational pastime for their owners. The majority of kennels can actually be classed as 'hobby kennels' and most are also one-man businesses. To keep

Bassets on this plane it is essential to retain only the number of hounds that can be comfortably managed by one person; if kennel assistance is available and can be afforded more hounds can be kept, but the number must be regulated by the amount of one's own time or the existence of outside help.

I have stressed the 'enjoyment' point because unless one is going to derive pleasure from one's Basset it is senseless to consider founding a kennel. Most established breeders enjoy their hounds, but they also take the matters of breeding, rearing, showing and so on most seriously and are all constantly trying to improve the quality of their stock. Quality, not quantity, must be the first consideration and the newcomer to Bassets should adhere to the maxim.

Once it has been decided that facilities are available for founding a kennel, some background knowledge of the Basset should be acquired. All the available literature on the breed can be studied and visits to shows and kennels arranged. A visit to a championship show gives a good idea of show procedure and the handling and judging, just as a visit to a working meet would give an insight into the Basset at work. Probably the best source of knowledge would be a visit to a kennel, where some idea of the housing and general management of Bassets could be obtained. Hounds at various stages of development could be seen and most owners would answer questions and give general advice on the Basset.

Hardly anyone purchases a kennel of hounds *en masse*; the orthodox beginning is the acquisition of one or two young hounds or a mated bitch. It is, I think, the best policy to start modestly and build up a kennel on a small but sound basis. The purchase of foundation stock should be carefully undertaken; the future of a kennel depends on its quality and the eventual breeding programme. Most breeders supply 'foundation stock', and the term means that the hound or hounds have been suitably bred, are typical of the breed and have the potential for producing good progeny. Properly mated, such stock invariably produces honest, sound hounds. Foundation stock is not usually superb from the show point of view, but there is an absence of serious faults, and the stock is constructionally and temperamentally sound with an impeccable ancestry. The pedigree of a hound intended as the keystone of a new kennel is very important and on a par with the quality of type. From the pedigree can be determined the method of descent. This falls into three basic categories, and the hound can be the result of:

1. Outcrossing, i.e. the breeding together of stock having no relationship with one another.

2. Inbreeding, the breeding together of closely related stock, i.e. matings between father x daughter, mother x son, etc.— incest matings.

3. Line-breeding, the breeding together of related stock, i.e. matings between cousins, grandsires x granddaughters.

In Bassets the first method of breeding is rare because, as is the case in most breeds, the best dogs can all trace their ancestry to a few common denominators. In Britain outcross blood has been introduced from France (five hounds), the U.S.A. (five hounds) and Canada (one hound). The five French hounds all had a common ancestry, and that of the five American hounds and the Canadian hound was also much the same. In many strains the blood of all the outcrosses has intermingled, and the chances of finding a really good outcross today would be very rare. The reasons for the introduction of outside blood are given in Chapter 3.

Anyone using outcross blood does so in an attempt to rejuvenate the strain or introduce some particular point, and once the outcross has been effected, quickly resorts to a programme of inbreeding or line-breeding. The two methods are used for the same end, the perpetuation of certain desirable characteristics and the continuation of a recognisable strain. I have explained how difficult this is to achieve in Bassets. One never knows what a litter will produce colour-wise or type-wise. The production of blue mottles is a mystery, and so is the occasional emergence of long-coated puppies. As a result of concentrated breeding the Artois-Norman is the most standardised of the three basic Basset types, but for some reason the same methods of breeding have not, in the main, resulted in overall standardisation in Britain or the U.S.A.

However, despite the setbacks, most British and American hounds are produced on a line-breeding plan, and when selling a puppy the breeder will usually suggest, in the case of a bitch, suitable matings, based on the hopeful assumption that the new owner will continue the line of breeding. The advice should be followed unhesitatingly, because no one knows the potential of stock better than its breeder. Nobody knows for certain what the results of any mating will be, but with inbreeding or line-breeding it is uncommon not to be able to distinguish the types of puppies produced and identify them with known ancestors. The outcross mating is necessary if prolonged inbreeding or line-breeding has taken place, as in the case of British Bassets after the war and the subsequent French imports, and the only thing required from such matings is the new blood. Once the outcross has been used, the previous breeding programme should be followed with the inclusion of the progeny of the outcross mating.

Most authorities are agreed that the Mendelian laws of genetics cannot be applied in full to dogs, and point out that Mendel conducted his experiments with plants and small animals whose powers of reproduction are greater than those of the canines. Besides, to follow the theories all the progeny of matings must be retained, and I doubt if any Basset Hound breeder could do this. The only law the average breeder can follow is the 'type will produce type' theory: selection of hounds with the type considered desirable and the mating together of these hounds, in the hope that they will produce their like and eventually establish a line. The old breeders attached great importance to 'purity of race', an essential point in those days when Beagle blood and unidentified French hound blood were being used. Today, I think, purity of strain is essential, and close breeding with the occasional infusion of outside blood is the best method of producing a strain. Even when purchasing additional hounds or introducing an outcross it is better for one's strain if there is a 'link' between the pedigrees of the hounds and one's own.

The pedigree of a stallion hound should be impeccable in that he is descended from a line of sound hounds, and not a

Fauve de Bretagne Basset, Lassie du Mas de la Londe

Bleu de Gascogne Basset, Eldorado de Bois Yvon

Australian Ch. Sykemoor Hopsack, 1964, as a puppy

Australian Ch. Chevalier Nicole, 1961

hotch-potch of hounds from every kennel under the sun. Of course, nobody should consider using a hound purely because his pedigree is excellent; if the actual hound is not typical then the pedigree becomes worthless. By 'typical' I mean an above-average specimen of the breed, sound, handsome and temperamentally stable. One can forgive minor faults, but any unsoundness of feet, limbs and body should debar a hound from use. One can produce faults galore without adding to them gratuitously!

The stud dog is expected to be a masculine, hard-conditioned hound, a forceful mover and having the essential points of his breed. The Basset Hound stud dog also needs some size and substance of bone. Although tricolours are most fashionable, the colour of a dog should not influence the decision about using it. 'Handsome is as handsome does', and this is the real test of a stud dog, his ability to produce the goods: the pedigree conformation, etc., become secondary to the quality of progeny. The prominent champions and show hounds are not necessarily the most successful sires, but because of their prominence they attract the greatest number of bitches from breeders. Because of the number of bitches served the law of averages is in the dog's favour and some good progeny is produced, but in direct ratio the average hound who produces good-class progeny in frequent sequence from a few bitches is the more successful sire.

The proven stud hounds are easily evaluated by their progeny but the young hounds are difficult to assess. They may or may not have inherited the ability to pass on virtues, and only trial can prove this. The young hound should be given the opportunity of mating an older bitch, preferably a proved brood and one that has been easy to mate. Twelve months is a good age for a dog's first service, and it is beneficial if it can be easy and trouble-free for the dog. Once the yearling dog has successfully mated a bitch he can be left for several months to develop, and then start serious stud work after the age of two. Many young dog-hounds are very sensitive and need lots of patient handling and encouragement in the early stages of stud work. In Britain the stud fee charged varies from

K

ten to twenty pounds, and it is more expensive in America. Fees in France are low and often no fee at all is charged for matings of hounds from the top kennels.

Unless his mate is of good quality and suitably bred, the best dog-hound in the world cannot be expected to produce his best, and therefore the real strength of a kennel and its future lies with the females. The bitch contributes equally with the male in the formation of productive genes, and for this alone should be given equal consideration. Most novice owners underestimate this simple fact and feel that if the dog-hound is good enough this fact will cancel out all the faults of the bitch. For breeding success—and not guaranteed success, for all breeding is uncertain—the female must be conformationally and typically as good as the male, and if possible better. Nothing is more pleasing to a stud-dog owner than to receive for mating a bitch that is a credit to the breed; conversely, nothing is more galling than to have one's dog used as a 'hopeful' improver of stock.

Small, weedy bitches are useless, and not only are they untypical of the breed but they are ill-equipped for producing and rearing a litter. The bitch must be large, have spring of rib in plenty and some length of body, and good wide quarters. As the dog-hound should be masculine, so the bitch should be feminine and sweet-natured, with a kind eye and expression.

The average Basset litter is eight puppies, and in order to carry, whelp and successfully rear this number, the health and vigour of the bitch is important. Naturally during the period of gestation correct diet and exercise are essential. However, even if the bitch is a good brood and regains condition quickly after maternal duties, she should not be made into a 'puppy factory' and mated every season. Every other season is sufficient for a bitch to be mated, and four or five litters in her life span should be considered ample.

Mentally, both dogs and bitches should be stable, not nervous or unduly aggressive. The correct Basset temperament is calm, gentle and somewhat serious, and always dependable with children and livestock.

From the very outset the foundation should be carefully

chosen and a plan of future progress via matings and additional purchases well considered. The building-up of a good kennel consisting of sound, typical stock is a long-term project, especially with Bassets, so notoriously difficult to breed. There is no short cut to success, and to purchase winning hounds without considering their background might well fill a kennel with good dogs, but to merge the many differing bloodlines successfully one would have to be a student of advanced genetics. Careful planning and control of one's bloodline are the safest ways.

Unsuitable matings on paper do occasionally produce excellent progeny, but it is infrequent and such progeny is correctly termed 'a flash in the pan'. They often achieve show-ring success, but because of the uncertainty of their ancestry are seldom used or are unsuccessful as stud-dogs or brood-bitches.

In all countries the influential kennels have been established in this way by a line-breeding programme, and authorities on Bassets like Millais, Verrier, Heseltine and the American Carl Smith have all advocated the use of this method. They set a good example to the modern breeder, not only by demonstrating the best way to breed Bassets, but also by stressing the importance of maintaining breed type and soundness. In Britain and France, Millais and Verrier quickly realised that the Basset quickly degenerates if the breeding is not controlled. Millais' phases of experiments and the final Bloodhound cross, with reversion to Basset stock afterwards, succeeded in combating the ill-effects of improperly used inbreeding. Verrier had the opposite problem, that of merging several basically good bloodlines and two types, the Le Couteulx and the Lane, into one composite and improved breed, the Artois-Norman.

The present-day problem is the lack of standardisation. There are many really excellent hounds, and over a period of ten years some great Bassets have been produced that combine breed type with soundness. However, a large number of varying types seem to be appearing all the time, and the whole policy of continued line-breeding seems to fail. One would have imagined that with so few actual outcrosses being introduced the breed type would stabilise.

One great problem does seem to have been overcome: hounds are being produced today that are clearly capable of a dual-purpose role, show and sport. The first dual champion was recently produced in the U.S.A., a dog-hound Ch. Kazoo's Moses the Great, and although no dual championship title exists in Britain or France, the top show-hounds are sound enough for prolonged hunting and in Britain many attend the B.H.C. working branch meets. The French hounds, show specimens and all, are fully expected to hunt well.

In the 1920s the controversy already described raged in Britain between the Basset Hounds hunting fraternity and the showing devotees. A rift of such proportions should never occur again, because the breed clubs and the breeders are fully aware of the need to combine type and soundness, and it is safe to say that at shows today ninety-nine per cent of the awards go to hounds that excel in both. It is agreed that exaggeration of breed points and ignoring soundness is as harmful as the breeding of 'semi-Beagles' which lack breed character but have structural soundness and speed. If the true Basset is found to be lacking in speed for modern hunting, this must be accepted and no attempt made to change the breed. Equally, the difficulty of obtaining the many desired features must not cause the standard to be amended in order to accommodate hounds lacking the essentials.

The Basset is unique in that it is the only surviving slow-hunting hound, and of course the breed is singularly quaint in appearance. In the *Kennel Gazette* of October 1882 an unknown author wrote: 'Like all field dogs the Basset Hound appeals to two classes, the sportsman and the fancier. With the former they must rapidly ingratiate themselves for their remarkable powers of hunting, their marvellous scent and deep melodious voices; and the fancier must admire their strange old, weird looks, the Bloodhound's head, the low-hanging ears, the long flews and full dewlap, their bright colouring and the curious crooked forelegs and massive paws over which the loose skin hangs in folds like the wrinkles in a mousquetaire glove.' Since its introduction into Britain the Basset has had many ups and downs, and has resisted change and attempts to change it. It must continue to do so, with the support of the breed societies, the breeders and the judges.

The breed societies and most breeders are well aware of the importance of retaining the correct breed type, and fortunately most judges are aware of their responsibilities. Some, however, certainly accept invitations to judge Bassets whether they are qualified to do so or not. It was not unusual at one period to be approached by puzzled judges and asked what sort of dog one's Basset was. Now that the breed society in Britain has compiled approved lists of judges the situation need never arise where a complete outsider to Bassets is appointed to judge. The Basset is rather more complex than other breeds and does need careful and knowledgeable judging.

Despite the fact that the breed needs rather more attention than is normal regarding breeding, rearing, etc., it is undemanding over accommodation. As long as the basic kennelling principles are looked after, there is no need for elaborate housing. Essential requirements of kennelling for any breed are space, warmth and cleanliness, and all must be draughtproof and waterproof.

Bassets can be kept indoors in a house, but I think they are better and much more happily kennelled outdoors. At least they can have some degree of freedom outside, and the open-air life is more in keeping with a hound breed.

Kennels vary in size and manner of construction, but most breeders try to organise things so that the hounds have a maximum of space inside and out. Although one's area of land and the number of hounds governs the scope of a kennel, it should regardless of size be as comfortable as possible, and for one's own convenience, planned for ease of cleaning and maintenance.

If possible the kennel itself should provide space, apart from the bed or bench area, to enable the hounds to exercise or relieve themselves, and to be fed indoors during really inclement weather. The kennel should therefore be divided into bench area and floor area. A rough guide for a bench size is one square yard per dog, and it is best made of a wooden platform raised off the floor to prevent floor draughts. Sides no less than three inches in depth also prevent draughts and help to hold in the bedding material. The floor area is usually of wood or concrete; the latter is probably more easily washed and more hygienic. A covering of sawdust absorbs the water and prevents droppings adhering to the floor. As well as space indoors, light and air are essential, and therefore an adjustable window is a necessity in any kennel.

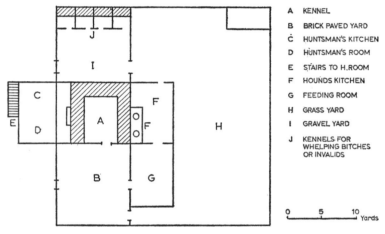

A   KENNEL
B   BRICK PAVED YARD
C   HUNTSMAN'S KITCHEN
D   HUNTSMAN'S ROOM
E   STAIRS TO H.ROOM
F   HOUNDS KITCHEN
G   FEEDING ROOM
H   GRASS YARD
I   GRAVEL YARD
J   KENNELS FOR WHELPING BITCHES OR INVALIDS

FIG 10   Plan of a kennel for 16 to 25 hounds

Bedding should always be clean and sweet, and I think good straw is the best and warmest. Wood-wool is also hygienic, and I have seen hounds happily bedded on bracken. All these materials are cheap and easily disposed of. Any form of sacking quickly becomes soiled and smelly.

Kennels must be kept clean and washed out and thoroughly disinfected weekly. The bedding, walls, etc., are easily sprayed with disinfectant or insecticide aerosols, and the floor should be washed out with a good deodorising disinfectant. Then dry fresh sawdust should be put down. Walls can be whitewashed annually and the woodwork treated with creosote and any maintenance seen to; roofing felt may be repaired or doors mended. It is surprising how a bad winter takes a toll on kennels, and Bassets can be pretty boisterous and bound against doors and so on. Because of this wear and tear it is necessary for any type of kennel to be soundly constructed, and the conversion of stable-blocks and outhouses is excellent.

The kennel runs or yards need to be roomy too—as large as possible to allow the hounds opportunity to exercise and play together. Bassets do not take kindly to restrictions, nor do they like solitude. They are happiest in a small pack with plenty of room in which to enjoy life. Except in cases of illness, heats or return from a show, Bassets should not be kennelled solitary.

Despite their low stature Bassets are agile and any fence surrounding the kennel run must be an efficient and practical barrier of over four feet. Iron railings are ideal but very expensive, and so are brick or stone walls. Chain-link fencing is probably the best alternative and it is easily erected and maintained. Chestnut paling is also good, but over a shorter period because it tends to rot away at the base and break away from the wire holdings. I always thought the Scandinavian-type fencing of larch posts, well tarred, looked efficient and very attractive, but it would be expensive in Britain, I imagine.

The kennel run needs a surface because earth or grass is unsuitable as it rapidly becomes damp and muddy and is not good for the hounds' feet. Concrete, and compounded ash or clinkers, are the two best materials and once laid down require little or not maintenance. Concrete can easily be washed down and the droppings removed. Although it is good for keeping nails short, some breeders feel that because it holds the moisture too long, concrete is not helpful to the correct formation of the Basset's front legs. I have not experienced this in Bassets, but I do know that it did tend to malform the front legs of Dandie Dinmont Terriers whose front assembly resembles the Bassets. Ash or clinkers should be laid to a depth of one foot, and evened out and beaten down. This type of surfacing drains exceedingly well and is good for keeping hounds well up on their feet. It is easily raked and then disinfected with a sprink-

ling water-can. Hounds love to dig the ashes, and therefore
additional quantities must occasionally be put into the run.

All runs, whatever the surface, are better if a wooden platform or a couple of sandstone flags are made available for the
hounds to lie on. If one has space to spare a grass run is very
useful, especially in summer. There the hounds can be allowed
to spend a few hours every day, out of the ordinary dusty runs.

Drinking water should be available indoors and out and
some shade provided where hounds can escape the sun.

The basic kennelling requirements are normal kennels plus
the runs, a shed for storing straw, sawdust, travelling boxes,
etc., and which may be utilised as an office or grooming place;
a whelping kennel; and if possible a smaller kennel situated
away from the main kennel block, to be used for invalids or
visiting bitches.

The whelping kennel need not be much different from the
normal type, except that some breeders like to provide a source
of heat. The bench should be large, at least four square feet,
raised from the floor, of course, and with deep sides and a
removable front made up of loose boards that can be raised or
lowered according to the agility of the puppies. More details
of whelping requirements are given in Chapter 10.

Obviously some equipment is needed. For kennel cleaning
a good sweeping-brush, shovel and bucket are required, also
a rake and watering-can. For the inmates of the kennel, a good
supply of collars and leads, hound-gloves, combs, brushes,
etc., are needed. Good-quality leather is unbeatable for collars
and leads and is serviceable and better to handle than chains,
which are very functional but play havoc with one's hands.
Choke chains are unsuitable for Bassets because they tend to
catch up in the loose skin of the neck. A short coupling lead
for linking two hounds together is useful, too, and some finer
leather or nylon leads are better for showing hounds. The
bright colours of the latter can enhance the looks of a hound
a great deal.

Grooming is best done with a round-toothed comb and then
a stiff brush, followed by a session with a hound-glove, and
one's equipment is incomplete without these three items.

A large lightweight travelling box for sending bitches to stud-dogs, or railing hounds to a show, is a good investment and the overall measurements should not be less than three feet by two feet by two feet. It must be well ventilated. A couple of smaller boxes for sending puppies to new homes are also most useful.

As I have said, one cannot possibly suggest a kennel layout or set of kennel requirements that would find universal favour, and I have based the ideas given on what seems to be the general type accepted by British and French breeders. In the U.S.A. I believe there are zoning laws which restrict the size of kennels, and also because of climatic differences it is obvious that the robust weatherproof kennels of Britain would be unsuitable for Bassets in, say, southern California.

10

Mating, Whelping, and Care
of the Bitch

AFTER establishing a kennel the next logical step is breeding
and the matings should be planned well in advance. Naturally
if a mating is planned between inmates of one's own pack,
hardly any preparation is needed. However, when a mating
involves the use of an outside stud-hound, the owner must
have prior warning and a firm booking should be made, and
he should also be informed as soon as the bitch begins her
season. Arrangements for her visit can then be made; most
stud-dog owners prefer a visiting bitch to have a few days' stay
at their kennels, arriving a day or two before the eleventh day
of season and departing a day or so after mating. This gives
the bitch time to settle in strange surroundings and to famili-
arise herself with the stud-dog and his handler. It is expecting
a great deal to achieve a successful mating within the space of
an hour or so; it is possible, of course, but most people prefer
not to rush the mating.

The female comes into season for the first time around six
months; some bitches vary and often it is nearer twelve. It is
not usual to mate a Basset before the third season, by which
time it is eighteen months to two years old. The first mating
should take place if possible in the spring or summer; I think
it a great mistake to allow a young bitch to cope with the
rigours of a winter or late season litter. About two years is the
ideal age for a first litter; the hound is by that time fully
developed and mature in body and mind.

The signs of heat are a red discharge from the vulva and a
gradual enlarging of the area. Gradually the colour of the discharge lightens, until by the tenth and eleventh day it is watery

and pinkish-tinged. The vulva is by then large and soft and the eleventh day is considered the correct one for a successful mating. In bicoloured hounds the nose loses colour and often becomes very pale and pink, and the body markings seem to become more prominent.

The duration of a heat is about three weeks, but although many instances of early or late matings are recorded, the tenth, eleventh and twelfth days are the most usual for an effective one. On first introduction to the dog most bitches are somewhat coy and flirty and will not settle to allow the dog to mate them, but after this initial period of courtship the bitch will usually allow the dog to mate. However, because of the weight of a Basset dog it is often necessary to support the bitch by holding her up under the body, and also steadying her for the dog. This is a very different matter from a 'forced mating', where the bitch is forcibly restrained and held until the mating is effected. I am not an advocate of forced matings, and this view is endorsed by Miss Keevil of the Grims Hounds, who maintains that a litter seldom materialises.

As I have said, most bitches accept the dog in the end; some, however, are impossible to mate except when forced, because they refuse all contact with the dog, but may well accept an alternative dog quite happily. Most dogs on the other hand will mate any bitch and the experienced studs are unconcerned by the antics of the female.

Even if it is plainly visible that the pair will mate easily, someone should always be present and on no account should the pair be left unattended after the tie. Bitches tend to become restless and apart from moving about often wish to lie down; if allowed to do so they could possibly injure the dog. The tie is not essential for a productive mating, but most breeders are much happier about the outcome if a tie is effected. The length of time the hounds are tied is no indication of the size of a litter; in duration the tie can vary from a few minutes to a couple of hours, but the average period is probably twenty minutes.

After the mating the hounds should be separated and kept away from their other companions for about half an hour. The bitch should, of course, be prevented from mating with another dog by confining her until the termination of her heat. After a successful mating it is found that the heat ends quickly. If a second mating is required it can be done on the following day or two days after. One mating is enough to fertilise the bitch, and it is usually found that she conceives to the first one.

In the wild most animals mate in the early morning or evening, and domesticated animals also show a preference for these times. The procedure is best carried out in a quiet place, only one or two people known to the dogs being present.

The average stud fee of a Basset is twenty pounds, but many hounds stand at fifteen, and prominent champions and imported dogs can have fees varying from twenty-five to seventy-five pounds. Most stud-dog owners are reasonable enough to concede a 'Free return service if no litter' clause or even a 'No puppies, no fee' arrangement. This is purely at the discretion of the stud-dog owner; he is under no legal obligation to return a fee or offer another mating if the bitch does not conceive. The fee is charged for the mating, successful or not, and not for the results.

The gestation or pregnancy of a bitch is sixty-three days, but as with the length of time for a heat some degree of variation exists, and it is possible for a bitch to whelp a few days prematurely or to delay whelping for two or three days. Bitches that have whelped early or late before usually continue to do so. Some have been known to be a week or ten days overdue and whelp easily after the delay, but if whelping is overdue always call in the vet and ask him to ensure that there is no obstacle to normal delivery.

For five or six weeks after mating the bitch should lead her normal life, exercising and generally conforming to the daily routine. Her diet and number of daily meals should remain the same, but she should have an addition of vitamins and calcium. These are necessary to permit the bitch to build up reserves and promote the production of strong puppies. A product called 'Abidec', in capsule or liquid form, is extremely useful in that it contains the vitamins A, B, C, D and E. The essential calcium is best administered in tablet form, and

'Osteocalcium' is typical of the balanced form of calcium, phosphorus and vitamin D. Calcium powder alone is virtually useless, and for correct assimilation must be balanced with vitamin D and phosphorus. There are several forms of additives and all are easily obtained from chemists; although they may be slightly more expensive than preparations made specially for dogs, they have the virtue of being readily available. Cod-liver oil is a common addition to the diet of a pregnant dam, and so is radiostoleum in capsule form, or cod-liver oil and malt extract. The beauty of capsules and tablets is that the owner knows exactly what amounts are being fed to the bitch.

From the sixth week onwards the expectant dam should be moved into the whelping quarters and kept away from other hounds. Her exercise should be curtailed and all jumping and other violent activities stopped. She should be allowed freedom to wander about the premises, enjoy herself rolling in grass and generally have a carefree time. The diet must be increased and the ration of vitamins, etc., doubled so that the bitch may meet the growing demands being made on her. Bassets usually have large litters—eight is probably the average, but nineteen in a litter have been recorded in England—and in order to carry such a litter, whelp easily and rear the puppies well, the dam must be well and properly nourished.

The daily diet of a bitch in the six-to-nine weeks' stage should be on the following lines:

Morning   Warm milk (or Lactol) and egg, with honey or glucose powder added.
Midday   Cooked and raw meat, gravy, and hound meal, or fish, plus the vitamins and calcium product.
Evening   A soup, of gravy; or milk.

Needless to say, the bitch should have water available at all times, and Parrish's Iron Tonic or rose-hip syrup may be added to the water. Goats' milk is undoubtedly the best but is not always available, in which case cows' milk or Lactol are good alternatives. The amount of hound meal should gradually be reduced until by the final week the meals do not contain it at all. Like every other living thing the dog welcomes a change of diet, and this can be provided by adding vegetables to the meals, or substituting fish for meat, or varying the type of meat.

For a week before the whelping date the bitch should be given a spoonful of liquid paraffin daily, and this acts as an internal cleanser and lubricant. Many breeders also worm the dam at least once late in pregnancy, say the seventh or eighth week, and at the same time an injection of vitamin D is useful and beneficial to the bitch immediately after whelping.

In late pregnancy most Basset dams become very heavy and distended with the litter, and because they are normally low to the ground, it is often found that the teats are touching the ground and liable to be scratched and become inflamed. A good antiseptic and soothing cream should be applied, and Savlon or Vaseline are both excellent. If the teats must be washed only the mildest soap should be added to lukewarm water. Any sign of mastitis, hard lumps in the teats, should be looked for and attended to by the vet immediately. Some bitches are prone to the disorder, but it can be cleared up quickly and with no after-effects.

The whelping quarters should have been prepared in advance and cleaned out well. Prior to whelping the bench need not contain much bedding because the bitch is always scratching it out and always seems to prefer to whelp on the bare boards. Restlessness is a sign that the time is approaching, and the bitch is constantly wandering about, in and out of the bench. To make sure she whelps indoors she should be kept in. When the whelping is imminent one can do nothing except observe quietly and leave the bitch to get on with things, with the owner making periodical checks. Most bitches, even the old hands, like a comforting word every so often, and the first-time bitch may not even settle unless the owner is present. Nature's way is the best and the bitch that has proved capable of whelping alone and consequently attending to the new arrivals herself is worth her weight in gold; but such hounds are few and far between, although generally speaking the Basset makes an excellent dam.

At the birth of a puppy the bitch will usually break open the enveloping membrane or 'sack' and bite the cord short, and proceed to lick, wash and dry the new arrival until it becomes active and begins to search for the teat and warmth of the dam's body. When the afterbirth appears the bitch normally eats it, or it can be removed immediately from the bench. Should the bitch delay in opening the sack, the attendant should release the puppy, sever the cord about three inches from the body, rub and dry the baby with a piece of towelling and when dry place the puppy on a teat. It is amazing how puppies only minutes old can grasp a teat and begin to feed almost immediately.

The period between arrivals can vary; sometimes only minutes pass and the whole whelping can be concluded in an hour or two, and on the other hand a long, lazy type of whelping can take up a day, and in extremes two days. Bassets are fairly large in the passage and seldom have difficulty in whelping a correctly presented puppy, but if a puppy is coming abnormally and thereby blocking the passage some assistance from the vet should be sought. The experienced owner can often correct things by manipulation, but the novice owner is well advised to call in the vet if a puppy appears to be stuck. In all but extreme cases the puppy can be safely removed without harm to the dam. If it is thought advisable by the vet a lazy whelper can be speeded up with an injection of Partuatrin. There is no need for panic if the delays are not unreasonable and if the bitch appears at ease.

Depending on the temperament of the bitch, it is occasionally necessary to remove the whelps from the bench as they arrive, and this enables a good whelper to get on with things without worrying about the earlier arrivals squirming about beside her. Some dams, however, become very agitated if puppies are removed: in such cases the pups should be left in the bench, but to prevent their being crushed when their mother moves about a very careful watch should be kept. Because the Basset dam almost touches the ground there is real danger of puppies being swept under or behind her by the teats and being crushed when the dam settles. Great care is needed to prevent this at the time of whelping and until the puppies are about three weeks old. However, despite almost constant vigilance accidents do happen, and it is a common hazard in the breed, crushed and suffocated puppies accounting for many deaths.

A bitch will seldom eat or drink during a whelping but food and liquid refreshment should be offered. The same applies to the bitch relieving herself, but she should not be fussed to do this or to eat; she will do both in her own good time. She is often seemingly grateful for a sponge down with mild antiseptic in lukewarm water, as of course it must refresh and keep her sweet-smelling. The bedding of the bench should be kept clean, and during a whelping old newspapers provide ideal bedding, as it can be changed frequently and absorbs all the moisture and discharge present at every whelping.

Throughout the whelping the temperature of the kennel should be a constant 65°F or thereabouts; no great amount of heat is needed. During spring and summer no form of artificial heat should be required, but the British climate often dictates otherwise. Winter-born puppies always require warmth but Bassets are best whelped in spring and summer. Whatever form of heating is used, safety is the keynote, and the appliance and fixtures must be carefully checked and correctly fixed.

If the vet has had to remove puppies or examine the dam internally it is usual for him to inject her with penicillin or some other antibiotic, and an injection of vitamin D, if not administered prior to whelping, should also be given as a guard against eclampsia, a condition where the dam collapses and is incapable of nursing the puppies. Usually this only occurs if the pre-natal care of the birth has been neglected.

After whelping the bitch will rest and sleep deeply; the puppies continue to feed and the satisfied ones sleep. This gives an opportunity to place smaller puppies on to vacant teats and make sure they feed, and also, if puppies outnumber teats, the unsatisfied puppies; usually the noisy ones can be accommodated. Nothing is more satisfying than to see and hear a litter of strong puppies feeding off a sleeping dam. The sight alone is recompense for the anxiety of the owner during a whelping.

11

Care of the Young Basset

MR. SHEPHERD, an old breeder of Basset Hounds and a former secretary of the Basset Hound Club, once said that the Basset is 'made or marred in fifteen weeks', and he meant the nine weeks' period of growth in the foetus and the succeeding six weeks after birth—the correct nourishment of the dam and the puppies during these times. The two stages must be attended to with great care if the production of strong, healthy hounds is the aim. The feeding is just as important as the breeding. Two very heavy-boned hounds may be mated, but they themselves do not pass on heavy bone to the progeny, only the ability for the puppies to produce heavy bone if promoted by correct nutrition. Small-boned hounds can produce stock which, if properly fed, will eventually mature into well-boned hounds. In other words, the breeders must assist nature by ensuring that their stock is fed in such a way that its full potential is revealed.

We have discussed the subject of choosing hounds with good pedigree and the types of dogs and bitches most desirable, and Mr. Shepherd's first period of making a good Basset has also been covered. Attention must now be given to the feeding and rearing of the young stock.

Once the bitch has recovered from the whelping and is more or less settling to the new routine of coping with several permanently hungry puppies, the youngsters can be closely examined, notes made on the division of sex and colour, and any puppies having major faults removed. The Basset is not prone to many inherent faults, cleft palates, etc., but, of course, deformities can occur and these are best eradicated as soon as possible. One recurring fault is the 'kinky-tailed' puppies; the tail is deformed by one or several kinks. Little can be done

L

with the seriously malformed tail, but only one or two minor kinks can often be 'eased out' by daily massage. The fault was known to Millais, who blamed the fault on inbreeding on the dam's side.

Litters average eight and often attain double figures—most breeders prefer to have a below-average litter. However, if a large litter does emerge I am not in favour of killing off any healthy puppies for the sake of reducing numbers. A Basset bitch, well nourished and cared for pre-natally, can cope with twelve puppies quite easily, and all healthy puppies should be left with the dam. Taken as a whole the mortality rate in Bassets, due to puppies being crushed at birth, is high, and this is a form of culling. Despite great care by breeder and dam, one or more puppies are liable to be crushed or suffocated in the three or four weeks after birth. Straw laid thickly round the whelping-bench is a good aid, in that if any puppies do get behind the bitch, they are pressed into the straw, and not the hard sides of the bench, and can therefore remain for some time quite safely in its refuge, until rescued.

The puppies are quite content to feed off the dam for about three weeks, and depending on the size of the litter they are adequately nourished. However, if the litter is a large one, some supplementary feeding is needed, and feeding should begin at the ten-to-fourteen days' stage. In any case, irrespective of the litter size, the puppies should have the opportunity of supplements and be feeding away from the dam at three to four weeks.

To begin with the puppies should be offered three meals per day, and these should coincide with their normal feeding times. It is little use offering milk to puppies who have just been satisfied by the dam. Not all whelps will accept food immediately but they should still be handled and offered it. The food at this stage should, of course, be liquid—warmed Lactol or goats' or cows' milk with the necessary amounts of the vitamins and calcium products added. Honey is also excellent and is, of course, sweetening. The milk used should be the same as that being fed to the bitch, and this identity of feeding should apply also to the vitamin additives. I have given details of these in the last chapter, and for simplification will refer to the additives as 'vitamins' from now on; the term will cover the full range of products.

The food should be placed in a small, round, shallow dish and should be lukewarm; cold or boiling milk should not be given. The puppy should be cradled in the right hand, supported firmly and held to the milk, and attempts made to encourage it to take the milk. As I have said, some puppies will steadfastly refuse to lap, but others will need no encouraging. If the puppy refuses, dip the muzzle in the milk, and once it has tasted the milk it will often start to lap it. For the first day or two the puppies must not be allowed to have more than a taste of the milk, and gorging must be avoided. They should be fed thrice daily, the size of the meal being gradually increased and the demands of each individual puppy carefully gauged. If overeating does occur, a spoonful of Dinneford's or milk of magnesia should be administered and the puppy relieved.

During the feeding the bitch can be let out into the kennel run and locked out, and the bedding changed in the whelping box. After feeding the pups can be replaced in the box and their mother allowed in. She will usually clean them and gradually settle down with them, and they will resume feeding from her. This method of doing several jobs at the same time, i.e. feeding puppies, dam outside being fed, bench cleaned, etc., is ideal in that it cuts down the number of times the dam and litter are disturbed. I think peace and quiet are best for all concerned. The fussed bitch naturally becomes strained and is unable to settle to feeding or caring for the litter.

From the beginning of feeding until four weeks the feed should be liquid, but after four weeks the meals can gradually become more substantial and the milk be thickened by Farex or Farlene. All meals, whatever the substance, should contain the vitamins, and this applies to the meals being given to the dam. The demands on her are great, and in order to make milk her diet should have the same attention as that of the puppies.

At three weeks the puppies should be wormed and the recommended dosage strictly adhered to; great care must be taken not to overdose. It is essential for the worms to be cleared out of the puppies before the rapid period of growth from four to eight weeks. Worming can be repeated weekly, and it will be found that although worms will continue to be emitted each time, the quantity will rapidly decline. The nails of the puppies need clipping weekly; this ensures that the foot has a chance to develop correctly, and the bitch is also relieved of the nuisance of sharp little nails scratching the udder. Dewclaws may or may not be removed according to the desires of the breeder.

The diet is gradually increased in quantity and around four weeks meat and fish can be added, plus Saval No. 1, a small-grained biscuit-meal. All meat should be finely minced or scraped and fish inspected and all the small bones removed. Meat should be the basis of a diet, but fish is a useful addition and provides a beneficial change. It is impossible to give a diet acceptable to everyone, but basically most breeders agree on four good meals per day for puppies of four to twelve weeks, consisting of two milk feeds and two meat meals. The following is a rough guide for a daily diet:

8 a.m.   Warm milk on porage oats, with egg, honey and vitamins added.

12 noon. Minced meat, cooked or parboiled with the gravy. Saval No. 1 (increasing the grade of Saval as the puppies grow), vitamins added. Bones or hard biscuits.

4 p.m.   Warm milk, as for morning meal, or Farex or Farlene. A spoonful of cod-liver oil and malt each, or Brand's Essence of Beef.

8 p.m.   Meat meal again, followed later in the evening by a warm milk feed.

The puppies are best fed individually, thus ensuring fair shares and correct amounts for all. Bones are beneficial but they are best fed to the puppies in the dam's absence. If she is allowed to feed at the same time she will inevitably snap at a puppy who ventures near her bone.

Drinking water should always be available for the dam and litter. Rose-hip syrup or Parrish's Iron Tonic is easily added to the water and is useful for improving pigmentation.

The diet given can safely be followed through from twelve weeks to twelve months, simply by increasing the quantities. Individual feeding all through the dog's life is best, but in large kennels this is not always possible. However, in the average-sized kennel all young stock should be fed separately. Frequent worming is necessary, but by twelve months the results of a worming should be negative.

I should add at this stage that it is my own personal view that Basset puppies should never be weaned from the dam, but should be allowed to stay with her as long as she will tolerate them. I think Bassets are very sensitive hounds, and young stock especially respond to comforting, and the presence of the dam, especially at nights, is one way of giving contentment. Bitches are often weaned early in order to get them back in show condition, but I think that all thoughts of showing a bitch should cease when she is mated and plans made accordingly. After all, what is more important, the successful rearing of a litter or a show? Definitely the former. Most Basset bitches are good mothers and content to have their puppies around them for months.

Young hounds gradually tire of milk meals, and when this happens increased quantities of meat and hound meal can be given, so that at the twelve to eighteen months period they are on at least three substantial meals per day, and at two years old are down to two meals daily. The Basset grows and develops for two years, and therefore the great care given to the feeding also continues for two years. The full range of vitamins must be given for at least this time. Some youngsters naturally develop sooner than others, but early maturity should not signify that the correct feeding should be terminated—it must be continued, to ensure that the heavy bone one has developed becomes 'strong, heavy bone'. Heavy bone, minus strength, is a liabilty to a hound. The sudden reduction of diet or withdrawal of vitamins from a young hound can, and frequently does, result in malformation, especially in the forelegs.

Mr. Shepherd, at the beginning of the century, was fully aware of the need to feed well, and sixty years later his ideas are being endorsed by prominent modern breeders. In *Dog World* of 1 July 1966, an article on Bassets contained comments by two breeders. Miss Keevil, of the Grims Hounds, said: 'A Basset bitch in whelp is often preparing for twelve or thirteen puppies in contrast to the five or six of other breeds, and they should be fed accordingly.' Mrs. Wells, breeder of the Fredwell Hounds, said: 'Good feeding is vitally important in rearing sound, well-boned Basset hounds. In-whelp bitches and young puppies should have plenty of raw meat, eggs, milk, vegetables and a wholesome biscuit meal.'

The cost of providing the Basset bitch and then the litter with the proper diet is not low, but it must be fully understood that there is no alternative. Such a diet cannot be cheap, and it is, of course, a 'luxury' diet, because the breed is more demanding than most other breeds. Certainly hounds can exist on a moderate diet, but the growth rate of the puppies cannot be supported by a diet deficient in good food and vitamins.

No Basset puppy should be sold at less than eight weeks old, and probably the best age for allowing pups to leave for new homes is ten to twelve weeks. By that age the breeder has had ample opportunity to establish their diet and routine and set them well on their feet. Most breeders provide customers with the puppies' diet sheet and general information about feeding and rearing, and in all cases the instructions should be followed, especially the insistence on dietary additions. The diet may be altered to allow for differing local food supplies, but the number of feeds and, as I have said, the vitamin additives should be unchanged.

Basset puppies begin to walk fairly steadily at three weeks, and from the very earliest stage should be allowed to walk about indoors and go outside if the weather is favourable. In really hot weather some form of shade should be provided, as unscreened sun can distress very young puppies and cause sickness. Fresh air is essential to all growing stock, and even on cold days the pups should be allowed to go outside, but they are best kept indoors if it is wet. If they are caught out in a sudden shower they should be thoroughly dried before being put back in the kennel.

In cinder-surfaced or grass kennel runs the puppies will have to be carefully watched, and prevented from chewing on stones and sticks. It is a habit with them and, of course, there is a possibilty of puppies swallowing stones.

The puppies should have regular checks made on their teeth, nails and general condition, and by doing this the breeder is also getting them used to being handled and examined. They can be taught to pose in a 'showing position' at a very early age and can even begin very simple lead-training at the same time. The ears should be checked frequently, and cleaned inside and out if necessary. Several ear-cleaning products are obtainable, but ordinary surgical spirit is as useful as anything. The coat can also be cleaned with the spirit.

All breeders are unanimous in the opinion that Bassets should definitely not be exercised until they reach at least six months. The only exercise needed before that age is what can be had by walking and playing in or round the kennel. This should be unrestricted, and the puppies given all the freedom one's premises permit. The litter should not be permanently confined to the kennel run all the time but have opportunities to explore the world outside, hear strange sounds and see and smell new objects. This method of allowing freedom to puppies has been the policy of foxhound packs for centuries, giving the young hounds a carefree early life and education before they return to the pack proper and the necessary disciplined life. The same policy should be followed for Bassets so far as the breeder is able.

Lead-training can begin very soon; five minutes daily is all that is necessary to train a puppy, and one should not be in any hurry to complete the training. Puppies usually jump about at first, but with encouragement and titbits they soon settle down and learn to walk steadily at one's side. Combined with this training should be the puppies' first instruction on show procedure—walking steadily and being taught to stand for the judge's inspection. It is a good help if some other person can then be present and examine the puppy as a judge would, so accustoming the youngster to being handled by someone other than the owner.

Once lead-trained, the puppy or puppies should be taken out on to a street or road and allowed to watch the passing traffic and people. All that is required is five minutes daily, and no attempt must be made to walk the puppies more than about fifty yards. Before exercising proper begins the puppies, if all has gone well, should be lead-trained and fully prepared for the sights and sounds they will see outside the kennel.

The reason for deferring the beginning of exercise proper is to give the youngster a chance to develop steadily and to let the massive bone strengthen. It must be remembered that the Basset is a large hound, and the youngsters grow at a tremendous rate and are often very heavy in early life. The bone at this stage is heavy but not strong, and therefore it is important not to tax the bone by exerting undue pressure on it before it strengthens and the joints knit more soundly. One has only to watch a young hound walk to see how loose the joints seem, and there appears to be a total lack of co-ordination in the limbs.

The process of exercising and bringing the young hound to a sound, well-muscled condition should begin at six months and take at least twelve months to accomplish. One must not despair when the puppies pass through several unattractive 'ugly duckling' stages, and complete soundness should not be expected in a matter of weeks. An injection of vitamin D is very beneficial at this period: it ensures that the calcium is fully absorbed into the body, and therefore the bone is being aided at a time when more stress is being placed on it.

The nails should be kept well trimmed to ensure that when the hound does come up on to the toes with the exercise, the weight will be evenly distributed and supported by all parts of the foot. Before exercise most youngsters are well back on the pasterns and down in the hock, but this is simply a result of their age and the exercise will remedy the condition.

A quarter of a mile is far enough for the first walk, and for the first week or so the emphasis should be on helping the youngsters to enjoy being out, talking to them and generally making a fuss of them. The puppies should be allowed to dictate their own speed and pace, and without being allowed to wander anywhere be generally free to go where they like and stop whenever they want. Discipline and guidance and exertion of the owner's will should be gradual, and all harsh checking and pulling avoided.

When exercising on roads, the puppies should be kept on leads and walk to face oncoming traffic. On the highway the owner has a duty to keep dogs under control at all times, and even old traffic-experienced hounds are safest on a lead. On open ground the hounds may be released and allowed to have a good gallop. Stock-chasing should be checked at once and the culprits reprimanded. Bassets are sensitive hounds and usually respond to vocal admonition. No Basset owner or breeder need ever possess a whip except for controlling a pack. The best professional huntsmen and whippers-in use the whip only on the rarest of occasions.

As the puppies get used to the routine of regular daily exercise, the length of the walk may be gradually increased and the hounds kept on the hard road surface for longer periods. At some stage a short halt or a break for a run in a field should be allowed, and for owner and hounds it is much better if the exercise never becomes boring or irksome. Some variety should always be available—the walk should cover different routes and not continually go over the same stretch. As the duration of the exercise increases so should the discipline or training, and the hounds should be kept at a regular pace and held on the course required by the owner. Dog and owner should walk easily side by side, and any attempt by the dogs to pull ahead, straining on the leads, should be discouraged.

On returning from exercise, the hounds should be checked over with great attention paid to the feet, and any small stones or thorns must be removed. After exercise in fields or woods, the ears and eyes must be inspected and any seeds dislodged. A quick grooming or rub down with a hound-glove is particularly beneficial after exercise, as the circulation is already toned up and the muscles especially respond to massage.

In kennels and out at exercise the young hounds must not

be allowed to run up and down steps or stairs, and all jolts and jars of the front legs should be regarded as potential dangers. The front-leg formation of a Basset is composed of delicately assembled joints and they are prone to dislocation and sprains. Any sign of stiffness should be given attention by the vet, and in cases of a simple strain an injection or course of Cortisone usually clears the trouble up quickly.

Bassets should never be lifted by their front legs—children and 'non-doggy' people tend to lift all dogs in this way. It would be most harmful to Bassets and in time would completely dislocate the shoulders. Very young puppies should be lifted by grasping the loose skin behind the neck with the left hand and lifting and supporting the body with the right. Old hounds, because of their weight and long bodies, are difficult to lift: one of the best ways is to put the left forearm well under the chest of the dog so that the hand holds the body side; the right forearm and hand cradle the hindquarters, and the hound is held to the body when lifting so that it is firmly supported both sides and below. Some judges insist on inspecting hounds on a table, so it is just as well to accustom them to being lifted on and off a table and also to teach them to stand still there.

Regular grooming is essential for good coat and skin condition, and the hound-glove or bare hand massage is especially good for muscle development. A good combing followed by a brush with the hound-glove is all that is required for the orthodox grooming, but some extra work is needed when preparing hounds for show. This is dealt with in the next chapter.

Not until a hound is at least eighteen months old should it be asked to take part in hard exercise, and for regular hunting two years is probably the most sensible age for entering him. The condition of a young hound should be hard and muscular but with the ribs and body structure well covered with firm flesh. Fat, flabby Bassets should be dieted by cutting down on the meal part of their feeding. Bitch hounds tend to put on weight faster than dogs; the latter can occasionally be difficult to keep bodied up, and it may be found necessary to feed dogs at least one extra meal a day.

Although the growth rate of the Basset is fantastic in the early stages, the actual process of development from young puppy to adult hound is slow in body and in mind, and not until the hound is two years old should it be considered as mature. For the full two years it is essential to pay great attention to diet, exercise and general welfare.

Some breeders of other breeds would probably scoff at the almost 'mollycoddling' methods used by Basset Hound breeders in the rearing and breeding of their stock, but experience is a hard master and it has taught Basset breeders that there is no cheap or rough and ready way of producing sound, strong, well-developed stock. The cost of providing the diet for dam and litter has to be borne, and the long job of bringing young stock to maturity patiently and diligently adhered to. Sir Everett Millais once said: 'The Basset is a gentle dog and must be treated gently, they are slow-thinking and slow-moving and their owners must be patient and understanding with them.' Perhaps some of today's Bassets are not as slow as they were in Sir Everett's day, but they do still require lots of understanding and are a dog for the connoisseur who is fully prepared to accept the demands made on the bank balance, time and peace of mind!

12

Showing and Show Procedure

NOTHING seems to be easy with Bassets. One of the greatest and most challenging difficulties a breeder has to face is the choosing of a show-prospect puppy from a litter. The cause is that there are so many specialised points to consider that are essential if the breed type is to be retained, but also the soundness required in any working breed must be present and combine with the breed type to form the whole hound. Breed type minus soundness is useless, as is soundness minus breed type.

The assessment of adult hounds is easy compared with the appraisal of immature ones; on the old hounds the breed points and soundness are present or absent, but on the youngsters they are hidden by tenderness of age, and the future development can only be partially forecast. It must be emphasised that there is no 'fool-proof' formula for choosing the best puppy out of a litter.

The safest and by far the best method is to delay selecting a puppy as long as possible. This, however, entails the running on of, if not the whole litter, then at least a couple of the pups. Because of the cost, time demanded and space needed, very few people can afford to retain a full litter of possibly eight or more puppies, and so most breeders settle for the best alternative of keeping some and making a final choice from them.

The process of choosing which puppies to keep is one of gradual elimination, and this can begin as soon as the litter is born, because some faults can be seen at birth. These include lack of bone and size, deformities and bad coat texture.

Many very small and puny puppies fail to survive more than a day or two, but naturally some do, and with extra care and attention can often turn out quite useful hounds, but they always lack the size of body and substance of bone that a Basset needs if premier show awards are contemplated. In the show ring small hounds are always handicapped, and the virtues of substance are also needed in the hunting field and in the breeding programmes.

Severe cases of deformity can be detected at birth, and the unfortunate puppies are best destroyed immediately. In all forms of life freaks and deformities are constantly appearing, and some abnormalities in Bassets include recorded cases of a Basset born minus one ear, puppies minus nails, and puppies having the long limbs of a larger hound type instead of the shortened Basset limbs. The latter cases are thought to be throwbacks to the old French hounds the Basset is descended from. Tails deformed by kinks are not uncommon, and I dealt with this fault in a previous chapter.

Long-haired and woolly-haired puppies are occasionally produced and these faults can usually be detected at birth, although some cases do not develop the faulty coat until a later stage of puppyhood. In the Basset Hound and Artois-Norman Basset any other form of coat than the smooth is a definite fault, and hounds having it should never be considered for breeding. Incidentally, both the long and woolly coat are considered faulty in the Griffon-Vendeen Basset, and any attempt to try to breed Griffon-type coated hounds from them would be folly.

At a later stage of puppyhood the mouth and jaw formation can be judged. Many excellent puppies have been cursed with a bad mouth, but the temptation to keep them in the hope of improvement should be resisted. Mouths that are incorrect, overshot or undershot to any extent will not improve, and even in less serious cases the fault usually becomes worse instead of better. A hound with the least suspicion of a faulty mouth will always be by-passed by judges. British breeders spent years eradicating the faults (overshot jaws especially), and now the condition is fortunately rare in British stock, so it can be understood why the judges are so uncompromising on faulty mouths and jaw formation.

The process of elimination must not depend on faults only,

because in the early stages some desirable features also appear, and if the breeder is fortunate the litter may contain puppies showing none of the aforementioned faults but definite virtues. These include bone and body substance, ears and skin texture, colour and coat.

Every breeder likes to see the arrival of a very even litter; well-developed and substantially bodied puppies present no obstacles. Occasionally litters arrive that are not so even: some of the pups are large, some medium-sized and others small. As the litter develops it is usual to find that the medium-sized puppies gradually grow and eventually become almost as well grown as the puppies which were larger at birth. This means that the large and medium-sized whelps may be judged equal, but the smaller puppies should never be seriously considered for retention.

The only drawback with the very big puppies is that they are liable to turn coarse in the latter stage of puppyhood, and this is most evident in head points. The body of a new-born puppy should be long and the ribs well rounded. The limbs should be short, thick and very heavy-boned in the upper arm, and the feet large and well padded. The substance and strength of foreleg on a new-born Basset puppy never ceases to amaze me, and the rate of development of this point is fantastic. The tail should be short and very thick at the base, and old Basset breeders used to say: 'Choose the puppy with the ugliest head and the thickest tail.' They also held the belief that if the bone was not heavy in the tail it was seldom heavy elsewhere in the Basset's anatomy. Certainly the long, spindly-tailed hounds always seem to lack substance, so there was something in what our predecessors said.

The quality of the ears can be assessed at birth, and to be ideal they should be set low on the skull, V-shaped and very thin to feel. The inward curl or corkscrew effect cannot be judged until later, but the V-shaped ear always turns well inwards with maturity, while the U-shaped or round-ended ear always fails on this important point, tends to hang too flat from the skull and thus spoils the whole appearance of the head. In outline and profile the skull of the Basset should never resemble that of a Cocker Spaniel, which is what happens when the ears hang flat and are thick-textured.

Closely allied to ear texture is the overall texture of the body skin, and this should be as fine as possible, without of course impairing the weatherproofing. Because of the rigours of the British climate the native hounds naturally develop a thicker skin and denser coat than the French Artois-Normans, who have a very thin, supple skin and a fine, short coat. Whether the coat is dense or fine the skin must be elastic, and when tested should pull out easily from any point of the body, not just from the neck where it is always loosest. A tight, close-fitting skin is a serious fault and can be detected very early in the hound's life.

Unless one or more puppies in a litter really stands out, the final selection of the 'chosen few' should not be made too soon, and one should always be ready to change a formed opinion. Such changes are usually inevitable because there are two important points of the Basset that change constantly as the hound matures. Both skull and soundness alter frequently and are best judged in the later stages of puppyhood.

Soundness, meaning the correct structural conformation of the limbs and the correct motivation of the hound by the limbs, is extremely difficult to judge on a hound under four months. In the young hound there is a looseness of the limbs and an unsteadiness associated with all young animals, and when in motion a definite lack of co-ordination. Until the puppies begin to muscle up and tighten in front and rear, any decision regarding soundness and movement should not be made.

From a very early age the nails should be kept well trimmed, for the comfort of the bitch and also, of course, to enable the feet and pads to form correctly when the puppies come on to them. In early puppyhood the nails grow quickly and will need trimming weekly.

The degree of crook should not be overdeveloped under four months and in fact the young hound is better if the forelegs tend to be straight as this gives all the bones and joints in the forelegs time to strengthen before too much weight and pressure is put on them.

Good strong knees and well-padded feet are essential to any hound and any tendency to knuckle over must be viewed with misgiving. It is natural for the young hounds to be back on their feet, and usually with increased activity and maturity they come forward and up on to the toes in the proper manner.

The loose-elbowed puppy will usually improve by tightening with age, but the wide, deep-chested puppy nearly always finishes by being too wide and 'Bulldoggy' in front. Contrasting with the wide front but equally incorrect is the very narrow chest completely lacking in depth or substance, and this fault is accompanied by forelegs that touch at the knee when standing. The forelegs should never be so narrowly set or the degree of crook so exaggerated that the knees touch.

The sternum, or keel bone, is present at an early age even though the chest is underdeveloped, and this is one of the points often overlooked but which is a feature of the Basset. The body should be long and rounded, especially in the rib-cage. Any flat-sides should not be considered, not only because flat-sides are faults but also because this fault is usually associated with flanged ribs. This is a condition where the ends of the ribs turn out and form a ridge along the bottom of the body, and the condition can also be so bad that the ends of the ribs are so twisted that they entwine and knit together under the body. The rib-cage must be round and deep and extend well back into the flanks and loins, which must also be deep and strong.

Until the hindquarters are muscled little can be done to assess hind action. In moving away the youngster is very loose and shaky on the hocks, but chronic cases of cow-hocks and bowed legs stand out, and even with unsteady hocks a potentially sound hound can be fairly accurately spotted. There must be a reasonable amount of space between the legs, and when moving away they should be thrown back straight and not be thrust out to one side. The 'throwing of a leg' is a fairly common fault and it seldom improves with exercise or age.

The hocks should be prominent, well pouched with loose skin and well bent, thus preventing the long straight-stifled

Thomas Fall

Breightmet Charity and Ch. Breightmet Chimer, 1958

Basset Hound Club working pack, 1967. Hounds with Mr. Alex McDonald

Ch. Wingjays Ptolemy, 1964, Ch. Sungarth Phoebe, 1960,
and Ch. Wingjays Fabulous, 1963

Walhampton puppies

look that is wrong. High-set hocks are also faulty and usually found on tall hounds or hounds with a topline that slopes up from shoulder to quarter.

Just as the soundness of a young Basset is very difficult to judge, so too is the skull, for the same reason, in that it is constantly changing. Final judgment should be delayed as long as possible, but some features show up in the early stages and can be a pointer to the eventual quality of the head. Points that the skull must have at an early age if a decent headpiece is to develop are dark eyes, low-set and fine-textured ears, correct mouth, good depth of lip and an overall oblong shape.

The eye begins by being blue, and a useful and well-tried guide to eventual eye colour is: the darker the blue the darker the eye will be later on. The pale blue eye usually changes to a light brown, which is of course undesirable. The eye must never be prominent nor too deep set but more or less level with the face; the looseness of skin above and the haw below give the eye its deep-set appearance, and these same points give the eye-setting the correct but very rarely seen diamond or lozenge-shape.

I have discussed the ears and mouth, but in conjunction with the latter point is the muzzle and the depth of lip. The Basset is not a killing dog in the terrier sense of the word, and it may be argued that strength of jaw is not important, but I feel it is and think that the Basset foreface and muzzle should consist of something more than a mass of lip and pendulous flews. The weak-jawed hounds are inevitably snipy and lack lip, and the fault is often accompanied by a light, prominent eye, and thus the whole skull and expression are incorrect and ugly. This appearance can be seen on young puppies. The best type of puppy muzzle is the well-cushioned one, deep and broad and short from nose to stop, so that when the head does lengthen the muzzle loses none of its depth and substance. With this muzzle the stop appears to be deep but with the refining of the head this fills in and slopes nicely up on to the skull.

The occipital peak bone is seldom present in young hounds and most often does not appear until much later. Occasionally

M

it appears soon in life and then disappears for a while, only to develop again later. Like the sternum bone it is a feature easily overlooked and, in order not to lose it, it deserves more attention from breeders.

The wide, flat skull is a fault and this can be seen on puppies. In order to have a chance of becoming a domed skull in later life, the puppy skull should be curved at a very early age and fall away well at the sides.

The eventual width of the skull is almost impossible to forecast under four months, but certainly the very narrow-headed puppies below this age should be avoided because they eventually become very fine and snipy, and the lip is cut away under the nose so that the skull is more like a Borzoi's.

I stressed at the beginning of this chapter that there is no certain method of choosing the best puppies from a litter, and it is true. Nearly every breeder has his or her own way and many will no doubt disagree with the methods of elimination I have described, but I know agreement would be unanimous on one point—luck. It plays a large part.

Apart from the constructional soundness and the correct proportion of desirable breed features, the chosen puppies must also have good temperament. Some character is needed if the hound is going to make the best of itself in the show ring, and hounds with a good temperament are infinitely easier to handle and exhibit. The Basset has always been known for its docility and gentle nature, and hounds with any aggressive tendencies should be corrected very early in life. A dog-hound is all the better for having some dash and a touch of fire, but these are far removed from vice. Young puppies should be bold, inquisitive, gay and playful, and always ready for their food. Shy puppies can be improved by gentle handling and patience and can very often have distinguished show careers in later life.

Vicious hounds, snappy and cantankerous hounds, should not be shown. Not only have they the wrong Basset temperament, but their activities in the show ring will upset the other hounds and their presence is therefore unfair. Exhibitors pay good money and go to lots of trouble to present their hounds well, and they do not want to have any chance of winning endangered by bad-mannered hounds.

Any puppies retained should be in perfect health, glossy-skinned, bright-eyed and active, and all should be injected at the appropriate age with an anti-distemper, hardpad and leptospirosis serum. There are many such preparations on the market, and the veterinary surgeons usually keep good supplies and will advise owners on the additional booster doses that may be needed.

Once it has been decided which hound is to be retained, it should be given full and careful attention to prepare it for maturity and its show career. The previous chapter dealt with the rearing and feeding of young Bassets, but some additional feeding and care is needed to bring the hound into peak show condition.

The Basset, so slow to reach maturity, is not a breed really fitted for early showing, and most breeders and exhibitors do not expect much of a puppy before twelve months. A youngster may certainly be shown a few times to gain experience, but he must not be subjected to a campaign, the rigours of travelling and the clashing life of shows. Local shows are ideal for schooling a young hound; they are not too noisy, no travelling is involved and therefore it is not too tiring for the puppy. If one can find a local or nearby society that stages a class or series of classes for Bassets so much the better, because if the classification is good, the puppy will be competing with others of similar age and sex. The Basset Hound Club usually publishes lists of shows catering for the breed in its quarterly newsletter.

The young puppy should not be vigorously exercised before a show—this should not start until he is at least nine to twelve months old. However, lead-training should have been given well before six months and the puppy taught to stand and generally behave well on the lead. To prepare it for its first show it should be given some lessons in show-ring procedure, because it is useless taking a novice into the ring and expecting it to put up a reasonable performance if it has never been given any schooling.

All that is required is that the puppy should move well,

steadily and easily on the lead, away from and back to the judge, who assesses the movement. Then the youngster should stand still in the show position and allow itself to be examined by the judge. These rudimentary points can be taught at home.

The show position is well illustrated in this book; the hound stands true on all feet, presenting a good balanced outline to the judge. Some hounds will stand free or on a loose lead and need little or no handling, and this is how hounds should be shown. Unfortunately, however, Bassets are not, generally speaking, natural showmen and need some assistance and handling. To poise the hound, the handler has to kneel alongside and stand the hound, and then hold the tail out with one hand and the head up with the other. I said the free-standing method is by far the best, but on the other hand I see no disgrace in 'topping and tailing' Bassets. The critics of this method seldom show and therefore their views should not be taken too seriously.

The puppy should be taught to stand on the ground and also on a table. Some judges prefer to examine Bassets on a table, so one should have the hound prepared for that.

Owing to the individual character of each Basset it is impossible to describe a common method of teaching them to stand, but schooling should begin very early in life, even as soon as three or four weeks old, and the lessons should be short and frequent, say five minutes every day.

Puppies flop about and tumble down at one end if the other is raised, and the first lessons should be devoted to getting the puppy to stand without much regard to the head or tail. Standing behind the puppy, the handler should raise the front and with both hands hold the elbows in, more or less cupping the chest and elbows; one hand should then be drawn along under the body, gradually raising it and the hindquarters. The puppy is therefore being supported front and rear. The hand holding the front can be taken away and the head can then be raised and if necessary eased into the outward-facing position. All the time the puppy should be spoken to gently and encouraged, and given lots of petting after every short lesson.

Most puppies object to having their tail raised and flop down immediately it is touched, so the hindquarters should be supported with one hand while the tail is raised with the other. The tail should never be gripped and raised, but just supported in the open hand and raised into the 'sabre-shaped' position. Even adult hounds hate being gripped by the tail.

Once the puppy is used to being handled, the handler can set about working on the head and hind-leg position. The head should be held up under the jaw by the open hand—gripping the loose skin under the head spoils the outline of the muzzle. Any tendency to raise the ears should be checked by gently stroking down the side of the head and towards the top of the ears.

The hind legs should be drawn back only slightly, and the feet should always be under the hound and not stretched out from under the body. The long-bodied Basset must be soundly supported by all four feet. To get the correct space between the hind legs, put the hand up between them, raise them slightly and then set the hound down; the hand can then raise the tail and the other hand position the head. The hound is then being 'topped and tailed' but in no way supported by the handler. There should never be an appearance of the hound actually being held up. I think this is what confuses the anti-handling set, who imagine that the hound would topple over if the handler left.

In France exhibitors are forbidden to show their hounds by any method except the 'free-standing' way, and therefore one cannot hold the hound in the accepted British or American way. In the main the French hounds are much more active than the other national types and thus more showy in the natural sense.

While one is training a puppy it is a good idea to enlist the aid of friends to 'judge' the hound, and examine its mouth, head and body, etc., as a judge would. The dog must get used to being handled by strangers, and with this in mind it is a great help if a dog owned and handled by a man can get used to being examined by a lady, and vice versa. As I have said, before the puppy attends its first show it must be prepared by the experience of seeing and hearing as much as possible outside the confines of its secluded kennel life.

After the handling lessons the hound can be groomed and this involves three stages—combing, hound-gloving and finalising the grooming with a 'polish-up'.

The best type of comb is the round-toothed kind; it does not pull out the undercoat nor snag and catch the skin as much as the ordinary comb. The whole body should be combed, from the base of the skull down over the body to the very tip of the tail. Combing removes all the dead hair and also any seeds, grass or insects that may have been picked up on exercise. The skin should be held taut with one hand all the while, otherwise the loose-skinned Basset is not easy to comb because the comb catches in the folds of skin. Extra combing and pressure should be put on the parts where the coat is heaviest, that is over the neck and shoulders, down the hindquarters and at the base of the tail. Extra attention to these parts makes the coat lie even with the rest of the hair.

After combing the hound should be hound-gloved. The hound-glove is a mitt-shaped glove with one side covered with bristle or fine wire, the former being the best for Bassets. The glove is slipped on the hand and the hound brushed down. With the fine-bristle type of hound-glove the whole body from nose to tail can be covered, whereas the wire-covered glove can be rather harsh on the skull and ears. Rather vigorous gloving is necessary in order to penetrate the coat, and to obtain a gloss some drops of ordinary brilliantine or paraffin should be put on the glove. To bring up the gloss and really complete the grooming, a yellow duster or piece of silk is ideal.

Grooming provides a convenient opportunity of checking the inside of the ears and removing dirt or seeds that may have lodged in them. Despite his long ears the Basset is not prone to ear disorders; eye ailments are also uncommon despite the deep eye and haw. The nails may be filed or trimmed at grooming-time, which if possible should be at the same time every day. It is surprising how the hounds look forward to being attended to.

A good test of a well-attended coat is to run one's finger

through it against the lie of the hair. It should immediately spring back to the original state as though it had never been disturbed.

Basset Hounds should need no trimming, but it is sometimes necessary on harsh-coated hounds to thin out the long, harsh hair on the neck and rump by using a saw-edged trimming-knife. The coarse hair under the stern should be left untouched as it is required by the official standard.

One or two days before the show the hound should be washed, or if the weather is very cold, damp or frosty, simply sponged over and the dirt and dust removed from the coat. There are many similar dog-shampoos available, and also any household detergent does the job just as well. After bathing or sponging the hound must be well dried before being returned to the kennel, especially the inside of the ears, the legs and the shoulders. A good combing will then ensure that the coat lies correctly and does not 'stare' anywhere.

All the white markings on the hound should be chalked and the chalk allowed to remain in the coat until after the journey to the show. This ensures that any dust or dirt that gets on the hound en route comes away much more easily when the chalk is combed out.

Like 'topping and tailing' the chalking of hounds has its critics, but in defence of the practice it must be said that a clean hound reflects the owner's care and attention and the intention of presenting the hound for show to the best of his or her ability. There are no awards for dirty hounds, and no judge likes handling them.

Travelling to a show by car is the most common way, and travel sickness crops up frequently because Bassets on the whole are not good travellers. The causes are many: anxiety, stomach upsets, etc. I think that Bassets are easily upset because they tend to gulp down their food, and afterwards the least shaking about will cause sickness. Many exhibitors have theories on the best means of prevention, but as dogs are as individual as humans the common preventative is not known. One method works for some hounds but not for others. There are several canine travel preparations and also very many made for human aid; all are good, but care must be taken not to exceed the specified dose, as some of the tablets have a sedative effect and nobody wants a doped hound arriving at a show. Whatever form of tablet is given, they must be administered about one hour before the journey.

Before starting out for a show the hounds must have ample time to relieve themselves; this gives them a better chance of settling in the car. A useful stomach settling agent is glucose—a few spoonsful given with water are all that is required. It may also be given *en route* to the show, and frequent halts should be made and the hounds allowed to stretch their legs and relieve themselves. Many hounds refuse to do this at a show, especially an indoor one, and consequently are never as happy or show as well, so it is important to give them every chance before and during the journey.

Other travel sickness preventatives that have proved most successful for some breeders are bedding the dogs on newspapers, placing a sod of earth in the car and suspending a chain from the chassis. Needless to say the hounds should be allowed plenty of air and the car window should never be closed, especially if someone is smoking.

On arrival at the show one's first duty is to see that the hounds are accommodated comfortably. The Open and Championship Shows are usually benched and each dog has an individual bench. The smaller Sanction and Limited Shows are usually without benching and can often prove to be very tiring for the young dogs. Whatever type of show it is, one should always take a good rug for the dog to lie on and a strong bench-chain and collar for securing the hound to the bench. It is essential to let young hounds enjoy their first show, and with this in mind they should have lots of attention, a comfortable bench, plenty of titbits, exercise and petting. They should never be left unattended for long periods, and if they have to be left for any reason a neighbouring exhibitor will usually oblige by keeping an eye on them.

After the hound is settled the grooming should be completed well before the judging; last-minute hurried preparation only flusters hound and owner. Show-grooming is the same as that already described. Chalking should be done away from the benches, as one's neighbours may not always appreciate having clouds of chalk descending on their hounds or belongings.

Be ready to enter the ring when the class is called and to follow the instructions of the ring steward on positioning of the dogs. Stewards are voluntary assistants at dog shows, very essential and hard-working, and it is only courtesy to be mannerly and not treat them as a piece of furniture. The judge examines each hound individually for body and head points and movement, and his instructions must also be followed as to how one's hound has to move and where it has to stand.

During the judge's examination the hound must naturally stand still and allow itself to be judged, but before and after the judge's assessment one should not neglect to see that the hound is behaving and not upsetting others. Make a fuss of the youngster but also be firm if it attempts to sit or roll on its back in the ring; it should be kept moving about and made aware that it is on show all the time it is there. The coat can be kept free from sawdust and dust by occasional wiping with a cloth, and offering a piece of meat or biscuit will help the handler to hold the interest of the hound.

When moving on the judge's instruction the hound should be moved at an even gait in a straight path to and from the judge. Any attempt by the hound to break the gait rhythm should be checked. Bassets do not have to move like a terrier and there is absolutely no need to string them up tight. A loose lead allowing the hound freedom is best, but although the head should be carried up there is no need to check the hound if it drops its head and nose to the ground occasionally. When moving the Basset should carry the stern well up, and some fuss and encouraging words before setting out will often induce a shy or novice hound to do this. However, some hounds never move with the stern up and are often severely penalised.

The method of show preparation so far described applies equally to dog and bitch puppies, and it must be remembered that road exercise should be very sparingly given to youngsters, so that the nails must be given careful attention in order to keep the feet correct.

Adult hounds need exercise, especially before a show, and the object should be to exercise and feed in order to bring the hound to peak condition for the show. To achieve this it is necessary to begin about one month before the show date. Bitch hounds do not present many difficulties—they seem more easily satisfied and more placid than the dogs. There is no rule against showing bitches in heat, but most exhibitors follow the unwritten rule and do not exhibit females in full heat. Bitches tend to put on weight more quickly than dogs, and therefore the extra feeding given before the show need not be much and the hound should be prevented from gaining too much weight.

The conditioning of a dog-hound can often be difficult and if it is at stud and being shown frequently, extra feeding and exercise should be given daily even when there is no show coming off.

The framework of a dog-hound seems to take longer to develop than that of a bitch and one seldom sees plump young dogs or adults; consequently it takes two full years before a dog-hound begins to deepen and body-up. Whereas a female can look deep in body and furnished at about two years old, it takes a dog about twelve to eighteen months more.

A dog being constantly shown and used frequently at stud should have three meals a day: one main meal and two smaller feeds, and all meals should contain the required vitamin additives and if possible one egg a day. In winter a daily spoonful of sherry or brandy is beneficial and really keeps hounds on their toes. It must be realised that at maturity the dog-hounds are very powerful animals, weighty and very muscular, and they thrive on hard work. If hunting cannot be provided, then ample exercise should be given, not only road work but also lots of galloping in fields.

During their puppyhood dogs are usually very sweet-natured, but in maturity they change and require firmer handling than bitches. They do not become vicious or even bad-tempered but do tend to get wilful and strong-headed. This is, of course, natural because they are pack dogs and must assert some masculinity. It is therefore essential to have dog-hounds under close control at all times and never to let their will prevail; also, any signs of fighting must be stopped immediately.

There is the danger of infection at every show and on returning home it is advisable to take a few simple precautions. Hounds that have been to the show should not be re-kennelled with the others but kept in a separate kennel and run for at least two or three days, and during that time they should be washed or sponged well with an antiseptic such as Dettol or Savlon. The temperature can be taken and if there is a sudden rise the vet should be called in and the reason diagnosed. Fortunately it is very rare that an illness does develop, but one never knows.

Showing can be very expensive and any financial return should not be expected, as the prize money awarded is not too generous, and even if one is very successful it is doubtful if the money won would cover the bare essentials. Basically speaking breeders show their stock to build up a reputation for producing good Bassets, so that they can command a better price for puppies and also export hounds to overseas breeders. A stud-dog must have had a prominent show career to attract the attention of those looking for mates for bitches. I have said that successful show dogs are not always good sires, but in the main they are. Puppies by top sires, or out of winning bitches, are usually more expensive because of their illustrious ancestry. The economic price for a well-reared, good-quality puppy from first-class parents is about fifty to seventy pounds; naturally the price will rise with the quality of the puppy.

Many British Bassets are exported and the breed has one of the highest hound export records. Most of the exports are purchased by breeders in other countries who require them for showing and introducing new blood. In Basset exports Britain leads the world, and the stock in many countries is descended only from British hounds, but in recent years overseas breeders have also been importing from the U.S.A. and France.

The export business is one of trust and honesty between buyer and seller. Most hounds are bought unseen, and therefore the purchaser must be provided with as many photographs as possible, an honest assessment of the hound and relevant information on the pedigree. Naturally the price asked must correspond with the quality of the hound, and transport costs and pre-voyage expenses must also be quoted. The seller and buyer must both be fully aware of the type of hound needed, and everything must be done to ensure that the hound is going to prove acceptable. To achieve this, protracted correspondence may be necessary, but it is worth the extra trouble and time because it is essential that the business should be mutually satisfactory.

The buyer naturally has obligations concerning prompt payment, and all arrangements for payment must be made well in advance.

The travel arrangements, too, should be made well before the journey and the consignee kept informed of all the details. Because there is quite a lot of documentation involved in an export transaction it is often best to place all the arrangements in the capable hands of a livestock shipping agency. The agency can supply a list of forms and certificates needed by different countries (most require the Certificate of Health only, but some need oaths, etc.).

Hounds should never be shipped too young, and a good rule is 'the longer the journey the older the dog'. At three months a puppy can set out for almost any destination by air transport, but a sea voyage involving tropical travel should not be considered for youngsters under four months. Dogs entering Australia must arrive by ship; the journey out from Britain takes about six weeks and means passing through the Red Sea, an area notorious for canine deaths aboard ship. For this journey it is essential that the dog is at peak condition and is being transported by a reputable shipping company.

Air-freight livestock-boxes and ship kennels must be large enough, and in reserving space allow plenty of leeway for a Basset. The livestock shipping agencies can take care of everything, including the supply of travelling boxes, feeding and watering, informing the consignee of time of arrival, and insurance.

Not many Basset imports have been made into Britain, due no doubt to the cost of quarantine and its six months' duration. The quarantine rule is essential and its value has been proved by the freedom from rabies these islands enjoy. All incoming dogs, regardless of their place of origin, must go into quarantine. There are quarantine kennels near all the major cities in Britain, and all are pretty well standardised as regards accommodation and boarding fees. Most are designed to provide not only maximum security but also maximum comfort, and nobody need have any qualms about submitting a dog to quarantine. Visits by the dogs' owners are, of course, permitted, and when an in-whelp bitch is imported the puppies may be removed from quarantine at eight weeks.

No record exists of an in-whelp Basset dam being imported, and in recent years the only female hound to be brought into Britain was Miss Keevil's Cornemuse de Blendocques from France. The stallion hounds that have been imported in the last twenty years are Ulema de Barly, Aiglon des Mariettes, Hercule de L'Ombrée, and Q'Château de L'Ombrée, all from France; Lyn-Mar Acres Dauntless, American Ch. (and British Ch.) Bold Turpin of Blackheath, Long View Acres Rioter Braun, American Ch. Long View Acres Bonza, Brauns Clowverleaf Capers and American Ch. Lyn-Mar Acres Endman from America; and Barlindal Nebbish from Canada.

The Kennel Club have no record of any Blue-Mottled Gascon or Fawn Breton hounds being introduced into Britain, but the first importations of Bassets Griffon-Vendeen for many years were made in 1972 and 1973 and they came from France and Luxembourg.

13

The 'English' Basset Hound

THE English Basset, or Harehound, is not a breed recognised by the Kennel Club, and I doubt if its producers and devotees would ever wish it to be accepted by the governing body. It is a working hound and was evolved for that sole purpose.

The breed is manufactured in that it has been produced by mating together many hound breeds, and by simple process of elimination the desired end-product was evolved. It is, however, not such a recent introduction as many people imagine. The foundations were being laid between 1910 and 1920, the time of dissension between the B.H.C. and the M.B.H.A. Several members of the latter were breeding hounds not unlike the modern type, but I do not think they had used other hound breeds in their efforts to improve on the hunting ability of the pure Basset. The intention then, as it is now, was to reproduce the *Basset à jambes droites* (straight-legged Basset) which was mentioned so often in early literature. This type of leg conformation lost favour and gradually disappeared from every Basset breed except the Griffon-Vendeens, and today they are called *grands Bassets Griffon-Vendéens*. Quite naturally the Griffon-Vendeen has played a considerable part in the making of the English Basset. The pure Basset remained the basis of the crossbreeding with Vendeen, Beagle and Harrier, and it was always intended that the 'new' breed should retain many pure Basset characteristics. These can be observed in the tone of voice, scenting powers, substance, length of body-frame and depth of chest of the English Basset.

The hound stands about fifteen and a half inches and stands over more ground than the Beagle. The lines are very clean, with good reach of neck and sloping shoulders, but the substance is most apparent.

There is no official standard for the breed, but the accompanying photograph of Westerby Sabre (1956) vividly shows the type of hound required by the M.B.H.A. Sabre belongs to Lieutenant-Colonel Eric Morrison, M.C., M.F.H., and is an excellent sire and winner of shows held under the auspices of the M.B.H.A.

The Masters of Basset Hounds Association, formed in 1911, is responsible for the breed's welfare. Mrs. Groom is the present secretary. The society used to hold shows at Banbury in the White Lion Hotel yard, and the regular exhibitors included Lieutenant-Colonel Morrison, the Hon. Mrs. E. Greenall of Waltham, Major de Lisle Bush and Mr. Seymour-Williams.

The first show of the reconstituted M.B.H.A. was held at Aldershot on 22 May 1959, when it was honoured by the presence of H.R.H. Princess Margaret.

Many people in the pure Basset sphere considered that 'English Basset' was an unfortunate choice of name, and much discussion took place in the fifties about the confusion that would possibly arise in people's minds when confronted with English Bassets and Basset Hounds which were then only beginning to come into prominence. The M.B.H.A. debated on alternative names, and two suggestions were 'Leicestershire' or 'Morrison's Bassets', and it was also suggested that the pure breed should adopt the name Artois-Norman. However, all the names proved unacceptable and the position remained as it was. With the passage of time the fears about confusion proved ill-founded, and both the pure Basset Hound and the admirable hard-working English Basset have gone from strength to strength.

Among the packs of English Bassets are:

The *Westerby*, the successor of the pure Walhampton pack. Formed on English Basset lines by Lieutenant-Colonel Morrison in 1932. The pack hunts in the Midlands; the hounds are frequent winners at hound shows and have had great influence on every other English Basset pack.

The *West Lodge*, originally a Beagle pack but re-formed as English Bassets by Mr. Lionel Woolner in 1950. Mr. Woolner

prefers the title Harehounds for his pack. He recently introduced Petit Bleu de Gascogne, and some Castle Milk Griffon-
Vendeen blood is also apparent in this pack, which hunts in
the Home Counties.

Mr. R. E. Way, M.A., of Burrough Green, founded his *De
Burgh* pack on Westerby drafts in 1963, and they hunt around
Newmarket.

Notes on the conformation of Basset Hounds for the
guidance of judges

1. The hounds owned by Masters who are members of the
M.B.H.A. are either pure Bassets or what are now known as
English Basset Hounds, and should be judged in accordance
with the following criteria.

2. Pure Bassets are of the Artois-Norman breed as it has
been evolved in this country.

3. The English Bassets are hounds based primarily on Artois-
Norman, outcrossed substantially with stud-book Harriers and
to some extent with West Country Harriers, Griffon Vendeen
(rough-coated) Bassets and a little blood of other hound breeds.

Additionally the requirements and preferences of individual Masters have resulted in two somewhat different types
of English Basset Hound being evolved.

4. Some hounds (Type A) are of a type and general conformation which is nearer to that of a small foot Harrier than
to the Artois-Norman Basset. They are usually a little too short
in the leg to fit into the 'square' which approximately encloses
the conformation of the Foxhound, Harrier, and Beagle. They
do not, however, give the 'Basset' appearance of being long-
bodied, quite short-legged hounds. They have considerably
more bone and substance than the Beagle or Foot Harrier but
less than that of the Artois-Norman Basset. They should have
hound merits of good shoulders, necks, backs, loins, hocks,
feet and sterns. Their forelegs may be straight or show a slight
crook, indicative of their Basset ancestry. There must, however, be no obvious unsoundness. The forefeet should face the
front.

5. Other English Bassets (Type B) may be described as lying
roughly between the Artois-Norman Basset and Type A. It is
a noticeably short-legged hound but not as close to the ground

N

as the Artois-Norman Basset. It may have more substance than Type A but is not so heavy as the Artois-Norman hound and in consqeuence should show greater activity. In general its shoulders and other points mentioned in paragraph 4 should be the same as those in Type A except that, because in type it follows more closely the Artois-Norman Basset, the forelegs may have a more pronounced crook and the forefeet may turn slightly outwards. *There must, however, be no obvious unsoundness and a hound must stand squarely on its pads.*

6. Certain hounds of both types may, by reason of their Griffon ancestry, show rough or broken coats.

7. Artois-Norman Bassets, although having shorter legs and more substance than both types of English Basset Hounds, should have all the general hound points mentioned above. The crook in the foreleg may be rather more developed but, again, no unsoundness should result and the feet even if pointed slightly outwards should rest squarely with the whole pad on the ground.

8. Artois-Norman Bassets and English Bassets of both types, when competing in the same class, should be judged on their merits.

The above notes were kindly supplied by Mrs. J. Groom, Secretary of the M.B.F.A.

14

The Basset in Illness

ONE can forgive the uninitiated for looking at the Basset with misgivings about the soundness of its constitution, and thinking that a low-slung hound, with such ears and eyes, must surely be prone to more than its share of canine afflictions. Nothing is further from the truth; the Basset Hound is no more susceptible to and no less immune from disease and accidents than any other breed.

A great thing in the breed's favour is that it has not fallen heir to any serious hereditary disease. Some cases of hip dyplasia have been discovered, but it is true to say that this is rare. The Basset Hound Club has many eminent practising veterinary surgeons as members, and one, Mr. Robert Townson, M.R.C.V.S., caused a sub-committee to be set up to keep an eye open for any onset of hereditary disease in the Basset.

In the old days distemper and hardpad played havoc with Bassets and they were notoriously difficult to rear. Today these diseases, and hepatitis and leptospirosis, are unfortunately still present but kept under control by many excellent makes of serum. Not every breeder makes use of the injections and the diseases can still be passed on because of their negligence. As a safety precaution, periodical booster doses of the serum should be administered, especially to hounds that are being shown frequently.

Occupational hazards of all working breeds are sprains, strains, bruising and dislocations, and young Bassets are rather open to such injuries because of their soft bone, front-leg assembly and boundless energy. As I have stressed in a previous chapter, minor injury to the joints and knuckles in the front legs can be avoided if the puppies are prevented from running up and down steps, but older puppies can quite easily strain a leg or joint when playing.

Prime essentials in the task of keeping a hound in good general health are good, clean wholesome food, clean feeding and drinking bowls, clean fresh water, plenty of fresh air and ample exercise. It is also important to maintain a high standard of cleanliness in the kennel and provide dry and comfortable draught-proof sleeping quarters.

In dealing with the various ailments that can affect the Basset I have, because I am just a layman, concentrated on the more minor, yet nevertheless irritating illnesses that can be fairly easily diagnosed and treated by most owners. It must be stressed, however, that even with these ailments professional advice should be sought. Any delay in calling a veterinary surgeon to a sick dog is putting an obstacle in the way of a quick and successful cure, and, of course, to delay for any undue length of time may prove fatal.

The normal temperature of a dog is 101·2°F.

Stings. Hounds are frequently stung by a variety of insects, but wasps are particularly active in late summer. The best remedy is the application of a strong solution of bicarbonate of soda and water. Ordinary washing blue applied, or rubbing a freshly cut onion on the sting, are good time-honoured remedies. If the sting is in the mouth the vet should be called.

Cuts, scratches and bruises. After hunting hounds should be examined for cuts, etc., and any wound or injury must be promptly treated. The wound should be cleaned with a mild antiseptic in lukewarm water and plenty of antiseptic cream or powder applied. It is essential to check the injury every day, clean again and apply fresh ointment.

If the cut is deep the vet must be called in to stitch up the wound. If the hound sets about trying to scratch at the repaired cut it should be bandaged over.

Bruises can often be relieved by bathing alternately with warm and cold water. Antiseptic ointment should be applied liberally.

Cut pads are a menace at any time and should always have professional attention. For minor cuts the owner should clean well, removing all grit or glass, and apply tincture of iodine.

Wounds caused by bites need careful attention and there is

danger of poisoning. The wound should be kept clean and allowed to drain.

Dislocations, sprains and strains. These ailments, especially dislocations, should always be treated by the vet. In Bassets the injury is usually to the front legs and can be caused very easily. The patient must be kept warm and dry and only exercised for short periods. Frequent massage is required with embrocation or olive oil, and it is also beneficial to feed calcium and vitamin D. A series of cortisone injections or tablets prescribed by the vet usually proves a successful cure. No quick overnight cure should be expected, and when the hound shows signs of improvement the temptation to exercise normally should be resisted.

Diarrhoea can be caused by numerous things—cold, damp kennels or indigestible food, even a sudden change in the weather can bring on a bout. A change of food is helpful, and common porridge or boiled rice often acts as a settling food. It is advisable to isolate the affected hound, as diarrhoea can spread quickly to others.

Constipation. The affected hound should be well exercised and fed plenty of good meat and gravy mixed with vegetables. The cause is usually too much dry food and bones. Liquid paraffin is an excellent lubricant, but if the hound has great difficulty in moving the bowels, the vet should be called in to examine the hound for a possible stoppage.

Coughing. Kennel cough can be difficult to stop and nearly always requires veterinary treatment. It is infectious and affected hounds must be isolated. The hound coughs frequently and is constantly trying to clear its throat. The invalid usually loses interest in food and should be given frequent small feeds of warm milk, egg and honey. Exercise should be as normal and the hound should be in a good airy kennel. The weather seems to have little to do with kennel cough because it can appear at any time of year.

Obesity. This is not a condition commonly found among kennel hounds, but it is unfortunately common in single pet hounds. The cause is usually over-feeding and indolence. Bitches are more prone to it than dog-hounds. The food should be cut by half and fatty, oily and starchy foods eliminated entirely. Only lean meat, liver and occasionally eggs should be fed. The restriction in food should be accompanied by regular exercise and the opportunity of good gallops in a park or fields. A bitch due for mating or whelping should never be allowed to get fat. In the show ring the obese hound is always penalised.

Mastitis. Hard lumps can be felt in the teats, and they are often large and easily seen. It is important to call in the vet immediately they are observed and the condition is usually cured rapidly, although some bitches are always prone to it and it reappears annually. The lumps occasionally burst open and a large wound appears in the udder. This must be kept clean, washed frequently and well covered with ointment to promote healing and discourage flies.

Worms. It is important to worm Basset puppies early, and three weeks old is the best time. The puppies grow very fast and the growth rate and intake of food is severely hampered if worms are present. The youngsters should be wormed weekly from three to eight weeks, and then monthly from two to six months. Lack of worming can cause some severe ailments and eventually lead to the death of the hound.

Eye and ear disorders. Because of the extreme sensitivity of these organs all disorders connected with them should be treated by the vet. However, the owner can ensure that they are regularly inspected and any dirt or seeds that have lodged in the eye or ears removed. The pendulous ears of the Basset do not make it any more susceptible to infection than any other normal-eared hound. To clean out the ears, cotton wool soaked with surgical spirit is as useful as anything.

Draughts can cause a cold in the eye, which is indicated by a discharge. Golden eye ointment is excellent for stopping this condition.

Thorns lodged in the eyeball can often be easily removed by gently wiping over the eyeball with a piece of cotton wool.

Parasites. Lice and ticks are usually found only on neglected hounds, but they do occasionally transfer their attentions to healthy dogs. In cold weather a good dusting of D.D.T.

powder should be applied, and in warm weather a bath in lukewarm water containing Jeyes Fluid or Cooper's Wash will soon remove the pests. The kennels should also be sprayed frequently with insecticide, with special attention to the benches and all cracks and crevices.

Skin disorders. The most notorious of the skin ailments is mange. There are two types, equally troublesome and difficult to cure. Sarcoptic or red mange is very infectious and the infected hound should be isolated as soon as it is diagnosed. The hound is continually scratching, the skin takes on a red hue and little pimples appear, especially on the hindquarters, shoulders and behind the ears.

There are many treatments, but one of the easiest to administer is Sellene, which is made up in a wash and applied to the hound two or three times weekly. The hound should be soaked thoroughly and then semi-dried with a rough towel. Zemol ointment should then be applied and rubbed well into the damp skin, and the hound allowed to dry out in a warm kennel.

Sellene may also be used in the treatment of follicular mange. In this second type the hair comes out, leaving bare patches of grey, wrinkled-looking skin. The affected parts are usually the face and hindquarters. There is also an unpleasant 'mousey' smell. The affected hounds rub themselves against kennel walls or railings, but there does not seem to be the irritation that accompanies Sarcoptic mange.

The hound must be washed all over with Sellene, and after drying sulphur, Zemol, or Liverine ointment should be applied to the bare patches. Eventually the wrinkled skin contracts to form a scab, which finally comes away, revealing healthy skin.

With both types of mange many patient weeks must be spent washing and dressing the affected parts, and great care must be taken not to relax the washings when the condition improves. It can flare up again quickly.

The invalids must be isolated, and attendants should change their clothes and wash after working among infected hounds. The kennels have to be kept clean and airy and the dogs exercised and fed as normal. The bedding should be changed frequently and the used bedding burned.

After curing the hound the kennels have to be cleansed, and the best method is to burn the benches, instal new ones, and go over the whole of the kennel interior with a blowlamp. The floors should be scrubbed and creosoted and the walls white-washed. Finally the kennel should be left vacant for a week with the doors and windows open.

Skin disorders are so complex and varied that it is always advisable to consult a vet and make absolutely certain of the exact nature of the ailment and the method of treating it. The range of skin disorders is extensive: eczema, dermatitis and various allergies can all resemble more serious diseases.

A common type of allergy affects the muzzles of young puppies. Large pustules appear, the whole muzzle becomes swollen and tender and the unfortunate puppy has difficulty in eating. The allergy is seldom infectious and it is common to find only one puppy affected in the litter. The first step towards a cure is to find and eradicate the cause of the allergy. Some-times it is the sawdust on the kennel floor or contact with various plants, or it can often be worms that have resisted attempts to remove them. Calamine lotion applied four times daily for about one month will usually clean up the unsightly spots, but unfortunately the face is always left scarred by black, hairless patches where the pustules have been.

Dry, brittle coats and dandruffy condition of the skin can be improved upon with frequent shampoos and the application of olive oil. A good, tried and tested skin tonic is a weekly spoonful of linseed oil and lime water. The tonic should be made up of one part linseed oil to three parts of lime water, the whole being well shaken before internally administered.

General remarks. Hounds should be severely checked if they are caught eating scraps or rubbish when out hunting or exer-cising. Dead birds and small rodents may have died by eating chemically treated seeds or rat poison. The poison can often remain active in the body and thus be transmitted to a hound. If there is vermin about the kennels it should be eradicated by using poison that is harmless to domestic animals and children.

If a hound has eaten poison a very strong dose of salt and water or soap and water should be forcibly given in order to make it sick, and the vet should be called immediately.

A phantom pregnancy is not an ailment but can be a great nuisance, especially if one intends showing the bitch. Even for hunting purposes a fully developed udder is hardly a suitable condition for work.

Unmated bitches suddenly develop an udder and the teats fill with milk just as they would on a mated hound, and the general impression given is that of a bitch in whelp.

One of the best cures for the condition is to give a good dose of Epsom salts, followed by smaller doses for about fourteen days. One dose a day accompanied by a reduction in food and plenty of exercise will usually clear up the trouble.

The same treatment will work for the bitch which has been mated, shown signs of pregnancy and then 'missed' (failed to produce). Before administering the treatment in this case, two or three days should be allowed to lapse after her supposed day of whelping and great care taken to ensure that she is really barren.

Some bitches continue to have milk even when the litter has grown out of feeding off them. To dry the udder up several applications of three parts vinegar to one of water should be made on the teats daily. Brandy is said to have the same effect, but who could afford such treatment today!

On the whole Bassets are healthy dogs and if kept well housed and exercised can live quite a long time. The Veterans Classes of the Basset Hound Club shows are always well supported and filled with well-loved old campaigners who belie their advanced years.

When senile decay does set in, and the old hound loses faculties and begins to have a series of petty ailments due to age, the kindest thing is to have it put to sleep. I think it is best to have the vet call and do the sad job and then have the old favourite buried on home ground.

Talleyrand is reputed to have said: 'When the old dog dies, forget the sadness by sending for a whelp.'

KENNEL CLUB REGISTRATION FIGURES

1909 —30	1931 —31	1953 — 20
1910 —15 (inc. two Roughs)	1932 —29	1954 — 64
1911 — 6	1933 —27	1955 — 81
1912 —18	1934 —20	1956 — 131
1913 — 6	1935 —39	1957 — 145
1914 — 7 (inc. one Rough)	1936 —20	1958 — 249
1915 — 0	1937 —10	1959 — 237
1916 — 2	1938 —41	1960 — 441
1917 — 0	1939 —13	1961 — 552
1918 — 0	1940 — 7	1962 — 839
1919 — 0	1941 — 3	1963 — 922
1920 — 2	1942 —17	1964 — 1529
1921 — 3	1943 —11	1965 — 1687
1922 — 4	1944 —13	1966 — 1955
1923 — 9	1945 — 0	1967 — 2246
1924 —20	1946 —10	1968 — 2510
1925 —23	1947 —20	1969 — 2679
1926 —51	1948 —23	1970 — 2642
1927 —32	1949 —20	1971 — 2837
1928 — 2	1950 —25	1972 — 3173
1929 —27	1951 —24	1973 — 2875
1930 —13	1952 —34	

AMERICAN KENNEL CLUB REGISTRATION FIGURES

1930 — 65	1963 — 11,763
1940 — 241	1964 — 13,716
1950 — 479	1965 — 14,686
1955 — 2,103	1966 — 16,140
1956 — 4,013	1967 — 17,595
1957 — 5,207	1968 — 17,452
1958 — 7,008	1969 — 19,319
1959 — 8,055	1970 — 20,046
1960 — 8,782	1971 — 20,848
1961 —10,218	1972 — 18,989
1962 — 9,978	1973 — 17,843

THE BASSET HOUND BREED CLUBS

The breed has achieved great popularity throughout the world, and the few old-established societies have now been joined by many newly formed clubs. The clubs, their secretaries and date of foundation are:

The Basset Hound Club (1884, re-formed 1954)
Mrs. M. Seiffert, Chathill Cottage, Tandridge Lane, Oxted, Surrey.

Club du Basset Artésien-Normand (1910)
M. Leon Soutoul, 5 rue André Joineau, Le Pré Saint-Gervase Val d'Oise.

Basset Hound Club of America Inc. (1936)
Mrs. R. Bateman, P.O. Box 215, Warrenville, Illinois. 60555.

Basset Hound Club of New South Wales (1960)
Mrs. C. Garvin, 66 Runyon Avenue, South Wentworthville, N.S.W.

Basset Hound Club of New Zealand (1962)
Mrs. M. Mckenzie, 438 Richardson Road, Mt. Roskill, Auckland 4.

The Basset Hound Club of Ireland (1965)
Mrs. E. Mitchell, Tinna Park, Kilpedder, Co. Wicklow

The Basset Hound Club of Northern Ireland (1974)
Mrs. I. McFerran, 34 Four Winds Park, Belfast BT8 4GD.

The Basset Hound Club of South Africa (1966)
Mr. M. A. Blackburn, 20 Haley Avey., Germiston, Transvaal.

The Basset Hound Club of Scotland (1966)
Mrs. P. Moncur, South Brae, Dunlop, Ayrshire.

Club du Griffon-Vendéen (1907)
M. Hubert Desamy, La-Chaize-Le-Vicomte, Vendée.

Club du Basset Fauve de Bretagne
M. Pambrun, rue Carnot, Dinan, C.D.N.

Club du Chien Bleu de Gascogne
M. Bachala, 74 Ave Saint-Michel, 82 Montauban.

Basset Hound Club von Deutschland (1967)
  Herr H. Hausner, 6601 Eschringen, Grafinthaler Str. 27.

Basset Hound Club Français (1967)
  Mme. A. Peress, 17 Av, du Maréchal-Lyautey, Paris 16.

Basset Hound Club of Canada
  Mr. L. R. Bowman, 11th Street South, R.R.3., St. Catherines,
  Ontario.

Basset Hound Club of Finland
  Mrs. M. Massingberd, Untamontie 9c17, Helsinki.

Danish Basset and Beagle Club
  Mr. I. C. Christensen, Gribskovhus, Esrum, 3230 Graested,
  Denmark.

In the U.S.A. there are many regional Basset Hound clubs, and
most are affiliated to the B.H.C. of America. The regional clubs
hold shows and organise field trials, and among the more prominent
are:
B.H.C. of Southern California (1953)
B.H.C. of Northern California (1955)
B.H.C. of Greater Detroit
B.H.C. of Sacramento
B.H.C. of Northern Alabama
B.H.C. of Maryland (1960)
Long Island B.H.C.
Buckeye B.H.C.
Susquehanna B.H.C. (1955)
Fort Dearborn B.H.C.
Pilgrim B.H.C. (1953)
Gateway B.H.C. (1960)
Rancocas B.H.C. (1955)
Timberline B.H.C. (1957)
Potomac B.H.C. (1959)
Kentuckiana B.H.C.

The affairs of the packs of English Bassets or Harehounds are
looked after by the Masters of Basset Hounds Association, Mr. R.
Hudson, Hampden, Andoversford, Cheltenham.

CHAMPION BASSET HOUNDS 1904–74 (12 June)

Year	Name	Sex	Birth	Sire	Dam	Breeder	Owner
1904	The Queen of the Geisha	B	30-3-98	Ch. Paris	Fair Star	J. Stark	J. W. Proctor
1906	Loo Loo Loo	D	17-6-01	Ch. Louis Le Beau	Sibella	Mrs M. Tottie	W. W. M. White
1907	Sandringham Dido	B	13-9-04	Tarquin	Viola (Unregistered)	Col. J. H. Annand	Queen Alexandra
1909	Waverer	D	12-7-04	Major (Unregistered)	Daisy (Unregistered)	A. Croxton-Smith	Sir M. Bromley-Wilson
1913	Mentor	D	3-7-10	Ch. Waverer	Ch. Melanie	J. P. & W. Roberts	J. P. & W. Roberts
1913	Melanie	B	25-7-07	Ch. Loo Loo Loo	Mirette	Miss E. Wright	J. P. & W. Roberts
1915	Warrender	B	26-7-10	Ch. Waverer	Sandringham Pamela	Queen Alexandra	Queen Alexandra
1925	Walhampton Andrew	D	20-6-22	Walhampton Ferryman	Walhampton Actress (Unregistered)	Major G. Heseltine	Major G. Heseltine
1926	Walhampton Gratitude	B	23-6-24	Walhampton Linguist	Walhampton Grizel	Major G. Heseltine	Major G. Heseltine
1931	Patience	B	9-2-29	Walhampton Lingerer	Walhampton Pardon	Major G. Heseltine	Mrs E. L. Grew
1931	Walhampton Ambassador	D	7-5-28	Walhampton Lymington	Walhampton Amber	Major G. Heseltine	Mrs E. L. Grew
1932	Walhampton Lynnewood	D	22-5-28	Walhampton Musket	Walhampton Lyric (Unregistered)	Major G. Heseltine	Major G. Heseltine
1933	Walhampton Nightshade	B	28-6-30	Walhampton Grazier	Walhampton Nicknack	Major G. Heseltine	Mrs. N. E. Elms

Year	Name	Sex	Birth	Sire	Dam	Breeder	Owner
1935	Orpheus of Reynalton	D	9-12-33	Ch. Walhampton Lynnewood	Ch. Walhampton Nightshade	Mrs N. E. Elms	Mrs N. E. Elms
1936	Pigeon	B	9-10-33	Walhampton Grazier	Walhampton Nicknack	Mrs E. L. Grew	Mrs E. L. Grew
1936	Plover	D	9-10-33	Walhampton Grazier	Walhampton Nicknack	Mrs E. L. Grew	Mrs E. Robinson
1936	Venus of Reynalton	B	9-12-33	Ch. Walhampton Lynnewood	Ch. Walhampton Nightshade	Mrs N. E. Elms	Mrs N. E. Elms
1937	Minerva of Reynalton	B	9-12-33	Ch. Walhampton Lynnewood	Ch. Walhampton Nightshade	Mrs N. E. Elms	Mrs N. E. Elms
1937	Monkshood of Reynalton	D	1-5-35	Loyalty of Reynalton	Ch. Walhampton Nightshade	Mrs N. E. Elms	Mrs N. E. Elms
1938	Narcissus of Reynalton	B	9-12-33	Ch. Walhampton Lynnewood	Ch. Walhampton Nightshade	Mrs N. E. Elms	Viscountess Chelmsford
1950	Grims Warlock	D	26-9-46	Grims Worship	Grims Waspish	Miss M. M. Keevil	Miss M. M. Keevil
1950	Grims Wishful	B	14-5-40	Marquis	Wick Welcome	Miss M. M. Keevil	Miss M. M. Keevil
1950	Grims Waterwagtail	B	30-4-49	Grims Doughnut	Grims Watercress	Miss M. M. Keevil	Miss M. M. Keevil
1952	Grims Doughnut	D	11-8-47	Westerby Rennet	Grims Daisy	Miss M. M. Keevil	Miss M. M. Keevil
1952	Grims Useful	B	9-7-50	Grims Ulema De Barly	Grims Wallflower	Miss M. M. Keevil	Miss M. M. Keevil
1954	Grims Wideawake	D	1-11-51	Grims Ulema De Barly	Grims Waterlily	Miss M. M. Keevil	Miss M. M. Keevil
1954	Grims Willow	B	1-11-51	Grims Ulema De Barly	Grims Waterlily	Miss M. M. Keevil	Mrs A. Hodson
1954	Songster of Reynalton	D	1-1-48	Sovereign of Reynalton	Miranda of Reynalton	Mrs N. E. Elms	Mrs N. E. Elms

1956	Grims Whirlwind	D	5-5-54	Grims Ulema De Barly	Grims Wanda	Miss M. M. Keevil	Mrs W. M. Jagger
1956	Grims Gracious	B	18-7-54	Ch. Grims Wideawake	Grims Garrulous	Miss M. M. Keevil	Mrs M. Rawle
1957	Grims Westward	D	5-5-54	Grims Ulema De Barly	Grims Wanda	Miss M. M. Keevil	Miss M. M. Keevil
1957	Rossingham Amber	B	1-7-53	Ch. Grims Warlock	Ch. Grims Willow	Mrs A. Hodson	Mr G. I. Johnston
1957	Rossingham Anxious	B	1-7-53	Ch. Grims Warlock	Ch. Grims Willow	Mrs A. Hodson	Mrs A. Hodson
1957	Rossingham Badger	D	20-2-55	Ch. Grims Doughnut	Ch. Grims Willow	Mrs A. Hodson	Mrs J. Townson
1957	Grims Vapid	B	19-6-56	Grims Emblem	Ch. Grims Useful	Miss M. M. Keevil	Mrs M. Rawle
1958	Fochno Trinket	B	29-4-57	Ch. Grims Whirlwind	Sykemoor Gossip	Mrs J. Lorton	Mrs W. M. Jagger
1959	Barnspark Rakish	D	7-7-57	Ch. Grims Westward	Ch. Grims Gracious	Mrs M. Rawle	Mrs MacArthur-Onslow & Mrs Kewley
1959	Brockhampton Soloman	D	8-8-56	Ch. Grims Westward	Grims Minx	Mr. G. W. Dakin	Mr G. W. Dakin
1959	Rossingham Cosy	B	7-8-56	Ch. Grims Doughnut	Ch. Rossingham Anxious	Mrs A. Hodson	Lt-Col. A. Biss
1959	Mariseni Rarnee	B	12-4-58	Ch. Rossingham Badger	Barnspark Rustic	Mrs P. Warren	Mrs P. Warren
1960	Jamestown Generous	B	22-7-55	Rossingham Ambassador	Grims Gainful	Mrs J. F. Eisenman	Mr W. W. Wells
1960	Fochno Trooper	D	29-4-57	Ch. Grims Whirlwind	Sykemoor Gossip	Mrs J. Lorton	Mr G. W. Dakin
1961	Sykemoor Aimwell	D	3-6-59	Ch. Grims Whirlwind	Ch. Rossingham Amber	Mr G. I. Johnston	Mrs B. M. Prior
1961	Sykemoor Wiza	B	5-6-58	Sykemoor Garnet	Sykemoor Jealousy	Mr G. I. Johnston	Mr G. I. Johnston
1961	Bashful Bert	D	24-6-58	Grims Charlie	Lucy of Morcombelake	Countess of Craven	Mrs Lloyd Jones & Mrs Greenwell

Year	Name	Sex	Birth	Sire	Dam	Breeder	Owner
1961	Kelperland Baneful	B	7-6-59	Grims Emblem	Kelperland Amanda	Mrs J. Townson	Mrs J. Townson
1961	Barnspark Vanity	B	23-4-59	Ch. Grims Westward	Ch. Grims Vapid	Mrs M. Rawle	Mr B. N. Ghent
1962	Breightmet Chimer	D	15-3-58	Grims Charlie	Grims Vanish	Mrs M. E. Baynes	Miss M. M. Keevil
1962	Kelperland Artful	D	11-11-57	Ch. Rossingham Badger	Rossingham Amorous	Mrs J. Townson	Mrs J. Townson
1962	Crochmaid Bold Turpin of Blackheath	D	12-7-57	Santana Hounslow Highwayman	Santana Kate Hardcastle	Mrs C. Babson, U.S.A.	Mrs Macarthur-Onslow &Mrs Kewley
1962	Stalwart Debbie	B	2-6-59	Grims Varlet	Stalwart Thoughtful	Mr E. J. Evans	Mr E. J. Evans
1962	Mariseni Breightmet Wessex	D	5-5-59	Ch. Grims Westward	Grims Vanish	Mrs M. E. Baynes	Mrs J. Wells
1962	Dreymin Appeline Coral	B	8-9-61	Grims Lager	Appeline Dawn	Mr & Mrs D. Appleton	Mrs A. Minto
1962	Fredwell Varon Vandal	D	21-11-60	Ch. Fochno Trooper	Rollick of Fredwell	Mr E. Roberts	Mrs J. Wells
1963	Appeline Rochester	D	29-5-61	Ch. Grims Westward	Solemn Melody	Mrs J. M. Milne	Mrs C. Appleton
1963	Hooksway Cheeky Checkmate	B	8-10-61	Ch. Sykemoor Aimwell	Peardrop Princess	Mrs B. Symonds	Mrs J. Thompson
1963	Sungarth Phoebe	B	30-9-60	Ch. Sykemoor Aimwell	Aesops Able	Mrs B. Prior	Mrs J. Rowett-Johns
1964	Sykemoor Emma	B	16-5-62	Fochno Trumpeter	Sykemoor Jealousy	Mr G. I. Johnston	Mr. G. I. Johnston
1964	Wingjays Fanciful	D	22-11-61	Ch. Sykemoor Aimwell	Sungarth Jasmine	Mrs J. Rowett-Johns	Mrs J. Rowett-Johns
1964	Avenwood Dulcis	B	4-4-63	Ch. Breightmet Chimer	Wingjays Beautiful	Mrs M. E. Ashton	Mrs M. E. Ashton
1964	Barnspark Clarion	D	5-11-60	Ch. Breightmet Chimer	Ch. Grims Gracious	Mrs M. Rawle	Mrs P. J. Benge Abbott

Year	Name	Sex	Date	Sire	Dam	Breeder	Owner
1964	Pointgrey Suss's Folly	D	24-1-62	Lyn Mar Acres Dauntless	Julie of Aldbury	Mrs A. M. Reed	Mrs P. J. Benge Abbott
1964	Chantinghall Flaxen	B	19-3-62	Grims Lager	Mariseni Goodness Gracious	Mrs B. Greensmith-Downes	Mrs M. Seiffert & Mrs D. Langmead
1964	Chantinghall Jemima of Maycombe	B	13-11-62	Grims Lager	Chantinghall Bramble	Mrs R. McKnight	Mrs M. Seiffert
1965	Wingjays Fabulous	B	22-10-63	Ch. Fredwell Varon Vandal	Ch. Sungarth Phoebe	Mrs J. Rowett-Johns	Mrs J. Rowett-Johns
1965	Chantinghall Ancestor	D	24-6-64	Ch. Pointgrey Suss Folly	Chantinghall Harmony	Mrs R. McKnight	Mrs R. McKnight
1965	Fredwell Ideal	D	1-12-61	Ch. Mariseni Breightmet Wessex	Fredwell Rennet	Mrs J. Wells	Mrs J. Wells
1965	Chantinghall Harmony	B	15-9-63	Chantinghall Cognac	Mariseni Goodness Gracious	Mrs R. McKnight	Mrs R. McKnight
1965	Chantinghall Kitebrook Barley	B	19-6-63	Ch. Breightmet Chimer	Kitebrook Lilliesleaf Helen	Mr & Mrs M. McDermott	Mrs M. Seiffert
1965	Chantinghall Fredwell Amber	B	1-4-64	Ch. Fredwell Varon Vandal	Musical Melodies	Mrs Bowen	Mrs A. Matthews
1966	Mapleroyal Avenwood Atalanta	B	18-4-64	Kitebrook Actor	Wingjays Lovable	Mrs M. E. Ashton	Mrs Stewart
1966	Fredwell Charmer	B	12-8-64	Ch. Fredwell Ideal	Fredwell Annuk	Mrs J. Wells	Mrs J. Wells
1966	Grims Fochno Charming	B	3-5-63	Ch. Breightmet Chimer	Ch. Fochno Trinket	Mrs W. M. Jagger	Miss M. M. Keevil
1966	Maycombe Vaisya	B	17-8-65	Ch. Fredwell Varon Vandal	Ch. Chantinghall Jemima of Maycombe	Mrs M. Seiffert	Mrs M. Seiffert

Year	Name	Sex	Birth	Sire	Dam	Breeder	Owner
1966	Wingjays Ptolemy	D	13-7-64	Ch. Breightmet Chimer	Ch. Sungarth Phoebe	Mrs R. Rowett-Johns	Mrs R. Rowett-Johns
1966	Bactona Jupiter	D	11-8-63	Ch. Fredwell Varon Vandal	Narrabri Andromeda	Mrs J. Lacey	Mrs B. M. J. White
1967	Fredwell Maitri	D	16-7-63	Ch. Fredwell Varon Vandal	Treasure of Fredwell	Mrs J. Wells	Mr M. Browne
1967	Vescou Phebe Jane	B	18-4-64	Ch. Fredwell Varon Vandal	Justice of Cherryrock	Mr & Mrs Tilley	Mrs Goodyear
1967	Brackenacre Annabella	B	4-7-64	Hardacre Sungarth Eager	Brackenacre Kierhill Oonagh	Mr & Mrs Nixon	Mr & Mrs Nixon
1967	Wingjays Polygamy of Maycombe	D	6-12-65	Ch. Wingjays Ptolemy	Mapleroyal Zelma	Mrs R. Rowett-Johns	Mrs M. Seiffert
1967	Fredwell Perfect	B	31-5-64	Fredwell Maestro	Blairgold Venture	Mrs J. Wells	Mrs J. Wells
1968	Bargriff Eden	D	18-12-66	Ch. Fredwell Ideal	BargriffRowynan Gigi	Mrs B. Griffiths	Mrs B. Griffiths
1968	Balleroy Chestnut	D	24-3-67	Ch. Chantinghall Ancestor	Chantinghall Beatrice	Mrs P. Moncur	Mrs P. Moncur
1968	Hardacre Valorous	D	23-10-66	Ch. Fredwell Varon Vandal	Chantinghall Quality of Maycombe	Mrs A. Matthews	Mrs A. Matthews
1968	Huckworthy Tankard	D	22-2-64	Sungarth Token	Goldies Token	Mrs J. S. Kynoch	Mrs A. Hall Parlby
1968	Rollinhills Wingjays Fabric	B	17-5-67	Ch. Wingjays Ptolemy	Ch. Wingjays Fabulous	Mrs J. Rowett-Johns	Mrs B. M. J. White
1968	Rowynan Lark	B	27-7-65	Rowynan Chantinghall Legacy	Rowynan Cindy	Mrs R. W. A. Goodyear	Mrs R. W. A. Goodyear
1968	Foyewyn Stroller	D	2-12-65	Ch. Breightmet Chimer	Rosudgeon Dido	Mrs S. A. Goodwin	Mrs M. B. Williams

Year	Name	Sex	Date	Sire	Dam	Breeder	Owner
1968	Manory Graton Gretel	B	21-12-65	Ch. Fredwell Varon Vandal	Doles Cleopatra	Mr M. C. Crabbe	Mrs E. P. Rigby-Sisterson
1968	Framlands Clover	B	22-6-66	Ch. Fredwell Varon Vandal	Framlands Blossom	Misses N. Guthrie-Reed & P. Taylor	Misses M. Guthrie-Reed & P. Taylor
1968	Tintally Dubonnet	B	6-6-66	Ch. Wingjays Ptolemy	Tintally Anisette	Mrs S. Blackler	Mrs S. Blackler
1969	Wingjays Polonaise	B	9-12-65	Ch. Wingjays Ptolemy	Mapleroyal Zelma	Mrs J. Rowett-Johns	Mrs J. Rowett-Johns
1969	Fredwell Symon	D	5-3-67	Fredwell Dimber	Axters Jezebel	Mr W. E. Galley	Mrs J. Wells
1969	Foyewyn Berenice	B	30-10-67	Rowynan Chantinghall Legacy	Foyewyn Diamond	Mrs S. A. Goodwin	Mrs S. A. Goodwin
1969	Verwood Mirus	D	25-4-68	Dreymin Duskie Knight	Verwood Chinook	Mrs V. Ross	Mrs V. Ross
1969	Fredwell Varon Fawkes	D	24-2-67	Fredwell Dimber	Fredwell Pickle	Mr E. Roberts	Mrs J. A. Wells
1969	Charford Hurtwood Grizette	B	13-10-66	Kitebrook Banner	Weirwater Grizelle	Mrs F. Bridger	Mrs A. Charman
1969	Chantinghall Beatrice	B	10-5-65	Ch. Wingjays Fanciful	Chantinghall Airs 'N' Graces	Mrs J. Rowett-Johns	Mrs P. Moncur
1969	Fredwell Varon Fichle	B	24-2-67	Fredwell Dimber	Fredwell Pickle	Mr E. Roberts	Mrs J. A. Wells
1969	Dowerwood Soames	D	20-11-67	Chantinghall Dynasty	Breedmore Mirabelle	Mrs D. Heslewood	Mr & Mrs F. G. Holdsworth
1969	Huckworthy Leader	D	19-10-66	Hellidon Lager	Huckworthy Hopeful	Mrs A. Hall-Parlby	Mrs A. Hall-Parlby
1970	Wingjays Parthenon	D	3-9-68	Ch. Wingjays Ptolemy	Wingjays Vanilla	Mrs J. Rowett-Johns	Mrs J. Rowett-Johns
1970	Fredwell Balleroy Faithful	B	29-4-68	Ch. Chantinghall Ancestor	Ch. Chantinghall Beatrice	Mrs P. Moncur	Mrs J. A. Wells

Year	Name	Sex	Birth	Sire	Dam	Breeder	Owner
1970	Maycombe Victoria	B	24-10-67	Ch. Hardacre Valorous	Ch. Chantinghall Kitebrook Barley	Mrs M. Seiffert	Mrs J. M. Rawle
1970	Langstone Pearl	B	10-6-67	Ch. Chantinghall Ancestor	Ch. Hooksway Cheeky Checkmate	Mrs J. Thompson	Mrs J. Thompson
1970	Fredwell Tolly	B	22-8-66	Ch. Wingjays Ptolemy	Fredwell Dreamer	Mrs J. A. Wells	Mrs J. A. Wells & Mrs M. Seiffert
1970	Rowynan Taro	D	31-12-67	Rowynan Chantinghall Legacy	Rowynan Chantinghall Marcasite	Mrs R. W. A. Goodyear	Mrs R. W. A. Goodyear
1970	Bargriff Kimble	D	9-9-67	Ch. Fredwell Ideal	Bargriff Rowynan Gigi	Mrs B. Griffiths	Mrs J. Blyth
1970	Huckworthy Lyric	B	19-10-66	Hellidon Lager	Huckworthy Hopeful	Mrs A. Hall-Parlby	Mrs A. Hall-Parlby
1971	Irish Ch. Ballymaconnel Forester	D	13-9-65	Ch. Chantinghall Ancestor	Ballymaconnel Boule de Suif	Mr & Mrs S. P. Bridgham	Mr & Mrs S. P. Bridgham
1971	Barnspark Frolic	B	18-8-64	Ch. Pointgrey Suss's Folly	Barnspark Charity	Mrs J. M. Rawle	Miss W. A. Thomas & Miss D. B. Basset
1971	Turberville Amaryllis	B	21-7-68	Ch. Wingjays Ptolemy	Turberville Kelperland Necessity	Mrs D. Shemeld	Mrs D. Shemeld
1971	Rollinhills Wingjays Phoebe	B	13-9-68	Ch. Wingjays Ptolemy	Wingjays Vanilla	Mrs J. Rowett-Johns	Mrs B. M. J. White
1971	Barrabooka Apple Pie	B	17-10-67	Ch. Fredwell Ideal	Grims Ready	Mrs J. C. Wilson	Mrs J. C. Wilson
1971	Rollinhills Camilline Cuckoo	B	16-12-69	Wingjays Prometheus	Bargriff Camille	Mrs J. Lawther	Mrs B. M. J. White & Mrs J. Lawther
1971	Coastal Winston	D	18-11-68	Montague of Aberthin	Coastal Agnes	Mrs W. Thomas	Mrs M. Gray

1971	Brackenacre Daisy Belle	B	11-10-69	Ch. Fredwell Varon Vandal	Ch. Brackenacre Annabella	Mr & Mrs J. F. C. Nixon	Mr & Mrs J. F. C. Nixon
1971	Hobcote Folly	B	20-6-69	Balleroy Fanfare of Towbridge	Chantinghall Promise	Mrs A. M. Hainsworth	Mrs A. M. Hainsworth
1972	Wellshim Cruiser	D	26-7-70	Dalewell Rambler	Stationhouse Honey	Mrs A. C. Shimwell	Mrs A. C. Shimwell
1972	Lymewoods Finese	B	31-12-71-	Watercrest Solo	Lymewoods Elegance	Mr A. Wood	Mrs G. Bent & Mr A Wood
1972	Balleroy Nero.	D	25-10-69	Ch. Balleroy Chestnut	Balleroy Elegant	Mrs P. Moncur	Mrs P. Moncur
1972	Tamsmorna Heinekin	D	8-10-70	Croswolla John Peel	Tamsmorna Cleo-patra	Mrs W. Trezona	Mrs J. Walker
1972	Fredwell Flick	D	4-10-70	Ch. Fredwell Ideal	Ch. Fredwell Balleroy Faithful	Mrs J. Meacham	Mrs J. Meacham
1972	Coastal Weaver of Aberthin	D	18-11-68	Montague of Aberthin	Coastal Agnes	Miss W. Thomas	Mrs J. Hallett
1972	Maycombe Merryman	D	30-8-70	Ch. Chantinghall Ancestor	Maycombe Merry Lass	Mrs J. Gurney	Mrs M. Seifert
1972	Wingjays Polygon	D	13-4-71	Wingjays Prometheus	Wingjays Polonaise	Mrs J. Rowett-Johns	Mrs J. Rowett-Johns
1973	Beacontree Vanessa	B	10-7-69	Ch. Hardacre Valorous	Beacontree Emotion	Mrs B. Golding	Mrs V. J. Laurie
1973	Stormfield Hugo	D	9-10-70	Ch. Ballymaconnell Forester	Stormfield Tansey	Mrs W. Burgis	Mrs S. McHardy-Young
1973	Rollinhills the Swan	D	24-6-71	Wingjays Prometheus	Rollinhills Rollick	Mrs J. Lawther & Mrs B. White	Mrs B. M. J. White
1973	Balleroy Elegart	B	3-2-68	Ch Wingjays Polygamy of Maycombe	Balleroy Chantinghall Dreamer	Mrs P. Moncur	Mrs P. Moncur

Year	Name	Sex	Birth	Sire	Dam	Breeder	Owner
1973	Tintally Debutant	B	31-7-71	Ch. Wingjays Parthenon	Ch. Tintally Dubonnet	Mrs S. Blackler	Mrs S. Blackler
1973	Tintally Deborah	B	31-7-71	Ch. Wingjays Parthenon	Ch. Tintally Dubonnet	Mrs S. Blackler	Mrs S. Blackler
1973	Cwmdale Kynaston of Aberthin	D	17-10-70	Badger of Cwmdale	Monklon Aphrodite	Mrs J. Hallett	Mrs J. Elliot-Jones
1973	Brackenacre Fino de Paris	D	18-9-71	Ch. Fredwell Ideal	Brackenacre Chime of Bells	Mrs J. F. C. Nixon	Mrs M. Bews
1973	Langpool Miss American Pie	B	18-3-72	Am. Ch. Long View Acres Bonza	Balleroy Barshaw Caprice	Dr E. Andrews	Dr. E. Andrews
1973	Wingjays Pippin	B	29-9-70	Wingjays Prometheus	Wingjays Peonie	Mrs J. Rowett-Johns	Mrs J. Rowett-Johns
1973	Lymewoods Howard	D	15-11-71	Brigantium Fredwell Flip-A-Coin	Lymewoods Elegance	Mr A. Wood	Mr A. Wood
1973	Balleroy Yasmin	B	16-11-71	Ch. Balleroy Chestnut	Balleroy Toffee	Mrs P. Moncur	Mrs P. Moncur
1973	Chalkridge Francine	B	27-4-68	Ch. Fredwell Varon Fawkes	Varon Eleanore	Mrs P.M. Stevens	Mrs T. Johnson
1974	Woodland Amber	B	22-2-69	Ch. Wingjays Ptolemy	Woodland Beauty	Mrs S. Phillips	Mrs B. Rowe
1974	Gaymel Gay Tamarisk of Drawdell	B	28-2-72	Gaymel Marcus	Framberleys Bellissima of Gaymel	Mrs M. A. Travis	Mrs M. Ledward
1974	Boarfield Cassius	D	24-11-70	Ch. Wingjays Parthenon	Boarfield Bonnie	Miss C. Freeman	Miss C. Freeman

TRADITIONAL HOUND NAMES

Most breeders are well aware of the great ancestry behind the Basset and the present-day custom of giving hounds the traditional names reflects the breeder's interest in the Basset's past.

Hound names should 'roll off' the tongue easily and enable the hunter to give great carrying power to his voice when calling a hound.

The following is a list of French names, all taken from old Basset pedigrees, kindly loaned to me by the French breeders.

Aiglon	Bourbon	Elissette	Gorenflot
Allo	Briffault	Eminence	Glaneur
Alto		Emir	
Almenèche		Emma	
Alva	Calabash	Eros	
Amiral	Calchas		Harabuse
Ariane	Cassoulet		Harem
Arlequin	Chanaan		Havaud
Arlette	Cinnemon	Fama	Hector
Artemis	Clochette	Fanchette	Hercule
Azur	Cocarde	Fanfare	Hérie
	Colonel	Farandole	Hispa
	Comète	Fauvette	Hopp
		Finaud	Hourvari
Bacchanal		Flambard	Hurleur
Bacchus		Foulette	Huttin
Baliveau	Dagobert	Frapotel	
Balthazar	Danic	Fricandeau	
Balto	Danseuse		
Bártolo	Dare-Dare		Ica
Bavard	Dauphie		Idole
Bayard	Dauphin	Garibaldi	Idyle
Bellevue	Déesse	Gaulois	Infernal
Bellone		Gavotte	Irams
Bémol		Gelinotte	Irka
Birribi		Gigot	Iroquis
Boléro	Eclair	Gino	Isette
Bolívar	Eclaireuse	Gitane	Ixia

Jacobin
Jaguar
Java
Javeline
Jerrykane
Jex
Jimbo
Joilette
Jonquile
Judo

Kabilène
Kadidja
Kalou
Katou
Képi
Kikite
Kilina
Kimono
Kouki
Kraque

Lampo
Larbi
Lascar
Laurette
Léda
Lilla
Limoges
Loupiot
Loustig
Lumino

Malicante
Matamore
Maya
Mephisto
Millefleur
Minerve
Mireau
Mirontin

Mistral
Moka
Monolo
Mousquetaire
Moussec
Myrhha

Naïf
Nana
Navarre
Navette
Négresse
Nemrod
Nénuphar
Neptune
Néro
Nipotte
Noirette
Noisette
Nougat

Ods
Ola
Olympie
Omer
Ondine
Oppien
Oragonne
Orange
Orion
Otahiti
Ottoman
Oural

Paillard
Pallas
Paola
Paris
Pécadille
Péonie

Pervenche
Phideaux
Picador
Pilote
Pistache
Ponticou
Porto
Pschye

Québec
Qui Vive
Quichotte
Quimper
Quo Vadis

Rachel
Raoul
Ravigotte
Risette
Romano
Roméo
Ronfleau
Roublard
Rubicon

Sahara
Samovar
Samson
Sappho
Savoyard
Senateur
Sirocco
Sodome
Sully
Sultane

Tambour
Tarquin
Tayaut
Ténor

Thibaut
Timbale
Tobie
Tondeaux
Tranan
Triton
Troubadour
Tullie

Ulric
Ulysse
Unique
Uriage
Urie

Valentin
Valkyries
Vallens
Varron
Vénus
Victoire
Volage
Vol-au-vent

Xantippe
Xato
Xenophon
Xero
Xourri
Xerxes

Yako
Ygamme
Yolande
Yselle

Zanzibar
Zéphyre
Zeuxus
Zoulou

Names beginning with 'W' are not given to French hounds.

ENGLISH HOUND NAMES

Like their French counterparts, some of these traditional English names are very ancient but still in use today.

Abigail	Denmark	Handsome	Kiskin
Active	Dimity	Harmony	Klondyke
Affable	Doriman	Hebe	Koran
Aimwell	Dowager	Hecuba	Kudos
Airy		Hero	
Ajax		Hesperus	
Amazon	Earnest	Honesty	Lawless
Argus	Edgar	Hotspur	Lemon
	Egremont		Lightfoot
	Elegant		Lionel
Bauble	Ella	Iambus	Looby
Bellman	Ember	Iceberg	Lottery
Benefit	Ermine	Ichabod	Lusty
Bluebell	Eros	Idler	Lydia
Bluster		Impetus	
Brazen		Indian	
Brisher	Fairplay	Indigo	Marmie
Buxom	Famous	Item	Maskwell
	Fashion		Matchem
	Fearnought		Melody
Caroline	Fencer	Jailer	Minor
Champion	Fiddler	Jason	Moppet
Chanter	Foxglove	Jasper	Mulciber
Chimer	Freeman	Jealousy	Music
Comedy		Jingle	
Comely		Joker	
Cruiser	Gallant	Joyful	Nailer
Cryer	Gameboy	Junket	Nestor
	Ganymede		Nibble
	Garnet		Nimrod
Dainty	Go-Boy	Keeper	No-Go
Damper	Goodwood	Keepsake	Norah
Dancer	Gossip	Keswick	Nosegay
Delver	Gravity	Khartoum	Novelty

Oafish	Ranter	Ultimate	Willow
Obelisk	Ravager	Umpire	Woodlark
Object	Rector	Unicorn	
Occult	Ringwood	Uproar	
Odeum	Roman	Urchin	
Oliver	Ruin	Ursula	Xenium
Ottoman	Rumsey	Useful	Xerxes
Outlaw	Rustic	Utmost	Xeus

Parasol	Sailor		
Pedlar	Saladin	Vagrant	Yankee
Pelican	Saraband	Valiant	Yapper
Pilgrim	Sidestep	Vanguard	Yawler
Piper	Sifter	Vanity	Yemen
Posy	Singwell	Vaulter	Yeoman
Puffin	Siren	Victor	Yielder
Pugilist	Sportsman	Vocal	Yoga
		Voucher	Youthful

Quadrant	Tapster		
Quarrel	Tattler		
Questor	Thisbe	Wanton	Zedoc
Quickaway	Tiffany	Westward	Zero
Quickstep	Trail'em	Whimsey	Zodiac
Quiet	Trimbush	Whirlwind	Zoë
Quilter	Tulip	Whynot	
Quiver	Tuneful	Wildair	

PACKS REGISTERED WITH THE MASTERS OF BASSET HOUNDS ASSOCIATION
May 1974

De Burgh — Suffolk, Cambridgeshire
Fourshires — Oxford
Leadon Vale — Worcestershire
Oaston — Coventry
Westerby — Leicestershire
West Lodge — Home Counties
South Wales — South Wales
Albany — Leicestershire, Lincolnshire

The M.B.H.A. published its first Stud Book in 1925.

BREEDS CLOSELY ALLIED TO THE
BASSET HOUND

The Basset Hound is to France what the Dachshund breeds are to Germany, the indigenous low-legged and long-bodied dog. Apart from the Dachshund, some other breeds appear to have similar characteristics and possibly the same origin.

The Swiss breeds that come under the heading of the *Niederlaufhunde* or low-to-ground coursing hounds are said to have originated in the Middle Ages, and it is recorded that large numbers were sold to French and Italian noblemen. They were first shown in Zürich in 1881. The group includes:

The Lucernese, a tricolour hound, very often mottled and similar to the Blue-Mottled Gascon hounds.

The Bernese, a tricolour, also yellow and white. All colours permitted except self-black.

Other low-set Swiss breeds are the Jura, Schwyz and rough-haired Swiss Beagles.

The Scandinavian type of low-set hound is called the *Strelluf-Stovere* and is used for hunting in the forests much in the style of *chasse à tir* or with guns. The breed was developed by crossing many hound breeds, of which the Basset was one. They are tricoloured or bicoloured, and extremely popular in Denmark and Sweden.

SOME MEASUREMENTS OF BASSET HOUNDS

DETAILS	*Model* *Tricolour Dog* 1874	*Ch. Walhampton* *Ambassador* *Tricolour Dog* 1928	*Ch. Grims* *Whirlwind* *Tricolour Dog* 1954	*Ch. Fredwell Varon* *Vandal* *Tricolour Dog* 1960	*Ch. Sykemoor* *Emma* *Tricolour Bitch* 1962	*Ch. Maycombe* *Vaisya* *Tricolour Bitch* 1965
Weight	46 lb.	55 lb.	56 lb.	56 lb.	49 lb.	55 lb.
Height at shoulder	12 in.	13 in.	14½ in.	14½ in.	12 in.	12 in.
Length from nose to base of tail	32 in.	37 in.	39 in.	35½ in.	35 in.	39 in.
Length of tail	11½ in.	11½ in.	13 in.	13 in.	12 in.	12 in.
Girth of chest	25 in.	27 in.	27 in.	28 in.	26 in.	26 in.
Girth of loin	21 in.	22 in.	21 in.	26 in.	21 in.	24 in.
Girth of skull	17 in.	17½ in.	16 in.	16½ in.	14 in.	15 in.
Girth of forearm	6½ in.	7 in.	7 in.	6½ in.	5¾ in.	7 in.
Length of head. From nose to occiput	9 in.	10¼ in.	10 in.	9 in.	9 in.	10 in.
Girth of muzzle	9½ in.	10 in.	11 in.	10½ in.	8½ in.	10 in.
Length of ears. Tip to tip	19 in.	23½ in.	27½ in.	26½ in.	24½ in.	27 in.
Height of chest from ground	2¾ in.	4 in.	4½ in.	6½ in.	3½ in.	4½ in.

AVERAGE AGE OF HOUNDS WHEN MEASURED, 5 YEARS

BIBLIOGRAPHY

Ash, E. C. *Dogs, Their History and Development*, Ernest Benn, London 1927.

Auger, Dr. Jean. *Les Chiens Courants de Vendée*, Vigot Frères, Paris 1942.

Blaze, Elzéar. *Le Chasseur au Chien Courant*, Garnier Frères, Paris N/D.

Bourbon, Alain. *Nos Bassets Français*, A Goupil, Laval 1911.

Caius, Johannes. *Of English Dogges*, Abraham Fleming, 1576.

Compton, Herbert. *The Twentieth Century Dog (Sporting)*, Grant Richards, London 1904.

Cox, Harding (editor). *Dogs, Part VII*, Fawcett, McQuire & Co., London 1908.

Croxton-Smith, A. *Dogs Since 1900*, Andrew Dakers, London 1950.

de Canteleu, Count le Couteulx. *Manuel de Vénerie Français*, Hachette, Paris 1902.

du Fouilloux, Jacques. *Vénerie*, du Fouilloux, Rouen 1650.

Gilbey, Sir Walter, Bt. *Hounds in Old Days*, Vinton, London 1913.

Lane, C. H., F.Z.S. *Dog Shows and Doggy People*, Hutchinson, London 1902.

Leseble, L. *Les Bassets,* Firmin-Didot, Paris N/D.

Millais, Sir Everett. *Two Problems of Reproduction* (Lecture delivered at St. Thomas's Hospital, 25 February 1895).

Smith, Carl E. *Training the Rabbit Hound, Bassets and Beagles*, Hunter, Trader, Trapping Co., Chicago 1926.

Société de Vénerie. *Standards des Races de Chiens Courants*, F. Bouchy et Fils, Paris 1930.

Turbeville, George. *Art of Venerie*, 1576.

Verrier, Leon. *Les Bassets Français et Leur Utilisation*, L'Eleveur, Paris 1921.

Index

Adams, Miss Ena, 55, 57, 118
Adams, Norman, 55
Africa, Basset Hound in, 108
Alexandra, H.R.H. Princess, 38, 44
Alexandra, Queen, 49, 51, 52, 53, 109
Allbutt, Dr. Clifford, 40
Allen, E., 62, 63, 120, 121
Allergies, 200
Alwar, Maharajah of, 55
American Field, Chicago, 113
American Kennel Club, 113;
   registrations, 202
Anderson, J. C., 105, 106
Annand, Colonel, 49
Appleton, Douglas, 63, 73
Appleton, Mrs. D., 73
Art of Venerie, 19
Artois-Norman Basset, 98-100, 147
Ashton, Mrs., 74
Australia, Basset Hound in, 105-7
Aylesford, Lord, 116

Babson, Mrs., 70
Baden Basset, 27, 28
Baillet, M., 113
Bardot, Brigitte, 72
Barton, A., 51
Basset-Beagle matings, 34
Basset Hound—American standard,
   82-5; analysis of standards, 87-98;
   boar and wolf hunting with, 24;
   body length, 95-6; body structure,
   92; breed clubs, 203-4; breeding
   the, 141-53; care of puppies, 161-8;
   care of the young, 168-71;
   champions (1904-67), 205-10;
   character, 135-8; closely allied
   breeds, 216; coat, 82, 96; colour,
   82, 97; comparison with Beagle,

128-33; crossed with Bloodhound,
41; diet of young dogs, 165-6; drag
hunting, 121; ear, 81, 90;
English names of, 213-14; extinct
breeds of, 26; eye, 81, 90; feet, 81,
93; first mention in British
literature, 32; forequarters, 81,
95-6; French, 128; Artois-Norman
standard, 85-7; future of breed,
138-40; general appearance, 87;
head and skull, 80-1, 87-90;
height, 82, 98, 217; hindquarters,
84, 94; hunting, 127-34; hunting
packs, 43; in Africa, 108; in
Australia, 105-7; in Belgium, 110;
in first French dog show, 26; in
France, 108-9; in Holland, 110;
in illness, 195-201; in New
Zealand, 107-8; in Scandinavia,
109-10; in U.S.A., 111-16; Kennel
Club standard, 80-2; lack of
standardisation, 147; legs, 93;
mating, 154, 155; measurements of,
217; mouth, 81, 90-1; movement,
97-8; neck, 81, 91; need for
knowledgeable judging, 149;
obedience training, 125-6;
occupational hazards of working
breeds, 195; origins and evolution,
17-29; packs, 191-2; pedigrees,
46-7; registered packs, 215; scale
of points, 79; showing, 186-7;
standards, 77-80; supervising
eating habits, 200; tail, 82, 96;
teeth, 91; the 'English', 190-2;
the working, 116-26; traditional
names of, 211-12
Basset Hound Club, 38, 43, 52, 71,
   72, 116, 119, 120; acquires
   American stallion, 69; area